Quick Start

The following questions are amo̶... ̶̶o̶st̶ frequently asked by prospective divers seeking info̶ ... ̶̶̶CUBA diving (RSD). See 'SCUBA Sc̶ ... more complete set of questions (115+) ̶ ... ̶̶ ed in

Also see the Table of Contents and Index for additional Q & A.

SCUBA Scoop

Answers to Your Commonly-Asked SCUBA Diving Questions

By Gary S. Shumway

First Edition

Ernest Hill Publishing, Grand Terrace, California

SCUBA Scoop

Answers to Your Commonly-Asked SCUBA Diving Questions

By Gary S. Shumway

Published by:

Ernest Hill Publishing
12056 Mt. Vernon Ave., #234
Grand Terrace, CA 92313-5116   U.S.A.

Shumway, Gary S., 1949-
SCUBA Scoop: Answers to Your Commonly-Asked SCUBA Diving Questions by Gary S. Shumway. – [1st ed.]
    p. : ill. : cm.
Includes bibliographical references and index.

ISBN 0-9629410-5-0 (pbk.)
Library of Congress Control Number: 00-091073

Dedication

This book is dedicated to my parents, Dr. Ord L Shumway and Phyllis Fillerup Shumway who, as authors should acknowledge, ultimately made this book possible. Their love has been unwavering, even though I didn't become a Pathologist. Thank you for some great chromosomal material and your sustenance and succor over these many years. I love you both, immensely.

About the Author

Open Water Cert Photo

Gary Shumway first became interested in underwater exploration during his gestation. However, he did not become a certified diver until later in life. With his three brothers and Father being certified aquaholics, he recently figured it was about time to get it done. Gary's Open Water Diver certificate was completed with open water dives in a Pennsylvania quarry near Pittsburgh. As the season was early, a dry suit was de rigueur. Since that time he has dove in West Virginia, California, Minnesota, Florida, Mexico, Tahiti, and Australia, with many more locations planned in the future. He is currently a Master Scuba Diver with specialties in Rescue Diver, Medic First Aid, Oxygen First Aid, Nitrox, Dry Suit Diver, Ice Diver, Altitude Diver, Boat Diver, Wreck Diver, and Cavern Diver.

The impetus to write this tome began when he was seeking information regarding SCUBA diving. Dive shop personnel, though generally helpful and knowledgeable, could not be expected to contribute all their time to answering his questions. Even after acquiring a small library of diving books, there just was not a single book that answered the type of questions a person inquiring about diving would ask. Thus 'SCUBA Scoop'.

When not scuba diving, Gary works as a contract computer programmer. He has earned Masters degrees in Psychology (MA), Biostatistics (MPH), and Business Administration (MBA). He has published research and technical papers and the book, 'Winging Through America, A Motorcyclist's Solo Journey Through the 48 States'. He has been a member of Toastmasters International via Grand Terrace Toastmasters for over 14 years and has obtained the Distinguished Toastmaster (DTM) and Division Governor of the Year awards. Gary has three children, Greg (deceased), Jeff, and Glenna and resides wherever he can find desk space and an Internet connection.

Acknowledgments

Many individuals were involved in bringing this book from a single thought to what you hold in your hand.

For professional diving critique and suggestions I thank Major Barry Lowen, Mr. Anthony Wiley, Mrs. Nancy Lawson, Mr. Frank Veenstra, and the authors before me. For the medical related questions, I relied heavily on the public domain contributions from Drs. Ernest S. Campbell, Samuel Shelanski, and Fred Bove. I also thank the 128 dive shop owners and personnel who took the time to complete and return the dive site survey. Without their help, there would be no survey.

I thank Mrs. Michele Lowen and Mr. Anthony Wiley for many of the photographs included herein. Their photos added immensely to this project. I also thank Mr. Mike Whitt, owner of Matthews Water Sports, Inc., for giving me the freedom to roam his shop and take equipment related photographs.

Manuscript proof reading and suggestions for improving my use of the written word were graciously contributed by Dr. Ord L Shumway, Mr. D. Brian Shumway, Ms. Glenna Shumway, Mr. Jeff Shumway, and Ms. Mary Ann Lystra. Professional proofing by Ms. Laura Pacek added significantly to the readability of 'SCUBA Scoop'. Thank you all!

Many of the images, as well as the cover design of 'SCUBA Scoop' benefited, from the able hands and eyes of Mr. Wesley Yates of Art's Engraving. I also thank Mr. Ryan McMurtry and staff of Vaughan Printing for a printing job well done.

Lastly, I again thank Mary Ann for putting up with me these past years and for her understanding and forbearance when I secluded myself in 'my computer room' for hours on end. Thank you, Sweetie.

Table of Contents

For the Love of SCUBA

Contents (continued)   **Page**

Staying Alive .. and a Few Other Lesser Concerns

Contents (continued)   **Page**

s c U b a

The U in SCUBA .. Personal Considerations

SCUBA U. - *Getting Your C-Card and E-Ticket*

<u>**Contents**</u> (continued)   **Page**

You Are Well Suited For SCUBA - Equipment Exposés

Contents (continued)   **Page**

All Suited Up and Thousands of Dives to Make

Contents (continued)   **Page**

List of Illustrations

List of Illustrations *(continued)*

List of Illustrations *(continued)*

Conversion Index

One of the things I dislike when reading a book where there are several different measurement systems being used, is the 44 lbs/20 kg or 130 feet (39 meters) type verbiage. It is really distracting. To avoid that problem, I have decided to standardize (unless the measurement is contained within a quote or is the usual measurement referred to by divers, e.g., wetsuit thickness) on the U.S. (Imperial) system in the text of 'SCUBA Scoop' and include the metric system equivalents in this Conversion Index. Conversions are ordered within each grouping in ascending order of magnitude. For future editions, I would appreciate your feedback via **ehp@ehpublishing.com** regarding this methodology.

Area
(sq km=square kilometer, sq mi=square miles)
63,800,000 sq mi =
    165,241,241.4 sq km
142,000,000 sq mi =
    367,778,311.7 sq km

Distance
(cm=centimeters, ft=feet, in=inches, km=kilometers, m=meters, mm=milimeters yds=yards)
    1/8 in = 3 mm
    1/4 in = 6 mm
    8 in = 20.3 cm
    1.8 in = 30.0 cm
    3 ft = 0.9 m
    3.3 ft = 1.0 m
    5 ft = 1.5 m
    6 ft = 1.8 m
    7 ft = 2.1 m
    10 ft = 3.0 m
    15 ft = 4.5 m
    20 ft = 6.1 m
    30 ft = 9.1 m
    33 ft = 20.1 m
    40 ft = 12.2 m
    50 ft = 15.2 m
    60 ft = 18.3 m
    65 ft = 19.8 m
    80 ft = 24.4 m
    90 ft = 27.4 m

100 ft = 30.5 m
Distance (continued)
    110 ft = 33.5 m
    130 ft = 39.6 m
    140 ft = 42.7 m
    150 ft = 45.7 m
    165 ft = 50.3 m
    220 ft = 67.1 m
    250 ft = 76.2 m
    600 ft (200 yds) = 182.9 m
    660 ft = 220.0 m
    1,000 ft = 304.8 m
    4,400 ft = 1,341.1 m
    8,202 ft = 2,500.0 m
    36,373 ft = 11,086.5 m
    15 mi = 24.1 km
    50 mi = 80.5 km
    1,200 mi = 1,931.2 km

Pressure
(atm=atmospheres, psi=#/sq in)
6 atm (88.176 psi) = 6.1 bar
    105 psi = 7.2 bar
    200 psi = 13.8 bar
    300 psi = 20.7 bar
    500 psi = 34.5 bar
    600 psi = 41.4 bar
    623 psi = 43.0 bar
    700 psi = 48.3 bar
    1,000 psi = 69.0 bar
    1,200 psi = 82.7 bar
    2,250 psi = 155.1 bar

Pressure (continued)
2,400 psi = 165.5 bar
2,475 psi = 170.6 bar
3,000 psi = 206.8 bar
3,014.7 psi = 207.9 bar

Temperature
(F=Fahrenheit, C=Celsius)
-40º F = -40º C
28º F = -2.2º C
40º F = 4.4º C
45º F = 7.2º C
55º F = 12.8º C
60º F = 15.6º C
65º F = 18.3º C
70º F = 21.1º C
75º F = 23.9º C
80º F = 26.7º C
85º F = 29.4º C
91º F = 32.8º C
96º F = 35.6º C

Volume
(cc=cubic centimeters, cf=cubic feet, l=liters)
350 cc = 0.0124 cf
0.5 cf = 14.16 l
1.0 cf = 28.32 l
1.5 cf = 42.48 l
2.0 cf = 56.64 l
2.7 cf = 76.5 l
8.0 cf = 226.6 l
13.0 cf = 368.2 l
13.4 cf = 379.5 l
14.0 cf = 396.5 l
16.0 cf = 453.1 l

Volume (continued)
16.6 cf = 470.1 l
19.0 cf = 538.1 l
40.0 cf = 1,132.8 l
50.0 cf = 1,416.0 l
65.0 cf = 1,840.8 l
71.2 cf = 2,016.4 l
80.0 cf = 2,265.6 l
103.5 cf = 2,931.2 l
328,000,000 cu mi =
    1,367,163,638.7 cu km

Weight
(g=grams, Kg=kilograms, lbs=pounds, oz=ounces)
9.2 oz = 260.8 g
0.0834 lbs = 37.8 g
5 lbs = 2.3 Kg
6 lbs = 2.7 Kg
6.7 lbs = 3.0 Kg
10 lbs = 4.5 Kg
21 lbs = 9.5 Kg
29 lbs = 13.2 Kg
33 lbs = 15.0 Kg
44 lbs = 20.0 Kg
50 lbs = 22.7 Kg
62.4 lbs = 28.3 Kg
64 lbs = 29.0 Kg
100 lbs = 45.4 Kg
106 lbs = 48.1 Kg
15 tons = 13,607.8 Kg
200 tons = 181,436.9 Kg

Exchange
All $ (dollars) used in text is U.S. dollars (USD) circa 2000, unless otherwise noted.

What 'SCUBA Scoop' Is and Isn't

This book contains answers to more than 115 of your frequently asked questions (FAQs) regarding recreational SCUBA diving (RSD). 'SCUBA Scoop' answers the questions most frequently asked by those wanting to learn more about recreational SCUBA diving before taking the plunge, as well as questions a novice to intermediate diver may ask.

'SCUBA Scoop' is NOT a training manual. Training manuals have been written for and by the SCUBA certifying agencies, e.g., NAUI, PADI, SSI, YMCA. Instruction involving a professional SCUBA Instructor using one of those training manuals is the proper way to be trained in recreational SCUBA diving.

Except for the 'All Suited Up and Thousands of Dives to Make' section, this book does not attempt to answer questions that a 'more experienced technical diver' might have (though it might be a refresher for many). There are many sources on more advanced and technical diving topics (see the 'Diving Deeper into SCUBA' section) but a perceived lack of information for the perspective to intermediate diver. Thus 'SCUBA Scoop'.

As to bias, I am very enthusiastic about recreational SCUBA diving. In this book, I try to convey that enthusiasm for, and love of, recreational SCUBA diving. With diving, you can never say you have seen it all, done it all, or know it all. Every time you dive, there is the opportunity to learn or see something new.

I have tried to include a modicum of humor in this text as an attempt to make this book more readable than a dry, scholarly question and answer tome. The use of humor is not meant to denigrate the importance of being properly trained and diving safely, and should not be taken as such. Note that any text enclosed within curly brackets { } is a wise crack or a clarification of an authority's quote {it is up to you, gentle reader, to decide which is which}. Material that is referenced in the 'References' section are denoted with a letter(s) enclosed in square brackets, e.g., [A].

In closing, let me remind you that over two-thirds of this planet is covered with water. Obviously, we were meant to be diving at least two-thirds of the time. Get certified and get divin'!

How to Read and Use 'SCUBA Scoop'

'SCUBA Scoop' is organized into sections, with the questions and answers most related to that section included therein. The sections are denoted in the Table of Contents and the body of the text in bold italicized characters. Each question is numbered and printed in bold type. Listing, figure, and table headings within the questions are lettered and italicized. To enable rapid dissemination of information, the main points relating to each question or list are italicized. Even so, you are encouraged to read the entire answer, as you will not get all of the information you need by just reading the italicized print.

One of the things I dislike when reading a book where there are several different measurement systems being used, is the 44 lbs/20 kg or 130 feet (39 meters) type verbiage. It is really distracting and confusing. To avoid that problem I have decided to standardize on one system in the text of 'SCUBA Scoop' and include a Conversion Index on page 18. Conversions are presented in the Conversion Index for usage of distances, pressures, temperatures, volumes, and weights in the text. The conversions within each group are listed in the approximate order of presentation in the text.

There are four ways to read this book. You can elect to browse the Table of Contents and select those questions that interest you. This will tend to leapfrog you around the book as questions come to mind. This method may make your initial study of SCUBA and the reading of 'SCUBA Scoop' a little disjointed.

Secondly, you can go through the Index and select the words that appeal to you and read the appropriate text. This method may be more appropriate for a review after having read 'SCUBA Scoop', or for the intermediate diver wanting to augment their understanding.

Thirdly, you can peruse 'SCUBA Scoop' straight through, reading the questions that most interest you. The sections and questions therein were sequentially ordered to most logically lead you through the exploration of recreational SCUBA using this method.

The fourth way is to use the 'Quick Start' section, found on page one. 'Quick Start' points you to the questions you initially are most likely to ask. This method is basically using a sub-set of the Table of Contents questions. 'Quick Start' is meant to whet your appetite for reading 'SCUBA Scoop' in more detail.

As I do not know which of the above methods you prefer, you will note some redundancy in the answers to your questions. Some of the answers cover portions of multiple questions. As you may elect to skip around from question to question, I need to answer each question as completely as possible. That said, you will also note the frequent use of '(see Question #)'. This is a reference to additional information regarding your question via yet another question.

Regardless of the method you choose it is my hope that your questions are answered to your satisfaction. Please write me at **ehp@ehpublishing.com** or Ernest Hill Publishing, 12056 Mt. Vernon St. #234, Grand Terrace, CA 92313 (addressed to my attention) if you have questions regarding recreational SCUBA diving that are not covered in this edition of 'SCUBA Scoop'. I will try to answer your questions as expeditiously as possible by return mail and reserve the right to include them in a future edition. The focus of 'SCUBA Scoop' is to answer questions which are non-technical and those which a novice to intermediate diver might ask. Please limit your queries to that genre of questioning.

My Lawyer Owns the Expensive Suit
and Now My Tale Is Covered

Disclaimer

It is a travesty that our society has reached this level of mistrust, lack of 'responsibility for self', and unbridled greed which has been engendered by a few real butts. Yet I have been advised to cover my behind thus the following disclaimer.

The information presented in this book is not infallible. This book should in no way be used as specific advice, or as recommendation for any particular individual, or adopted in any form, as any type of training in the use of SCUBA. The author is not a trained medical professional. The medically related information presented herein has been obtained from publicly accessible documents. The primary purpose of the medical information in this book is to give you an overview of current medical thinking on a subject of interest to you and to encourage you to seek professional medical advice regarding your specific situation. **Do not base your diving solely on the general medical opinions supplied herein. Get medical advice specific to your condition!**

The purpose of this book is to increase your understanding of what is involved in the avocation of recreational SCUBA diving and not to tell you what to do. In fact, I make it clear that if you want to become involved in recreational SCUBA diving, then you should get a complete physical examination and seek professional training. It is not my intent to tell you how to conduct any dive or whether you specifically should take up SCUBA diving in the first place. Although I may make suggestions in some of the text, these are not specific for any individual and should not be taken as such.

You, yes, you the reader, must recognize that no matter who you are and how well-trained you are, there are dives which are beyond your personal ability, physical condition, training, and/or equipment. I recommend that any question you have about any activity related to an actual dive should be discussed directly with a dive professional, i.e., SCUBA Instructor, qualified Physician, dive store owner, Divemaster, etc. The author, publisher, and printer of this book and the Physicians quoted herein are not liable for damage or injury, including death, with respect to your diving from information obtained herein.

If you want to SCUBA dive it is **YOUR RESPONSIBILITY** to:
- get a physical examination and seek specific medical opinions for you,
- get trained,
- apply that training,
- not dive beyond your training,
- keep your training up-to-date,
- maintain your equipment,
- get periodic physical exams,
- be physically fit,
- USE YOUR HEAD, and
- then your tail will be covered too!

If you do not wish to be bound by any of the above, you may return this book to the publisher for a full refund of the cover price.

1. What is SCUBA?

The term *'SCUBA'*, *is an acronym for 'Self-Contained Underwater Breathing Apparatus'.* SCUBA diving means using an apparatus that is completely carried by the diver and is not connected to the surface, thus it is self-contained. SCUBA gives a diver the freedom of an extended, completely mobile, underwater adventure unavailable to the free-diver (breath-holder or skin diver), surface supplied air diver, or submariner.

Modern recreational SCUBA diving got its start in 1943 by Jacques Cousteau and Emil Gagnan with the development of a commercially-viable, workable demand regulator. However, recreational SCUBA diving (RSD) did not begin to catch on until the mid-fifties. Today, the greatest utilization of SCUBA equipment is in RSD, as contrasted to 'commercial', 'professional' and 'technical' SCUBA.

Recreational SCUBA diving, as typically defined by the certifying agencies and as used in 'SCUBA Scoop', is delimited by the parameters found in Listing A.

Listing A. Parameters Defining Recreational SCUBA Diving.
1. *Only compressed air* (see Question 17) is inhaled at depth (this may change in the future with wider adoption of nitrox or increased levels of oxygen in the compressed air),
2. is *always done with a buddy (see Question 45),*
3. dives *never exceed a depth of 130 fsw* (feet sea water) (see Question 82),
4. has a depth of dive and immersion time dive profile that *does not require a decompression stop (see Question 84),*
5. the diver always has *unobstructed access to the surface* (no deep penetration of overhead structures, e.g., cave, wreck, ice, etc.), and
6. *requires specialized training* beyond the basic open water course *for more specialized diving.*

The basic or initial open water certificate is just that, basic (implying additional training for more advanced diving) and open water, which means unobstructed access to the surface. The open water certified diver (see Question 5) should not dive beyond their training and should dive in environmental situations similar to which they were trained.

Recreational SCUBA diving can be enjoyed as an avocation by just about any healthy teenager or adult who is comfortable in water and can swim. If you are in reasonably good health, e.g., no heart, lung, or ear impairments (also see Question 65), have the desire, and get the professional training, then you too can become one of the some 500,000 divers who get certified yearly (see Question 79).

I use SCUBA in all caps in 'SCUBA Scoop' to emphasize my enthusiasm for the sport but you will also see it used by others in lower case. Again, I use SCUBA to mean 'recreational SCUBA diving' (non-commercial/non-professional/non-technical), unless otherwise noted.

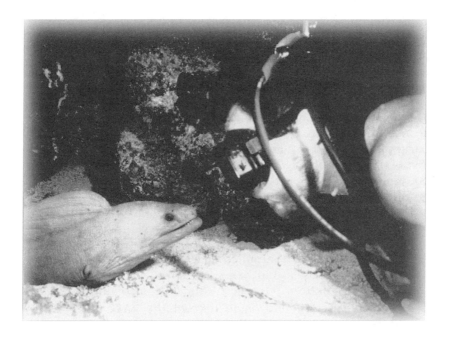

2. What's not SCUBA?

In addition to recreational SCUBA diving (RSD) there are a number of other ways of exploring our intriguing underwater world. For the purpose of this book, *recreational SCUBA diving does not include the following: sport surface-supplied air (SSSA) diving, breath-hold diving, diving enclosed in a submersible vessel or suit, professional, military, commercial, and technical diving.* Examples of what is not SCUBA follows.

In SSSA diving, the diver is tethered to the floating compressed air source by a hookah or long hose, regulator, and mouthpiece. The floating compressed air source is an air compressor and/or a tank of compressed air. SSSA is not SCUBA because the diver does not carry their own air source.

Typically, SSSA units, e.g., Brownie's Third Lung, serve pairs of divers (buddies) to depths of 30 to 90 fsw. SSSA is more akin to professional helmet diving except that no helmet is worn, the diving depths are typically less, only normal compressed air is used, and there is little if any surface support.

The pros and cons of SSSA as compared to RSD are beyond the scope of 'SCUBA Scoop', but SSSA does appear to be particularly useful in long duration, shallow depth, underwater dives such as lobster hunting, fish harvesting, cleaning the bottom of your yacht, etc. Divers using SSSA should be trained and certified. To dive safely, anyone breathing compressed air at depth must fully understand the operational procedures and inherent risks involved.

An extension of surface supplied air is, of course, the archetype of the diver, the suited and helmeted diver with an umbilical to the surface. For our purposes, this type of diving falls into 'professional' or 'commercial' diving, as the diver is paid and potentially uses special mixtures of air.

Breath-hold diving, because of its simplicity, is obviously the earliest form of diving and is still practiced for sport and commercial purposes, e.g., Ama divers of Japan and Korea.

Each dive is limited only by the individual's ability to breathhold and their acceptance of the risk of drowning from hypoxia (lack of oxygen).

Diving inside a walled vessel or dive suit which can maintain internal atmosphere at or near sea level enables the occupant(s) to descend without being physically impacted by the increasing external pressures. Such vessels are called bathyspheres if they have no means of mobility and are tethered to the mother ship, bathyscaphs if they have internal buoyancy control, and submarines if they can travel extensively in any direction under their own power.

A relatively recent extension of the diving suit is the selfcontained, armored diving suit. These suits are flexible, but can withstand pressures to depths in excess of 600 feet. One could argue that walled vessels and armored diving suits are SCUBA, but for now anyway, they are not used for recreational purposes and will not be classified as SCUBA in 'SCUBA Scoop'.

'Professional' diving is done for military, governmental, commercial, and/or scientific purposes and professional divers are paid to dive. Your Instructor as well as Assistant Instructors and Divemasters are classified as Professional Divers.

'Technical' diving, as used herein, is the term for all diving that exceeds recreational limits (see Listing A in Question 1) and is done as not-for-profit. Although some technical divers consider their diving as recreational, the advanced nature of their diving, the additional training involved, and the type of equipment used usually falls outside one or more of the RSD parameters. If we stick to the 'falls outside of RSD parameters' definition of 'technical' diving we can avoid unnecessary bloodshed over the term. Some of the diving which generally falls outside RSD parameters is shown in Listing B.

Listing B. Diving Requiring Additional Training.
(The specific RSD parameters exceeded (from Listing A) are in parentheses.)

- *Cave diving (5, 6 and often 1, 3, and 4)*,
- *deep penetration* wreck diving (5, 6 and at times 1, 3, 4),
- *ice diving (5 and 6)*,
- diving using a *dry suit (6)* (In cases where the diver is trained in the dry suit as part of their open water course, this may not be thought of 'technical' diving, though additional training is required. I was initially trained in a dry suit because of the low water temperatures in Pennsylvania.)
- serious *macro photographer* (2 and often 1 and 6),
- dives to *depths greater than 130 feet (3*, 6 and often 1, 4),
- *mixed gas diving*, e.g., nitrox, trimix (1), and
- diving with "closed circuit" or *rebreather* systems (1 and 6).

Some of the 'technical' diving specialties are taught by the open water certification agencies, while other specialties are taught by other agencies. As SCUBA technology matures, more and more divers will be included. What was once the realm of just technical diving, e.g., use of dive computers, has been expanded to include recreational SCUBA divers.

It is conceivable that some of today's more advanced technology, e.g., rebreathers, may one day be routinely used by open water recreational divers. Of course, by that time, further advances will make the science fiction of today the technology of tomorrow.

3. Why should I become SCUBA certified and dive?

If you want to dive, then you must be reasonably healthy and get the professional training that will lead to your becoming an open water certified SCUBA diver (see Question 79). To SCUBA dive without professional training is exceedingly risky. You need better survival odds!

Telling you why you should become a certified SCUBA diver is difficult. We each have our own reasons for doing what we do, but for me it has changed the way I think about life. Some of the reasons I enjoy being SCUBA certified are listed in Listing C.

Listing C. Reasons I Enjoy Diving.

☺ The *feeling freedom,*

☺ the *self-discipline, self-sufficiency, and self-esteem* SCUBA certification engenders,

☺ the opportunities for *exploration and travel and to meet a lot of great people,*

☺ diving a *paradoxically benign, yet potentially hostile, environment,*

☺ *expanding my capabilities, knowledge, and life experiences,*

☺ *learning more about myself,* and

☺ the opportunity to *understand more fully the inter-relatedness of life* on this planet. Being able to explore relatively unfettered, a totally new ecosystem is like going to another planet {yet being able to go back home and sleep in your warm bed}.

When other divers are asked why they dive, they respond:

☺ I dive because I love life.

☺ I dive so that I can be free and be with the greatest concentration of life on this planet.

☺ Once you go beneath the surface, you will never look at the water the same way. Going to the ocean and not diving is like going to the circus and standing outside of the tent. It's the "Greatest Show on Earth" but you have to pay the admission price to get in.

☺ SCUBA divers do not have the limitations that are imposed on snorkelers.

☺ I love fishing and SCUBA is a great way to check out the fish.

☺ I love diving on wrecks, especially when you know the history behind them. Being able to stand on the bridge and travel back in time on a ship that sailed 300 years ago is awesome.

☺ SCUBA is probably as close as I will get to the feeling of weightlessness in space. It is so cool to be suspended along a wall and look down into the dark, seemingly endless, void (see Question 51).

☺ Guess I am just an old adrenaline junkie.

☺ SCUBA diving is always different. It is a change of pace.

☺ SCUBA diving gives me the opportunity to try my hand at photography and videography.

☺ Diving is like traveling to another planet and marveling at the alien life forms so strange that you won't even recognize the animals as being animals.

☺ I am in awe of the beauty and mystery.

☺ The main reason I dive is to be underwater breathing air. The rest is just icing on the cake.

☺ Diving does not need a purpose. It is the objective and needs no justification.

Your reasons for becoming certified and diving may differ or parallel those of ours, but one thing is certain: giving SCUBA a try will expand your horizons!

Copyright 1998
Michele L. Lowen

Truck (Chuuk) horizon

4. Who should not be SCUBA certified?

As in any avocation, there are individuals who should not be involved in it. Just as some should not be on a motorcycle, or fly, or chew gum and walk, some should not be SCUBA certified. In my opinion, a non-exhaustive listing of those who should not SCUBA dive can be found in Listing D.

Listing D. Those Who Should Not Become SCUBA Certified.

☹ Those with *contraindicated medical conditions* (please get a complete medical exam from a Physician trained in dive medicine before diving - see Question 65),

☹ those who *use addictive or mind-altering substances* or medications such that they put themselves and others at risk,

☹ those whose *physical condition*, unless otherwise mitigated, puts them or their buddy at great physical risk,

☹ those *mentally impaired* or deranged,

☹ those who *think they are invincible* and that universal physical laws just do not apply to them,

☹ those with *no imagination or who lack the desire to learn* about and explore an exciting new ecosystem, and

☹ anyone who *exhibits thoughtlessness behavior which endangers themselves or others.*

5. What is certification and why do I need that C-card?

The basic 'C-card' is short for open water SCUBA diver certification card (see Question 11 for certification levels in SCUBA diving). SCUBA certification is akin to the certification process of hang gliding, pilot's license, etc., except that there are no governmental mandates or SCUBA police, yet. Without a C-card, that is, without certification, you should not SCUBA dive (unless, of course, you are under instruction by a professional SCUBA Instructor).

Recreational SCUBA diving certification entails being trained by a professional Instructor affiliated with one of a number of SCUBA certifying agencies and usually a dive shop. The training is roughly 30 hours in duration and generally consists of classroom, pool, and open water portions (see the 'SCUBA U.' section for cost and training required).

Upon meeting the relatively standard criteria set by the certifying agency (see Question 72 for a list of certifying agencies) you will receive your Open Water SCUBA Diver Certification, or C-card. A C-card is good for life, but if you take a lengthy break from diving, then you should take a SCUBA refresher course. Figure A is an example of a PADI (Professional Association of Diving Instructors) C-card.

Figure A. PADI C-card

Your C-card indicates that you have met the basic requirements (see Question 80) to SCUBA dive in water and situations similar to that in which you were trained. Without the C-card you should not be able to SCUBA dive from a commercial boat without an Instructor, get SCUBA tanks filled with air, buy certain equipment from a dive shop, or take more advanced training. The recreational SCUBA diving certification process is industry-monitored. Earning your C-card is for you and your buddy's protection. Do not dive without it!

6. Can I SCUBA dive without being certified?

Yes, you can SCUBA dive without being certified, but please do not do it unless you are with an instructor! In fact, you can also climb aboard a sport motorcycle and zigzag through freeway traffic, buy a hang glider and without training run off a cliff, or buy a personal submarine and set off to explore the Mariana Trench at 36,373 feet.

Yet, why in the hell would you do those things without proper training, equipment, and experience? There are no SCUBA police ... yet. The industry regulates itself well and so far 'Big Brother' has maintained a laissez-faire approach. We must keep it that way!

The only times you should dive uncertified is when you are undergoing certification training or taking a resort or similar course. Otherwise, PLEASE do yourself, your family, buddy, friends, and the industry a favor by staying alive. Do not SCUBA dive unless you are at least a certified open water diver or you are undergoing professional instruction. Thank You!

7. What is SCUBA diving like and why is it so popular?

The wide variety of diving possible makes your SCUBA diving experience very customizable. Some examples of SCUBA dives are shown in Listing E. Note that some of the dives in Listing E require additional training beyond open water certification.

Listing E. Examples of SCUBA Dives.
(Some of these dives require additional training beyond basic open water.)

≈ You can do a *beautiful and leisurely beach dive in warm water* in Bonaire while reveling in the splendid color of the flora and fauna.

≈ You can *ice dive* in the Alaskan waters or a Minnesota lake.

≈ You can do a *wreck dive* on the San Francisco Maruo off Truk (Chuuk) Island or the Regina in Lake Huron.

≈ You can do a *river dive* in the Colorado River as it comes pouring out of Lake Mead.

≈ You can *dive among kelp* off Catalina Island at night.

≈ You can do Pacific Ocean *blue water dives* while photographing sharks attracted by a chum trail.

≈ You can experience beautiful and fast paced *drift dives* off Palau and Cozumel.

≈ You can dive hundreds of feet back into a *cave* and explore the realm of the monster residing within each of us that encourages you to panic.

And the list goes on.

You can be as social as you want or totally immerse yourself in taking those fantastic underwater photos we all enjoy viewing. You can dive in water with over 100-foot visibility or in a fresh water lake with an algae bloom and count yourself fortunate when you can see your gauges held at arms length. You can travel to far off places, viewing sights and meeting people you never would have otherwise. Or, you can get in a quick dive after work in the quarry a few miles from your home.

SCUBA diving is enticing because it is an entirely different, varied, and for the most part, very beautiful world down there. It is a world that you can never entirely explore, thus it is always fresh and interesting. This watery world is truly hard to fathom until you have seen it. The plants and animals are very different, as is the physics of being surrounded by water 100 feet deep.

This underwater world is varied because of the differences in the inhabitants and the geography. These differences are due, in part, to global location and depth. It is also varied because of the different interests divers have, e.g., photography, wreck diving, night diving, deep diving, cave diving, fresh vs. salt water diving, etc. Just look at some of the excellent underwater photography and videos and you cannot help but marvel at the variety of life and the plethora of color far exceeding that of land based fauna and flora. And that hardly scratches the surface.

Come see for yourself!

8. How many SCUBA divers are there?

SCUBA diving originally began with military and commercial applications (see 'The History of SCUBA in Three Pages' section). However, currently and for the foreseeable future, its widest use, in terms of number of participants, is recreational.

No one knows exactly how many divers there are or how many dives are done each year. However, PADI (Professional Association of Diving Instructors), the largest (in terms of divers certified) SCUBA certifying agency, *estimates that there are some 8.5 million certified (includes all certifications) SCUBA divers in the U.S. and some 14.5 to 15.5 million worldwide.*[Z] The National Sporting Goods Association reported that in *1998 about 2,558,000 Americans went diving and 7,334,000 went snorkeling.*[HH] A Gallup study (via Leisure Trends Group) which was published in March of 1998, estimates there are 7,690,000 certified SCUBA divers in the U.S. Approximately one-third of those certified in the U.S. remain active participants (at least one dive a year) in SCUBA diving. It has been estimated that approximately 500,000 new divers were certified in 1998.[FF] The top six states for SCUBA certification training are: Florida, California, Hawaii, Texas, Illinois, and New York.[BB]

9. Who gets SCUBA certified?

Who is this person that changes from a bipedal creature of terra firma to a bubble-blowing aquatic adventurer? PADI (Professional Association of Diving Instructors) certifies more divers in the U.S. than any other certifying agency, and they state that 45 percent of their certified SCUBA divers are between 16 and 34 years old, 33 percent are between 35 and 44 years old, and 19 percent are 45 years or better (see Question 57).[AA]

Additionally, some 58 percent of SCUBA diving participants are married and 89 percent have had at least some college. Vocationally, 39 percent have professional/management jobs, 38 percent have service/labor jobs, 8 percent are in sales/retail, 6 percent homemakers, 4 percent retired, 4 percent are self employed, and 1 percent secretarial. The statistics show that you do not have to be rich to dive, as 38 percent of the participants have incomes less than $50,000 {probably SCUBA Instructors} and only 20 percent pull in greater than $100,000 per year {certainly not Divemasters}.

Where do you fit in?

10. Why is SCUBA attracting more women?

It is estimated that there are some 3 million Americans who are actively SCUBA diving with some 500,000 newly certified divers each year (see Question 8). Historically, most of these divers have been men, but the current trend is increasingly towards women and couples. About 35 percent of the new divers certified in 1999 were women.

In the beginning of recreational SCUBA diving, circa 1950s, most (but certainly not all) of the participants were men. Because of socialization and increased testosterone levels, men appear to be more amenable to taking the risks and meeting the physical challenges inherent in early SCUBA diving.

Yet as the sport has progressed, become safer (see Question 47), with SCUBA equipment becoming gender sensitive (with bumps and curves), training and facilities continually improving, increased numbers of women have become involved. According to PADI (Professional Association of Diving Instructors) currently some 28 percent of the SCUBA divers are female.[Z] About the only limitation for women compared to men is related to reproduction (see Question 61). Specifically, do not dive if pregnant or trying to get pregnant (see Question 59). According to Dr. Ernest S. Campbell, "In assessing fitness to dive in women, the same considerations applied to men regarding general health, physical capacity, mental stability, and training should be used."[X]

11. What are the certification levels in recreational diving?
Within recreational SCUBA diving (RSD), there are three diving
tracts, with multiple levels within each of those tracts. The
specifics of each tract and the level requirements are generally
dependent upon the certifying agency and the extent of the
diver's training and/or experience. *The three general tracts
offered by most of the agencies are 1) the pre-open water
certification, 2) non-professional certifications (including open
water), and 3) the professional certifications.*

The pre-open water certification tract includes the
bubblemaker, snorkeling, skin-diving, resort, and discover
SCUBA courses. This tract eases the hesitant or young diver-
to-be (see Question 58) into the world of SCUBA with minimal
expense (see Question 20). This tract is not actual SCUBA
training, but is introductory in nature.

The second tract is a non-professional tract. This generally
begins with the open water SCUBA certification. Open water
SCUBA certification is what most people think of when they
think of becoming a certified SCUBA diver. Yet the open water
diver needs additional training and experience in order to deep
dive, penetrate wrecks, ice dive, dive with enriched air, dive
with a dry suit, etc. This additional training is available
through specialty courses (see Question 12).

After specific specialty courses are completed and the additional
experience is gained, the open water diver can obtain what is
generally termed the Advanced Scuba Diver, Advanced Open
Water, or Open Water II certification. There may be multiple
levels within this Advanced rating, based on the number and
type of specialty courses taken.

The final level in the non-professional tract is typically termed
the Master Scuba Diver. The Master Scuba Diver generally has
taken a number of specialty courses (type and quantity is
agency dependent), has dove the required number of dives
(again, agency dependent), and generally has taken Medic/First
Aid and Rescue Diver courses. A diver can decide to go pro (the
third tract) sometime during their sojourn through the non-
professional tract or they can continue to take the specialty

courses in tract two. Taking these specialty courses is very satisfying in and of themselves.

The third tract is the professional or leadership tract. This tract generally culminates in the diver becoming an Instructor (though there are designations beyond Instructor). The initial certification within the professional tract is usually Divemaster, then Skin-diving Instructor (in some agencies), then Assistant Instructor, and finally Instructor. The Instructor certification is typically the minimum certification necessary to teach and certify a student as an open water SCUBA diver.

Unless Instructors have taken special training, they too are not trained to exceed recreational limits (see Question 1). Thus, they are not technical divers and would need further training to do mixed gas diving, deep diving, ice diving, etc. Of course, many SCUBA Instructors do obtain additional specialty training and certification in these and other technical diving skills.

The majority of recreational SCUBA divers never take more than the basic open water course. However, after making many dives over the years they can become very experienced and adept in the skills necessary in open water diving. In recent years, SCUBA agencies have created 'experience dive cards' that are bestowed upon divers who have reached various dive plateaus, e.g., 50, 100, 200, etc. dives. This 'experience dive card' facilitates the diver quickly showing the quantity of their experience when renting equipment or diving from a open water dive boat {obviously, you must be certified to get the experience dive cards and get specialized training for specialized dives}.

Agencies involved in certifying recreational SCUBA divers generally certify divers who are involved in recreational, technical, and professional diving. To become involved in commercial, military, scientific, aquaculture, journalism, etc., you will want to contact organizations that train specifically for that vocation (see Question 13).

12. In what SCUBA specialties can I get further training?
The different types of SCUBA specialties in which you can ultimately become trained are basically limited only by your imagination. Determine what interests you and seek out the training to dive safely while pursing those interests (see Question 48). The open water certifying agencies have a number of specialties. Additionally, there are organizations that offer specialties not generally found on the specialty list of the open water certifying agencies. Some of the specialties offered to recreational divers are listed in Listing F.

Listing F. Specialties Offered to Recreational Divers.

✓ *Photography*: underwater photography and/or videography are fantastic avocations in their own right and could become your vocation.

✓ *Wreck Diving*: learning the history behind a wreck and then actually diving it makes the wreck come alive. It comes alive not only because of the tangible artifacts, but because in most cases the wreck is literally alive with new inhabitants.

✓ *Night Diving*: night diving changes the ho-hum diurnal site to an excitingly new nocturnal one. Totally different fauna utilize the same ecospace; fascinating!

✓ *Boat Diving*: learning more about boat diving makes it more enjoyable and in deep open water can facilitate exciting encounters with large pelagic (of the open sea) animals. It stirs the imagination.

✓ *Ice Diver*: most shy away from the cold water but the increased visibility (in fresh water lakes) and the ability to get a closer view of underwater fauna, not to mention skiing back to the hole upside down on the underside of the ice, makes for an interesting specialty.

✓ *Cavern Diver:* learn the safe way to explore those caverns you often find. It also gives the diver a taste of what cave diving is about.

✓ *Dry Suit Diver:* your diving buddies are shivering and wet while you are warm and dry. Some 'purists' hiss through their chattering teeth that dry suit diving is not real diving.

✓ *Nitrox (Enriched Air Nitrox) Diver:* for a little longer stay at depth (but NOT for going deeper), and to help toward eliminating that 'after-dive headache', get trained in the use of the "old wheezing geezer's gas" or nitrox (compressed air (see Question 17) with an increased percentage of oxygen).

✓ *Search and Recovery:* everyone likes a challenge, and finding an item that has been dropped overboard makes for an interesting specialty.

✓ plus: *advanced buoyancy control, altitude diver, cave diver, computer assisted diving, deep diver, drift diver, equipment specialist, limited visibility diving, multi-level diving, oxygen provider, peak performance buoyancy, public safety diver, reef ecology, rescue diver, research diver, river diving, underwater archaeology, underwater ecologist, underwater hunter and collector, underwater navigation,* etc.

Regardless of the specialty that interests you, just be sure you get adequately trained. Being adequately trained increases your enjoyment, knowledge, and safety (see Question 48).

13. Can I make a living SCUBA diving?

Yes you can, but the self-fulfillment, necessary training, pay, and difficulty of the work varies widely, depending on your financial needs, your investment in training and equipment (see Question 92), type of diving required, and location. Because of the variety of diving vocations, discussing the depth and breadth of the subject is beyond the scope of this book. I will introduce the subject of *commercial diving* and give you some additional vocational ideas. Note that many of the diving related jobs can even be done part-time, e.g., Divemaster, Instructor, Search and Rescue, specimen collection, etc.

Commercial diving appears to be a mixed bag. Once you have the experience, then the pay is good. Yet the hours can be long and the work strenuous. The commercial diver is generally thought of as an underwater construction worker. The four primary ACDE (Association of Commercial Diver Educators) accredited schools are the College of Oceaneering, Divers Academy of Eastern Seaboard, Divers Institute of Technology, and The Ocean Corporation. There are a number of other schools, but the one that stands out is the Louisiana Technical College Young Memorial Campus as being inexpensive, but offering good training.

If you start working offshore as a commercial diver, expect to make about $6 to $8 an hour for the first couple of years as a Tender. The rate goes up to $10 to $15 an hour when you actually start to dive. Apparently, depth and saturation pay is the only way to make a good living and forget that past 40 years old. If you choose to dive inland waters, then you can get in the water after a month or so with higher pay, depending of course upon the location and type of job. Consider working for the Carpenter/Piledrivers union.

Commercial diving can be dangerous. The following quote is from the June 1998 weekly mortality report from the U.S. Centers for Disease Control and Prevention. "Of the 116 occupational diving fatalities reported to OSHA for 1989-1997, 49 occurred among an estimated 3,000 full-time commercial divers, ... The average of five deaths per year corresponds to a rate of 180 deaths per 100,000 employed divers per year, which is 40 times the national average death rate for all workers."

If you are still interested in commercial diving, you are advised to talk to those that are currently employed as such and get more information from such web sites as the National Association of Commercial Divers at http://www.naocd.org and Dive Web at http://www.diveweb.com/commdive/index.shtml.

The recreational SCUBA diving segment of the industry is undoubtedly the largest employer. This segment of the industry includes, but is not limited to, *Divemasters, Assistant Instructors, Instructors, sales personnel, dive shop owners, dive boat concessionaires, dive resorts, travel agents, dive equipment manufacturing and repair, and diver-related media personnel, including authors, publishers,* etc.

Underwater photography, videography, and cinematography can be both challenging and rewarding. Becoming a Mike Nelson or a James Bond *stunt double* is also a way to make a living while diving. Of course, *industry has need for divers, as does technical and research projects.* How about joining *the Navy as a S.E.A.L. or the Coast Guard as a Rescue Diver? Police departments and the government have need of divers.*

Freelance divers, who are appropriately trained, make a living from gathering golf balls, scraping boat hulls, maintaining and repairing boats, conducting surveys, salvage diving, specimen collecting, etc. You can also get a job diving for adventure programs and management training seminars. The list goes on.

However, one thing is very clear: a professional diver is trained as such. If you go beyond recreational SCUBA diving, then you must get the training, have the appropriate equipment and personnel, and not dive beyond your training and capabilities. Those who seek the services of a diver are often not aware of the special considerations involved. You, being the professional, must be. It is your life on the line.

Three of the basic open water certification agencies clearly state that being a certified open water SCUBA diver does not give you the training you need for commercial operations. To wit, NAUI (National Association of Underwater Instructors) in 1995 stated, "The official position of NAUI is that personnel training courses and resulting certification endorsed by this organization are intended solely for the practice of recreational diving. NAUI certification does not entitle an individual (unless other formal commercial diving training has been received as set forth in ANSI/ACDE 01-1993) to conduct commercial diving operations."[T]

PADI (Professional Association of Dive Instructors) in 1997 concurred by stating, "It is our opinion that individuals who hold PADI certification credentials and wish to enter into a commercial diving employment situation (i.e. underwater work including umbilical, light or heavy weight equipment, etc.) would need to demonstrate documentation or additional specialized training and expertise to do so safely. Recreational diving certification by PADI alone should not be considered as adequate training in bidding for underwater work of the nature described in your standards of operation."[T]

Additionally, the YMCA (Young Men's Christian Association) stated in 1995, "The recreational dive industry has established a criteria for a minimum standard of instruction and through its secretariat, RSTC (Recreational SCUBA Training Council), this standard was adopted by ANSI (American National Standards Institute). The commercial dive industry has established a criteria for a minimum standard of instruction and through its secretariat, ACDE (Association of Commercial Diving Educators), this standard was adopted by ANSI. The need for two different standards is as a result of entirely different training objectives, recreational and commercial. These standards are for the safety of the student plus define the level of certification the diver can safely perform. The YMCA SCUBA Program is dedicated to training recreational divers. We recognize and support the clear distinction of recreational diving and commercial diving as set forth by the standards in which they are trained. A YMCA recreational diving certificate does not represent the training required to safely perform in the commercial diving industry."[T]

Enough said.

14. How does diving in freshwater compare to saltwater?

When many think of recreational SCUBA diving, they think of saltwater diving. Yet freshwater diving can be just as rewarding and, for some, the only locally available diving. With additional training, freshwater diving can be done in caves, lakes, mines, quarries, rivers, sandpits, sinkholes, springs, swamps, etc. Dives in freshwater can differ from those in saltwater in a number of ways, but there are also a lot of similarities. Some of the more contrasting features of diving in freshwater vs. saltwater are presented in Listing G.

Listing G. Comparison of Diving in Freshwater vs. Saltwater.

☸ *Freshwater is about 3 percent less dense than saltwater* (a cubic foot of saltwater weights 64.0 pounds, whereas a cubic foot of freshwater weights 62.4 pounds). Thus, a freshwater diver should weight themselves about 3 percent less (3 percent of total weight, including gear) than when diving in saltwater {a heavy but smart dieter will weigh themselves in saltwater}.

☸ When diving *in freshwater,* the diver generally has to deal with *less visibility (vis) than when diving in saltwater.* However, do not tell that to divers who dive in crystal clear springs in Florida, as contrasted to low vis saltwater shore diving. Algae blooms may be a more common occurrence in freshwater but can also occur in saltwater, as does silting and pollution, all potentially affecting visibility.

☸ *Freshwater lakes tend to be colder than the oceans* that are commonly frequented by the vacationing recreational SCUBA diver. Yet, diving in thermal springs, shallow sun warmed waters of the Southwestern U.S., or lakes used in cooling power plants is thermally a more enjoyable experience than diving in some areas with 55° F ocean waters.

☸ *Thermoclines* (an abrupt change in temperature between two layers of water that can negatively impact visibility) tend to be *more predictable in freshwater lakes than oceans.*

☸ *Diving fresh water rivers may subject the diver to more current than open saltwater divers* commonly experience.

Here again, diving freshwater lakes vs. diving saltwater tidal flows, rip currents, downwellings, and some saltwater drift diving would reverse this generality. Note that the novice diver should not dive in significant current (greater than a couple of knots), whether it occurs in freshwater or saltwater, until they are adequately trained. Even prolonged swimming against a one knot (100 feet in one minute) current can exhaust a diver.

ⓞ *The flora and fauna is typically less diverse and colorful in freshwater as compared to saltwater.* Yet there certainly are dive sites (see Question 114) where the reverse holds true.

ⓞ *Altitude diving is more readily available in freshwater than saltwater.* The density difference between freshwater and saltwater amounts to a depth difference of about 3 feet for a 100-foot dive. This and many other factors make additional training necessary for altitude diving. Do not dive at greater than 1000 feet above sea level unless adequately trained in altitude diving.

ⓞ *Freshwater tends to preserve objects submerged in it much better than saltwater.* This enables the diver to find artifacts in freshwater that are hundreds of years old, yet they appear to be in near original condition.

Maybe the similarities between the two environments should be mentioned also. In both fresh and saltwater the diver can dive wrecks, engage in underwater photography, spear fish (check local regulations), ice dive, cave dive, deep dive, night dive, engage in search and rescue, hunt for treasure, use nitrox, etc.

The important thing to remember regarding either freshwater or saltwater diving is that either environment contains water. Though different to some degree, they both offer us the chance to dive and explore new worlds. Enjoy your dive!

15. How about some ocean trivia?

The world's oceans cover 71 percent of the surface of our earth, equating to about 142,000,000 square miles. In terms of volume, that is approximately 328,000,000 cubic miles of seawater. That is a lot of area to explore! The Pacific Ocean, at 63.8 million square miles, is the largest body of water on the planet and covers 40 percent of the world's surface. The Pacific Ocean is also the deepest with the Mariana Trench (36,373 feet), which is located near Guam.

There are three broad categories for life that call water home. One category is *plankton* which includes the plants (phytoplankton) and the animals (zooplankton) which drift about with the current. Plankton comprise some of the smallest life in the ocean. Another category is *nekton*, which consists of animals that can swim about under their own power (this includes some 13,300 species of fish). The final category is *benthos*, which includes the bottom-living (sessile) plants and animals. And, of course, it gets taxinomically a lot more complex within each of those categories.

The biggest fish on the planet is the whale shark, measuring to some 40+ feet and weighing 15+ tons. They eat plankton, the smallest stuff in the ocean...go figure. In the Sea of Cortez, near La Paz, Mexico, I had the opportunity to have a roughly 15-foot whale shark pass right underneath me, not 6 feet away. Talk about a rush! Very kewl. However, for really big, the blue whale is the largest animal ever to live on this planet and weights in at 200+ tons and measures some 110 feet in length (see Question 41).

16. What is in that SCUBA tank?

The air in the basic open water recreational SCUBA diver's tank (see Question 35 and Question 96) is simply the air you normally breathe that has been filtered and compressed. The contents of the air we breathe, and thus the contents of the basic open water recreational SCUBA diver's tank, is 21 percent oxygen, 78 percent nitrogen and about 1 percent other gases.

It is critical that the air being compressed into your SCUBA cylinder be filtered and unadulterated with carbon monoxide and other contaminants. Though a rare occurance, in 1997 two divers died by breathing from tanks contaminated with carbon monoxide from a malfunctioning compressor.[C] Be sure to obtain your air from reputable sources that have their air compressor facilities regularly checked.

With additional training, the diver can use a higher concentration of oxygen (nitrox or EAN (Enriched Air Nitrox)) and combinations of other gases suitable to more 'technical' diving. You must get the additional training because breathing elevated concentrations of oxygen at depth can cause oxygen toxicity. The probability of a diver experiencing oxygen toxicity increases substantially above 1.6 ATA (Atmosphere Absolute (see Glossary)) of oxygen (some use 1.4 ATA). Diving with 100 percent oxygen would subject the diver to oxygen toxicity below about 20 fsw (feet seawater), whereas the air we breathe (21 percent oxygen) can lead to the diver exhibiting oxygen toxicity at around 200 fsw.

Oxygen toxicity comes on quickly and causes seizures in a diver and may culminate in a drowning. Increase your likelihood of living to dive another day. Do not dive deeper than 180 feet on normoxic air![II] Fortunately, if the diver is able to ascend then the symptoms of oxygen toxicity will subside.

To further clarify, nitrox is any mixture of nitrogen and oxygen (though in diving the oxygen concentration is usually greater than 21 percent) and it is not the same as nitrous oxide (N_2O). Nitrous oxide is an anesthetic and is sometimes foolishly used as a recreational inhalant for 'getting high'.

17. Why is there air and what is air made of?

Mr. Bill Cosby once said many years ago in his "The Chicken Heart that Ate New York" LP album, the reason there is air is to blow up volleyballs. I would like to modify that slightly and suggest that *there is air so we can fill SCUBA tanks.*

The air we breathe, and with which your SCUBA tank will be filled, is *composed of 78.084 percent nitrogen, 20.948 percent oxygen, 0.934 percent argon, 0.031 percent carbon dioxide, and 0.003 percent other gases such as helium, hydrogen, krypton, methane, neon, nitrous oxide, ozone, and xenon.*

As you become a more proficient diver, you may want to become nitrox or Enriched Air Nitrox (EAN) certified, where the percentage of oxygen in your SCUBA cylinder is increased. Increasing the oxygen content tends to extend your bottom time a little. Nitrox alone does NOT enable you to dive deeper nor should you use it for that purpose (remember oxygen toxicity! (see Question 16)). Some (including myself) claim nitrox makes you feel a little better and gives you a bit more energy {some divers with less respect for their elders call nitrox the "old wheezing geeser's gas"}. See Question 85 for more information on nitrox.

18. Can I indulge in some of my vices underwater?

Even though recreational SCUBA diving is enjoyable, the advisability of indulging in your vices while diving is dependent upon what those vices may be.

If you are a heavy drinker, then another avocation would surely suit you better. Alcohol dehydrates you, there is the impaired mental capacity to contend with, the long and short term physical affects, and your pressure gauge is difficult to read if it is shaking. Sucking compressed dry air and being immersed for several hours a day is bad enough, but add alcohol and you are desiccated. Do not drink and dive. Even heavy drinking the night before is ill advised.

Obviously, smoking plugs up the alveoli {unless you are like Clinton and do not inhale ;p}, and it carries carbon monoxide that binds with your red blood cells, decreasing their oxygen carrying capacity. In fact, the average inhalation of a cigarette contains about 500 parts-per-million (ppm) CO. Smoking a cigarette just before a dive will make 3 to 7 percent of your hemoglobin unable to carry oxygen.[II] Your oxygen carrying capacity will be reduced at gradually lessening rates for 5 to 8 hours post cig. Smoking also decreases one's stamina. Smoking tends to increase the likelihood of lung over-expansion injuries due to emphysema and has also been shown to do bad things {scientific terminology} to the heart. *Smoking alone may not keep you from diving (consult a SCUBA savvy Physician) but it is counter-productive and could even be dangerous.*

For you Pot Heads, maybe watching the sunset on the beach would be better than going down when high. It has apparently been shown that marijuana decreases a skin diver's breath-hold ability by up to 75 percent and reduces heat loss tolerance by up to 90 percent. The effects of marijuana are greatly dependent upon the diver's depth.[L]

Illegal drugs, some prescription, and even over-the-counter drugs can get you into serious trouble if used in concert with SCUBA diving. Drugs that have one effect on the surface, may have entirely different or enhanced effects at depth. Drugs, including caffeine, decongestants, pain relievers, and stimulants, can cause cardiac dysrhythmias. The effect of drugs that induce drowsiness may be magnified to the point of unconsciousness in a diver when at depth.[K]   Consult your Physician or Pharmacist before diving while taking any drugs. You will learn more about drugs {but not how to obtain them} in your open water SCUBA class (see Question 76).

OK, I can hear you now, "Well that's fine but there are no vices left!" Well, actually there are a few. In your SCUBA class you will learn how to:

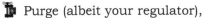

- Purge (albeit your regulator),
- be slothful underwater (that is relax, be one with the water (dive ala Zen), and of course being a drifter while drift diving),
- some of the best diving can be done on Sunday (but then any day is a great day) {after church of course!?},
- SCUBA will enhance your fishing skills or maybe you will lose interest in that 'vice'. Personally, I have found that when you are down there amongst them, eyeball to eyeball, catching them via hook and line seems to have lost some of its thrill. For others, it enhances it. To each their own.

OK, there are not a lot of vices {sex is not a vice unless you are a police officer} you can indulge in underwater, but think of the clean and healthy people you will be diving with!

19. Once certified, how do I avoid SCUBA burnout?

We all have friends who got certified, but for one reason or another eventually stopped diving. This could concern you, as you do not want to spend the time and money getting certified, buying equipment (see Question 70), etc. if you are eventually going to lose interest.

So why do divers lose interest? The answer to that question is likely as varied as to what motivates us. Some of the reasons people give up diving, along with ways to avoid burnout or to rekindle the diving flame, are found in Listing H.

Listing H. How to Rekindle the Diving Flame.

✳ Problem: Getting ready to go diving is a lot of effort.
Solution: *Store your gear properly and in one place.* Create a system and equipment lists (see Question 93) for gathering together gear that has to be stored separately or is consumable. Use protective liners, bungie cords, and plastic bins in your vehicle for transporting gear. Set up a system so that you can spend your time diving, not getting ready to dive. Of course equipment, tech, and organization freaks love the getting ready part. So, for them, take as much time as you like.

✳ Problem: It has been such a long time since I have been diving, my skills are just not up to snuff.
Solution: *Take a SCUBA refresher or review course.* These courses are very likely offered by the same agency with which you initially certified. These courses generally begin with a 'classroom' knowledge refresher and progress to in-water refreshing of primary SCUBA skills. The diver practices diving skills while supervised and after completion generally receives a SCUBA Review decal to be placed on their C-card. You do not need to get certified all over again, and you will find that your diving skills will quickly return. Contact your open water Instructor or local dive shop for more information.

✳ Problem: I love to dive, but I just do not like all the inconveniences of the outdoors that I have to endure to dive.

Solution: *Try a live aboard or sleep-aboard.* Find ones with warm running water, comfortable rooms, great meals, and beautiful dive sites (see Question 114).

✳ Problem: I just do not think about diving. I have gotten out of the habit of going.

Solution: *Keep your SCUBA gear by the front door so you almost have to trip over it; ah, trip, SCUBA dive-trip!* Not only will that keep you from forgetting about SCUBA, but it will also make for great conversation. You never know, that Jehovah Witness or door-to-door salesperson may like to dive and they could even make a good dive buddy. You might also clip photos from magazines and place them around your office as a reminder. Replace that Hooters or Studs calendar with a diving calendar; ok, have two calendars then. Subscribe to SCUBA diving magazines (see 'SCUBA Periodicals' section for addresses). Buy some diving-related books and place them on the coffee table. Better yet: read them.

✳ Problem: Been there, done that.

Solution: *If you have become bored with the same old diving, then take a road trip or get training in a specialty which can be used locally.* Wreck diving is very popular, particularly on the East Coast and the Great Lakes. If you are not wreck certified, then you are missing out on some great diving. How about underwater photography? To get you started, you can get a new underwater camera with flash for less than $160. Having a few of your better photos taped to the computer or refrigerator stirs the diving juices. Or maybe get further training and go night diving? Your local dive spot will be transformed. Plan some exotic trips and go dive them. How about some new equipment to play with such as underwater scooters. See your local dealer or check out http://www.torpedodpv.com and www.seascooters.com.

✳ Problem: I ain't got no buddy to call my own (see Question 45).

Solution: *Expand your circle of friends and talk up SCUBA.* You will be surprised who is certified but you just did not know it. Go down to your local dive shops and join their diver clubs. There are even national dive clubs. Scuba Duba at www.scubaduba.com has a pretty good list of diving buddies. Use one or more of the Internet searchers and search for "dive buddies". You will be amazed at how many sites there are. Talk it over with family members and get them involved in diving. If your spouse dives, then you have solved two potential problems (see Question 63).

✳ Problem: My gear does not fit or work or is outdated or ...
Solution: *Make sure you buy quality equipment that fits comfortably.* Fins that create blisters, wet suits that are too tight, BCs that are too big, and an ill-fitting regulator mouthpiece all make for an uncomfortable dive. Seek advice from your local dive shop and get good fitting equipment. Look for package deals or work out one of your own with a dive shop. It makes a big difference in your comfort and enthusiasm for SCUBA, not to mention being safer.

✳ Problem: I have a problem with an underwater skill and do not feel comfortable diving.
Solution: *Get remedial training or assistance* from a certified diving professional such as your Instructor, an Assistant Instructor, or a Divemaster. If you know what you are doing wrong, but just need more practice, then how about diving in the pool or a sheltered, shallow dive site?

✳ Problem: Diving is just too expensive.
Solution: *Diving need not be expensive,* see Question 113. Use business trips as the means of getting to the dive site and then all you have to bring is some of your gear (plan on renting what you need to minimize the hassles). A late afternoon business meeting means you have all morning to dive! When you go on that dive vacation, you can book reasonable accommodations and fix your own meals. If you need to save up, then put aside a percentage or fixed amount each pay day. You will be amazed at what $25 a week will add up to in a year with compounded interest or a good stock pick. One of the secrets of accumulating wealth (for whatever purpose) is to pay yourself first. Maybe use automatic payroll deductions or start a 'Christmas Account' at your Credit Union {they do not usually have 'SCUBA Accounts' – but should!}. Go on your dream dive in the 'off' season. To make your money go further, be prepared to go to places that may be experiencing a downturn in their economy. As groups often get significant price breaks, go

on that dive vacation with a dive group. You may even be able to start a business or become involved in tax-deductible activities or organizations, which would take some of the financial bite out of that shark-feeding dive vacation.

Using some ingenuity and forethought, most of the excuses for not diving can be solved. As stated in Question 4, SCUBA is not for everyone, but for those who can dive, it is a darn shame to give up an avocation that has so much to offer!

20. How can I e a s e into SCUBA certification?

For those not wanting to immediately take the plunge into SCUBA, there are a number of ways you can work up to it. Each of the certifying organizations has a little bit different terminology regarding the courses they offer, but they basically are: *snorkeling, non-certification resort courses, and introduction to or discover SCUBA courses.* Additionally, there is the  *referral system where you can complete your certification while on vacation.*

Snorkeling is popular because of the minimal equipment, training, and physical effort involved, and it introduces individuals and families to the beauty of the underwater world. For those who have not tried it, snorkeling is basically floating face down and breathing through a tube, or snorkel, that extends from your mouth to above the surface of the water.

 Even if you do not think you need the training, it is often helpful to know where to dive and have a guided tour of the area. Another great thing about snorkeling is that the mask, fins, booties, snorkel and even exposure suit (if any) you buy can be used when you decide to take up SCUBA diving (see Question 70). As there is no age requirement, snorkeling can be a recreational activity shared by the entire family.

The non-certification courses enable you to actually use SCUBA equipment, but under close supervision. Some of these programs even let you try SCUBA diving in the swimming pool. This takes a minimal amount of time and is popular in places that may not have an open water SCUBA diving area close by.

The Discover SCUBA or Resort courses enable you to make a shallow SCUBA dive while supervised by a certified Instructor. These dives are typically made after a short classroom and/or pool session to familiarize you with the equipment and techniques involved. These courses vary widely in length and content, but typically are only a few hours to a day in duration. These courses can be the quickest way to get in the water and see whether you like it. Another good thing about these courses is that when you do take your open water certification course, you will be just that much more familiar and relaxed with the equipment and breathing underwater. Prices vary, but these courses are usually in the $125 range.

The disadvantage of these Discover or Resort courses is that after you spend the money and time, you are not certified for open water SCUBA diving. Resort courses generally use no textbook and give you very little in the way of diving theory or skills testing. If you decide you want to pursue diving, then you will still need to take a full open water course to get certified. Resort courses are generally good only for that resort and for the time you are a guest there.

Another way to ease into SCUBA is to get certified while on that relaxing vacation. Those courses vary somewhat, but typically are three-to-five days in length with reading assignments in the evening. This is popular with workaholics who will not take the time unless it is vacation time or with others who just want to learn in a relaxing setting.

If you want to get certified while on vacation, a better way to do it may be to get the classroom and pool sessions out of the way at home while it is snowing outside. Then, get a referral from your Instructor for the open water portion of your training during your vacation. The referral from your Instructor states that you have completed the classroom and pool portions of certification. Most dive resorts have Instructors who would be happy to do the open water dives with you for a relatively small fee. This way, you will have the maximum amount of diving time in beautiful, clear, warm water. You may be able to rent most of your gear while on vacation, but you probably should at least bring your own mask, fins, booties, and snorkel.

A relatively new concept (as of May 1, 1999), is that divers who started their certification with IDEA, NASDS, NAUI, PDIC, SSI, and YMCA will be able to complete the required open water dives while on vacation at Club Med. Club Med is not just a dive resort, thus making this concept a hybrid between a resort course and getting a referral to a dive resort. It will be interesting to see how many divers avail them selves of this option.

If easing into SCUBA gives you the added benefits of being comfortable in the water then by all means e a s e on in.

21. What are my chances of getting back aboard the boat alive?

You are likely in greater danger driving to and from the dive boat or dive site (see Question 115) than actually diving. Certainly, there are potential hazards related to SCUBA diving but that is why you get the training and certification (see Question 69). As long as you get trained, dive smart and use common sense, recreational SCUBA diving (RSD) is relatively safe. In fact, for a trained and certified individual (see Question 6), *RSD has a lower incidence of injury than snow skiing, water skiing, racquetball, or volleyball, about the same rate as fishing, and just a little higher than golf and tennis.*[S]

It is estimated (as no one knows for sure) that there are somewhere in the neighborhood of 17,000,000 to 21,000,000 dives made in the U.S. each year. In data collected in 1996 for the U.S., Divers Alert Network (DAN) reported 85 RSD fatalities, and in 1997 there were 82 RSD fatalities. That is a fatality rate, during those two years, of approximately .0004 percent per dive or about one fatality for every 235,000 dives (see Question 23 for additional injury statistics). Experiencing recreational SCUBA diving is certainly worth the risks (see Question 3).

Please note that the above fatality rate is for <u>all</u> divers and applies most accurately to the 'average' diver. However, divers who dive more cautiously, dive with appropriate and well-maintained equipment, are physically fit, and are better trained to handle hazardous diving situations appropriately will have a much lower fatality rate (see Question 48). Hazards that every SCUBA diver must be aware of include: decompression sickness, air embolism, hypothermia, physical exhaustion, injuries from marine life, boating accidents (see Question 30), sunburn, entrapment, panic, and an out-of-air (OOA) (see Question 34) experience. The most serious problems, and how to avoid them, will be covered in your open water SCUBA certification course.

The primary factors that increase your likelihood of making it back up the dive ladder or shoreline are listed in Listing I.

Listing I. Primary Factors Which Decrease SCUBA Diving Risks.

🍂 *Be trained for the dive* (or dive with an instructor for that purpose),

🍂 *do not dive beyond your training and do not become overconfident,*

🍂 *apply the training,*

🍂 dive with *well-maintained and familiar equipment,*

🍂 *dive with a buddy* (see Question 45),

🍂 *do not dive if you have reservations about the dive* (environmental factors too extreme),

🍂 be reasonably *physically fit,*

🍂 *closely monitor your and your buddy's air,*

🍂 *do not panic* (use your head), and

🍂 for heavens sake .. *HAVE FUN!*

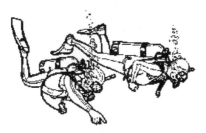

Recognize that no matter who you are and how well trained you are, there are dives that are not safe and are beyond your personal ability, training, and/or equipment (see Question 92). Finally, some dives are just flat-out more dangerous than others. Again, your certification course should train you to recognize your limitations and to dive within those limitations.

22. What one thing should I fear most in the water?

In my opinion, the biggest thing to fear underwater is a diver's inappropriate decision made before, during, or after the dive.

Running out of air, lack of buoyancy control, and entrapment are the primary factors affecting diving fatalities.[J]   To maximize diving safety, avoid or be prepared for out-of-air (OOA) emergencies, develop a high degree of buoyancy control, and avoid entrapment (see Question 48). These capabilities are introduced in your SCUBA course and reinforced and perfected by experience.

Following the admonitions in Listing J should help you decrease the likelihood of your making less-than-optimal decisions.

Listing J. Ways to Avoid Making Inappropriate Dive Decisions.
? *Be properly trained and stay current in your training.* Diving should be fun and relaxing. If you know what to do, then the likelihood that you will make the wrong decision decreases.
? If you are *not feeling good, stay out* of the water.
? *Do not do dives that are too advanced* for your training.
? If some *critical piece of equipment is malfunctioning, stay out of the water until it is repaired or replaced.*
? *If it stings or has big teeth, then do not touch it.*
? *Do not drink and dive.* One of the worst SCUBA diving accidents on record was due, in part, to heavy drinking and the use of illegal drugs. To make a long story short, after a night of heavy drinking and drugs, the eight Americans were hung over, unorganized, and only partially equipped. Regardless, they went for what was supposed to be a

shallow reef dive, but by the time everyone was 'ready', the boat had drifted off the reef and over the deep blue. The four pairs of divers (including a Divemaster and group leader) soon drifted apart and continued to <u>unthinkingly descend</u>. Finally recognizing the problem, the group leader alerted the nearby father and son pair who then ascended, then he dove after the male pair of divers. The group leader finally got them to begin ascending at nearly 250 feet! In the meantime, the Divemaster went after the female pair. After an apparent air-sharing struggle at immense depth, the Divemaster surfaced dead with a massive AGE (arterial gas embolism). The women divers were never found. Three dead and two survivors who had treatable DCI (decompression illness) - a totally unnecessary tragedy. If only they had paid attention to their depth gauges, the solution was that simple. Do not drink and do drugs if you dive! The complete story can be found on Rodale's Scuba Diving magazine web site at http://www.scubadiving.com/training/lessons/march.shtml.

? If conditions get *too rough, calmly get out.*
? *Stop, breathe, think, then act.*

Remember when you first learned to drive a car and how hard it was? The amount of concentration it took? I remember having to turn off the rock 'n' roll station when first driving with my Dad. I did not want to make an inappropriate decision with the 'key controller' in the auto. Now {hopefully} it is practically second nature. The same will become true with diving. However, just like in driving, do not become complacent, careless, or inattentive.

23. What injuries are most likely when SCUBA diving?

The good news is that, statistically, the accident rate for SCUBA diving is well below that of snow skiing or mountain biking and even lower than American football, baseball, water skiing, soccer, volleyball, and racquetball.[S] The not-so-great but obvious news is that because SCUBA diving takes place underwater, the consequences can be more severe. *Some of the types of injuries received while engaged in SCUBA diving are those associated with travel, being outdoors, inflicted by the underwater flora and fauna, and decompression illnesses.*

As most of us have to travel to get to that great dive site, there is a certain risk of injury during traveling. On the other hand, traveling enables us to get away from the day-to-day grind and enjoy that turquoise water and white sandy beach (or that little explored underwater cave (if adequately trained)). Take the usual precautions while traveling. Get the rest you need, keep hydrated, and be kind to your digestive system.

Injuries do happen at the dive site, or just being outdoors, which are not related directly to SCUBA diving. Such injuries include sunburn, boating accidents (see Question 30), and food poisoning. Some food poisonings include: 1) Ciguatera poisoning, which is the result of eating fish that ate specific species of algae, 2) Scomboid poisoning, which is the result of eating fish not kept chilled, and the most serious 3) Tetrodotoxin poisoning from eating fish such as the pufferfish or blowfish. Watch what you eat at that beach party.

Injuries can be inflicted by some of the underwater inhabitants simply because we come in contact with them, or worse, because we threaten or annoy them. The most common such injuries are from fire coral, anemones, jellyfish, some sea cucumbers, some sea sponges, bristle worm, etc. Most of these stings respond well to first aid. Check with locals regarding specific first aid but generally wash all wounds, bites, and stings (except jellyfish) with freshwater. Jellyfish stings should be washed in saltwater (though you will get arguments on that advice). Then soak the wound from the Coelenterates (corals, anemones, jellyfish, etc.) in white vinegar.[V]

The best way to protect yourself from the flora and fauna is to keep your body parts to yourself and cover up while diving (with a dive skin and gloves if nothing else). If you do not know what something is, then leave it alone. Look and take pictures, but do not touch. It is generally NOT a marine petting zoo down there! However, if an eel comes out and obviously asks for a belly rub it would be poor form not to oblige it. Otherwise, if it is poisonous then leave it alone!

Be careful of hand placement, turning over rocks {which some would argue you should not do anyway}, and diving at night. Maintain neutral buoyancy. Be wary of very colorful or conspicuous plants and animals as they likely show off with the brilliant displays because they are poisonous. If possible, get an orientation dive and consult local divers or dive shop about the local dangers and remedies.

As to the more specifically SCUBA-related injuries, DAN (Divers Alert Network) reports that of the decompression illness (DCI) accidents treated in 1996, there were 122 cases of Type I decompression sickness (DCS), 303 cases of the more serious Type II DCS, and 58 cases of arterial gas embolism (AGE). See the 'Glossary' section for the definition of terms and description of symptoms. For 1997 the numbers were 111 Type I DCS, 302 Type II DCS, and 39 AGEs.

Thus, for 1996, there were a total of 483 DCI accidents, and in 1997 there were 452. Of course, not all DCI accidents are reported and not all divers get treatment, but assuming (picking a number) some 750 DCI-type accidents per year and using 19,000,000 dives per year, that is an incident rate of 0.004 percent per dive, or one dive in about 25,500. If you will follow the advice given you during your SCUBA training, read further on avoiding DCI (see Question 39), and dive conservatively, you will further minimize the probability you will make DAN's DCI list.

24. What kills recreational SCUBA divers?

While reading the answer to this question, it is important to keep in mind that recreational SCUBA diving (RSD) has a very low dive fatality ratio of approximately 0.0004 percent (see Question 21). Of course, this low dive fatality ratio is of little comfort for those that make up that statistic. But for the rest of us, it is reassuring that done properly, RSD is relatively safe, though certainly not without risk (see Question 48).

In addition to their own experiences, a wise person learns from those of others (tragic though they are). It is my opinion that every diver should be a member of DAN (see Question 89 on DAN membership) and every diver should read through at least one edition of DAN's yearly report entitled, "Report on Decompression Illness and Diving Fatalities". Copies of the complete DAN report are available to DAN members for $22 (plus $5.75 shipping) and to non-members for $25 (plus shipping). Call (800) 446-2671 or (919) 684-2948 and get your copy. The title of the report accurately summarizes its content and it is tallied for all U.S. residents whether they were diving in or out of the U.S. While reading DAN's report, keep in mind the low dive fatality ratio and assimilate the information DAN presents to make you a better and more cautious diver, not a more paranoid one.

It could be argued that the information would tend to dissuade the prospective student or the new diver from continued diving, and that they should not read it until additional experience and confidence is gained. On the other hand, of the 11 student fatalities for 1997 (out of a total of 82), four occurred during open water certification, two were persons involved in a SCUBA familiarization class, and five were divers taking advanced training. This indicates to me that the student should be made aware of where the risks of diving occur so as to avoid them. This point is further supported as some 41 percent of the diving fatalities for 1997 involved divers with 20 or fewer dives. I believe the inexperienced diver would benefit from reading DAN's report, as long as the information was kept in perspective.

In addition to DAN's report, you can learn from Jon Hardy's column in Rodale's Scuba Diving magazine (see 'SCUBA

Periodicals' section for subscription information) entitled "Lessons for Life". In his column, Jon reports on SCUBA accidents and presents the lessons that can be learned from them. Some of the past "Lessons for Life" columns can be reviewed at http://www.scubadiving.com/training/lessons/. Additional information on diving fatalities can be obtained from the rec.scuba newsgroup (though one should verify the information presented before adopting it as truth).

Dr. Sam Shelanski at http://www.scubadiving.com/training/medicine/divesafety/ maintains that there are four factors behind the majority of the dive accidents. *Those four factors are: panic, not diving intelligently, overconfidence, and not being physically fit* (particularly the cardiovascular system). He makes a convincing case that even though these factors are important, they are preventable.

Dr. Shelanski points out that every year, a significant number of injuries and fatalities are because divers panic underwater. Particularly telling is that panic is the main reason divers make rapid ascents (ascents faster than 60 feet per minute) and some 60 percent of the AGEs (Arterial Gas Embolisms) are due to rapid ascents. He further states that panic was listed as a contributing factor in more than 20 percent of the 1996 dive fatalities (see Question 26 on dealing with stress and panic).

Dr. Shelanski states that the second factor is diving intelligently. Diving intelligently means not letting your exuberance or desires cloud your judgement. Even if you did spend $4,000 and six months of work to get to your paradise dive site (see Question 114), do not keep diving if you experience numbness, difficulty walking and speaking, light-headedness, and coughing up blood (signs and symptoms of actual divers who kept diving). Know the signs and symptoms of DCI (decompression illness) and seek medical treatment if you have them (you will be taught those signs and symptoms in your open water SCUBA class).

The third factor Dr. Shelanski believes causes accidents is overconfidence. In 1996, 46 percent of the DCI injuries and 33 percent of the fatalities were experienced divers, divers having more than 60 lifetime dives. Undoubtedly, some of those fatalities were due to complacency and "pushing the envelope" (diving beyond the diver's capabilities).

The final factor, according to Dr. Shelanski, is cardiovascular problems manifesting themselves while diving. For the past decade, some 26 percent of the diving fatalities involving divers over the age of 35 listed cardiovascular disease as the leading or significant contributing cause of death. Divers who do not get daily physical activity may not know their limitations. Well-known risk factors for heart disease are age (males over 45 and post-menopausal females), smoking, high blood pressure, diabetes, family members with heart disease, and high cholesterol. Get regular checkups and stay as physically fit as possible. See a dive Physician if you have any questions.

DAN's 1999 Report on Decompression Illness and Diving Fatalities, states that cardiovascular disease and inexperience are the two primary contributing factors in diving fatalities. This finding supports Dr. Shelanski's belief that panic and lack of intelligent decision-making, as well as cardiovascular disease, are among the leading factors in diving accidents.

A final thought on this subject: if you value any material thing more than your life, then leave it at home when you dive. You do not want to reflexively go diving in after a prescription facemask, a camera, or spear gun that you lose over the side of the boat. This behavior has caused death in divers who dive in with just their weight belts on, with minimal air, with air turned off, over very deep sites, or into nets snagged underwater. If there is a sign that says "Underwater Intake/Suction" then stay away from that area! Think about Dr. Shelanski's second factor: dive intelligently. Think before you act.

25. Won't sharks or giant squid eat me or want a taste?

First there was Jaw$ (and its sequal$), then Deep Blue $ea, and next Hollywood will have sharks running for congress. Then again, probably not ... too close to reality. Anyway, the Jaw$ genera of Hollywood flicks are just that, Hollywood flicks made to make a buck and raise the hair on the back of your neck (it seems most humans like to be frightened). However, according to noted shark expert, Dr. Eugenie Clark, "Driving your car to work in the morning if far more dangerous {than diving and being attacked by a shark}."[A]

It has been estimated that there are between 2.5 and 3.5 million Americans participating in recreational SCUBA diving, with another 500,000 becoming certified each year in the U.S.[EE] The Diving Equipment & Marketing Association (DEMA), a SCUBA trade group, estimates that there are some 17 million dives made in the U.S. each year.[D]

Let's leave all the hype behind and look at the facts. An excellent web site for those interested in shark attack data and from which the shark attack data presented herein was abstracted is http://www.flmnh.ufl.edu/fish/sharks/statistics/statistics.htm#divers.

Since 1980, there have been, on the average, 38 confirmed unprovoked shark attacks on humans per year, worldwide. Only about 13 percent of those attacks (19 percent for divers) resulted in death. Some 33 percent of the attacks were off U.S. waters, 22 percent off Australian waters and 19 percent off the Pacific Ocean Islands (particularly Hawaii and Fiji).

Worldwide, the incidence of shark attacks during the past three decades has increased dramatically for surfers, stayed approximately the same for swimmers, and increased moderately (2 percent per year) for divers. During the 1990s, surfers worldwide suffered the majority of the shark attacks with about 19 attacks a year. Divers were attacked about 7 times a year and swimmers about 5 times. *It can be seen that considering the millions of people, who venture into the ocean each year, shark attacks are very rare. More people are killed by lightning or bee stings each year than by sharks.*

Reviewing the data specifically for divers (includes all types of diving not just recreational SCUBA), it can be seen that in U.S. waters there are less than 3 fatalities a year due to shark attacks. If we use DEMA's estimates of 17 million dives made in the U.S. per year, and if we assume some 2 fatalities a year for recreational SCUBA divers. Then your probability of being fatally bitten by a shark while SCUBA diving in U.S. waters, averages some 0.000012 percent on any given dive. Of course, the average is much less in freshwater lakes {essentially zero}, lower in freshwater rivers flowing into the ocean, and higher in the ocean.

If you want to dive and just do not want to see sharks, then restrict your diving to landlocked freshwater lakes with no sharks. Yet if you do, you are missing out on a lot of great diving around the world.

Interestingly, if you want to further minimize your risk of ending up a shark's menu item, spend most of your dive time below 50 feet, as 86 percent of the shark attacks on divers occurred above 50 feet. Also, be aware that most of the shark attacks are by individual sharks, and they definitely do not have to circle you before attacking. Sixty eight percent of the time, the shark came directly at the diver or the diver never saw the shark before it attacked. One last consideration: some 82 percent of the shark attacks were in water where there was less than 50-foot visibility.

It is thought that when there are unprovoked shark attacks on humans, it is generally because sharks mistake the person for their regular meal of seal or sea lion (pinnipeds). Surfers are at a much greater risk of being attacked than SCUBA divers because their surface-splashing, dark silhouette resembles pinniped behavior and body form.

Of the some 360+ species of sharks that range in length from 8 inches to 60 feet, only a few species are responsible for most of the attacks. The three species responsible for 60 percent of the attacks on humans (worldwide) are the Great White, Tiger, and Sand Tiger shark. A few other shark species are

potentially dangerous, but I say "potentially dangerous" because first you have to find them. Divers pay good money and go to great effort to finally see sharks up close and personal. They generally come away awed by the experience.

Guided shark adventures and shark feedings (though feedings have been questioned ecologically) are growing in popularity. You have seen TV 'documentaries' where they have to actively chum for sharks in order to have any around to dive with. Many divers intentionally dive with sharks (with or without cages) and, if done correctly, are at minimal risk. Near La Paz, Mexico, in the Sea of Cortez, divers seek out hammerheads that circle a sea mount at some 150+ feet deep. Seeing a shark is far from an every-dive occurrence and for most of us, seeing a large shark is rare indeed.

To avoid being bitten by a shark (and most underwater creatures for that matter), do not spear fish. But, if you do, then remove the fish from the water quickly. Further avoid attack by not teasing or poking the wildlife. Do not grab sharks by the tail, it pisses them off. A boy in Florida found that out the hard way when a shark latched onto his belly and had to be surgically removed. Additionally, do not corner wildlife (give them an escape route), do not put your extremities where you cannot see, and use some common sense. If you see a shark that you would rather not then just remain calm and move slowly out of the area (do not panic or rapid kick).

From my experience, most ocean fauna basically look at you, the diver, and go through a 'thought process' something like this: "Is that SCUBA diver going to eat me?" Well, it does not act like they will now and there is no spear gun visible. "OK, is that diver something I can eat or do they have something for me to eat." Naw, it looks too big and chewy in that florescent green and purple wet suit (the diver obviously has questionable taste anyway). "Is that diver a competitor or someone I can mate with?" You're kidding, on a scale of 1 to 10 it has no scales. They then go about their business, mostly ignoring you.

It seems that the animals, particularly on a heavily populated reef, tend to be very busy trying to survive themselves (by not being eaten and getting enough to eat themselves) and, at times, reproducing. Sure, some are curious and/or are just hanging out at the corner of Morrey's reef. But once you are not placed in one of the above four categories, then you are forgotten until you do something to threaten them. Few animals kill for the 'fun' of it, and we SCUBA divers just are not natural prey.

26. I am prone to panic and stress. Can I SCUBA dive?

According to the U.S. Centers for Disease Control, more than half of all fatalities between the ages of one and 65 result from stressful lifestyles. Every year more than 800 million dollars are spent on 'anti-anxiety' medications. Americans account for five percent of the world's population, but consume 33 percent of the all the pills.

Yet, a moderate amount of stress can help keep a diver mentally and physically stimulated. A diver should know when the stress they are feeling is becoming overwhelming so panic does not ensue. Understanding that panic is a potential problem and knowing the causes, signs and symptoms, and solutions for stress and panic will make for a safer diver and a more enjoyable SCUBA experience.

According to a recent study out of the Sport Psychology Lab at the University of Wisconsin, more than half of the experienced divers surveyed said that they had experienced panic or near-panic while diving.[DD] Further, the National Underwater Accident Data Center (NUADC) attributes 19 percent of the SCUBA fatalities from 1976 to 1988 to panic, with another 22 percent resulting from unknown causes. *A good portion of the divers who have drowned were found with adequate air in their tanks (see Question 35) and no obvious problems with their equipment. It is thought that a large number of these fatalities are the result of panic attacks.*

Panic is also implicated in many cases of arterial gas embolism (AGE), which usually occurs from a rapid, uncontrolled ascent. A small number of these cases are the product of inadequate training or equipment malfunction. However, the majority of the cases are due to divers who experience panic and go straight to the surface. *Many instructors teach that if it all possible, problems should be dealt with at depth and not by rapid ascents (see Question 98).*

Panic while diving can come on gradually from repeated stress cycles, or instantly if sudden and extreme fear is experienced. There are some obvious underwater situations that would cause a diver to become stressed and potentially panic. Turning around and being face-to-face with a large Great White or Tiger shark could produce incontinence. Experiencing an out-of-air (OOA) situation underwater, going on that first night dive, and becoming repeatedly entangled in fishing line or kelp can all contribute to increased stress. We each have situations that can increase our stress levels. According to Dennis Graver, probably the number one factor causing diving stress is the diver becoming cold.[1]

It has been shown that humans vary in response to stress. Some people, like the astronaut whose heart rate increases only six beats per minute at lift-off, are essentially immune to stress-producing qualities of the environment. Others are very susceptible to stress. In fact, Dr. William Morgan, in a study published in the December 1995 issue of Sports Medicine, believes that divers who score significantly higher than other divers on a test that measures "trait anxiety" (as opposed to "situational anxiety") are potentially at greater risk of experiencing a "panic attack". Dr. Morgan states that it is possible to predict panic behavior in beginning divers with 88 percent accuracy. Studies like Dr. Morgan's may produce ways that a prospective diver and their instructor can assess the student's risk for panic and produce training to mitigate the problem or encourage the panic prone student to reconsider diving instruction.

In your open water SCUBA course, you will learn the signs and symptoms of stress (particularly pertaining to diving). Some of those signs and symptoms of stress are listed in Listing K.

Listing K. Some Signs and Symptoms of Stress.

💣 *Increased heart rate,*

💣 *rapid breathing,*

💣 *increased sweating,*

💣 *irritability, defensiveness, and aggressiveness,*

💣 *dry mouth,*

💣 *talking too fast or too loud,*

💣 *cool skin, hands, and feet,*

💣 *tense muscles,*

💣 *repetitive behavior,*

💣 lots of air bubbles, shallow breathing, rigid vertical posture, flailing arms, jerky movements,

💣 impaired analytical abilities,

💣 decreased awareness and perception,

💣 feelings of nausea,

💣 constantly adjusting and fiddling with gear,

💣 inability to sit still, yawning, nail biting, and

💣 increased urination and diarrhea.

So how does a diver beat stress and avoid panic? *Many experts suggest the diver should be both physically and mentally prepared for the dive.* Physical preparation involves having the proper equipment and making sure it functions correctly before diving. While this is obvious, fatalities cited in the 1996 DAN study, included a diver who started his dive with only 1,000 psi in his tank. Additionally, there were two incidents of divers entering caves without the means to locate the exit and one diver who tried to retrieve a fishing net but became entangled in it and drowned.

If you are not physically fit to handle demanding situations, then you put yourself at risk for increased stress and panic. Continuously fighting a strong current can be physically stressful and lead to over-breathing of the regulator (trying to breathe in more air than the regulator can produce - see Question 34). This, I can attest, is stressful and can lead to panic and breath holding ascents, with a potential AGE (Arterial Gas Embolism).

Mental preparation is also critical. If you do not feel comfortable diving in a certain situation, then do not dive. Do not let your ego get in the way of safety. Pass on the dive, and make sure you are around to do it another day. If you do not have the training to dive under certain conditions, then do not dive.

A buddy's training does not substitute for you being properly trained (see Question 77). In 1996, 10 SCUBA fatalities involved certified open water divers who were performing dives (cave, wreck, deep) that they were not qualified to do. Each year, five to fifteen divers die trying to dive beyond their limits. If your buddy is certified for more technical dives and you want to join them, then first get the necessary training (see Question 79).

Mental rehearsals can reduce stress when a previously anticipated problem arises. Because your body may react to your thoughts, it is generally best to avoid unnecessary visualization of the dangers you have mentally pre-rehearsed during your dive. After all, you are already mentally prepared and diving should be fun. Reduce the importance of some nonessential issues such as kick technique in open water or forgetting a snorkel. Recreational SCUBA diving is recreational; do not get stressed out.

Fear, all too often, is the fear of the unknown. Reduce that fear by keeping your diving techniques current, dive frequently, get additional training, dive safely. When you dive, "plan your dive, then dive your plan".

Take a clue from speakers who reduce the stress of speaking by PMR (Progressive Muscular Relaxation). PMR involves progressively tensing, holding, then relaxing your muscles (start with your toes and work up), concentrate on your breathing, have a positive mental imagery (everyone in the audience being naked {ok, not everyone!}), and visualize the stress flowing from you.

To help the diver deal with stress, Dr. Ernest S. Campbell at www.ismax.com/cgi-bin/cgiwrap/ismax/htmlow.cgi/00578.1. 42939483333 suggests that adopting the suggestions in the book Stress and Performance in Diving by Bachrach and Egstrom has helped quite a few divers who had difficulties with stress. For those that have problems with stress and diving, he also recommends a progressive exposure to snorkeling skills, i.e., mask, fins, snorkel, BC (buoyancy compensator), etc. The diver should become comfortable at each progressive level before undergoing SCUBA training.

When you have control of your stress factors and the propensity to panic, you should be instructed on how to deal with panic in other divers in your open water SCUBA certification course. Succinctly, communication, i.e., verbal, eye and facial contact, hand signals, etc., is essential when dealing with a stressed diver. You should take control of the situation if possible, but do not endanger yourself! Rescuing two divers (one of them being you) is more difficult than rescuing the original one.

Take the Rescue Diver certification course. *Learn self-rescue, dive with competent buddies, rehearse scenarios with them, know what to do, and be prepared to take charge if necessary.* After all that, you may never have to use any of it because SCUBA diving is, in fact, relatively safe (see Question 48), but you will know how! That fact will reduce stress and increase your enjoyment of SCUBA diving.

27. I know nothing about SCUBA, won't they laugh at me?

Guess what. Everyone who dives was at one time a beginner. A lot of this SCUBA stuff is not information or skills that are innate or stuff you need to survive on land. Though not difficult to learn (see Question 67), SCUBA obviously entails submerging yourself in an entirely new environment with a fair amount of equipment. *Do not take yourself so seriously that you cannot have a little fun with the mistakes we all (including you and me) make when learning. If you have a sincere desire to learn SCUBA and are not obnoxious or cocky about what you already know {or think you know, but do not}, you will find most other divers will go out of their way to help you.*

In fact, as SCUBA is a very buddy-oriented avocation (see Question 45), divers have a tendency to want to help each other {isn't that partly what a buddy is for?}. Someday it  may be our turn to ask for help. No one knows it all. Most divers appreciate tips or suggestions {offered in the right spirit} from those that have 'been there and done that' and have the knowledge.

One warning: never touch another diver's equipment unless asked to do so or unless there is an emergency. Most divers have their equipment set up to their liking and your well-intentioned adjustment may put them at risk. Communicate your question or concern, but do not touch unless asked to or it is an emergency.

If you have questions or problems, please ask your instructor, the Divemaster, or a more experienced diver. Get additional SCUBA certifications, dive frequently, read all you can about SCUBA {'SCUBA Scoop' is a good start}, dive with reliable and safe buddies, and before you know it, you will be the one others will come to for assistance. There are no dumb questions in SCUBA. Ask your question and dive safely.

One last paragraph on this subject. Remember, recreational SCUBA diving is supposed to be fun. You do not need a perfect water entry, the perfect kick, the most expensive equipment {appropriate equipment, yes}, or that fancy wet suit to have fun.

Get and keep yourself in shape and learn proper techniques, but most of all enjoy SCUBA. If SCUBA becomes a burden, you are more likely to give it up. It is a far too compelling avocation to let that happen!

28. I do not like cold water! How do I stay warm?

Over time, divers can become hypothermic (decreased body core temperature) even if they are diving in 85 degree water. Truly isothermic water (water in which a person can be immerged indefinitely with no appreciable change in body temperature) for a diver without an exposure suit is 91° F.

Water has a capacity for heat some 1,000 times greater than air (see Question 17) and the body loses heat 25 times faster in water than in air. Therefore, seemingly warm water drains heat away from a diver faster than the person can generate heat. If you become cold in the water, then get out and get warm.

A few tidbits regarding diving in cold water would be appropriate here. Exercising in water colder than 60° F will cause you to lose more heat than if you just remained motionless. When you are insulated against heat loss, then moderate exercise can delay hypothermia. Insulating your head is wise because of the amount of heat lost there. Additionally, you can lose 15 to 24 percent of your heat-producing capability via respiration. The human body maintains thermal balance by metabolic rate, circulatory control via vasoconstriction and vasodilation (the shunting of blood from the body extremities), respiratory control, shivering, and perspiration.

If you do not like cold water, then how about diving in water so warm that if you wear even a thin wet suit you could be uncomfortably warm. It is tougher to find isothermic water, but diving locations such as Florida, Cozumel, the Red Sea, the Caribbean, Bahamas, Great Barrier Reef, Tahiti, Hawaii, etc. are great places for the cold-adverse diver. These warm water locations are home to some of the most abundant underwater life on this planet. As we become more senior, places such as these make for easier diving, as less gear and weighting are required and they are often done via boat or an easy shore dive.

On the other hand, even in the winter you do not have to fly to exotic places or hang up your dive gear. *The resourceful diver can find lakes with natural warm water or water used by a power plant for cooling (be sure you get an area orientation and seek permission if necessary before diving).*

One of the more unusual dives I have done was in the middle of winter in West Virginia at Vepco Lake on Mt. Storm. Even though there was snow on the ground, we had a reasonably comfortable pre-dawn dive in the 70° F water. Dry suits were worn to protect us more from the below-freezing air temperatures than from the relatively warm waters. During the summer, Vepco Lake almost seems too warm to dive for extended periods, even with just swim trunks. If you do not like cold water, you can certainly find enough warm water to keep you satisfied. Note: do not dive at altitude or in adverse weather conditions unless adequately trained and equipped.

It is interesting to note that fear, apprehension, illness, hyperventilation, and other mental and physiological factors all contribute to the loss of body heat. Thinking and feeling abnormally can bring on hypothermia faster than normal behavior. If you do not feel right, then abort the dive, especially when the water is cold.

Prolonged shivering is a serious symptom. You should get out of the water if you cannot suppress sporadic shivering with voluntary movements. You do not want to become chilled at depth as this may contribute to a DCI (decompression illness) hit. After long, cold, deep dives, avoid anything that might excessively increase heart rate and blood pressure, such as heavy exercise and hot showers (warm is OK).

Shivering, increased respiration, and numbness are early warning signs of hypothermia. When your body core temperature drops below 96° F, you start losing muscle control, have difficulty speaking, experience amnesia, confusion, sluggish reactions, idea fixation, and hallucinations. Get warm! Females generally have a smaller muscle mass and generate less heat, so they should be doubly on guard for signs of hypothermia. Which they usually are, as they seem more in tune with what is going on with their bodies while men figure they will just tough it out.

Regardless, do not sell colder water diving short. A dry suit (see Question 100) worn with adequate clothing underneath, a heated tent, and hot chocolate or soup can even make ice diving a treat. Note: do not dive with a dry suit or ice dive without additional professional training.

One last word of caution: a heavily perspiring diver preparing to dive can experience heat exhaustion. Take steps to cool yourself down immediately if you feel like you are becoming overheated in your exposure suit.

29. Won't I get trapped or sucked down to the bottom?

Getting trapped underwater and drowning is a subject most divers have at least thought about. However, the real questions are: trapped by what? and what course of action should be taken to avoid or rectify the situation? *Getting trapped by underwater fauna is rare at best.* The giant clams of Australia close so slowly that the diver would really have to try to get caught, not to mention that the clam probably closed long before a diver could begin to harass it.

There was an instance where a diver was messing around with a large octopus and the octopus tried to pull the diver's head into its rock crevice. The biggest danger during this experience was loosing the regulator, which the diver kept a hold of while prying the mollusk's arms from around his head. Yet who precipitated that situation? Answer, the diver. So, if you are prepared for other forms of entrapment and keep your hands and feet to yourself, you do not have much to worry about from the animals.

It certainly is possible to get entangled in kelp, long eel grass, etc. Either avoid diving in those areas (but you would be missing some great diving) or be familiar with how to handle the situation. The prime thing is not to panic and not to start twisting and turning. Do not make the situation worse. Your buddy (see Question 45) can help untangle you, or as a last resort you can use a knife (see Question 105) to cut the offending flora. Be careful not to cut yourself or your gear!

If you read DAN's Report on Decompression Illness and Diving Fatalities (which is recommended reading) *the vast majority of instances where a diver is detained and succumbs underwater is due to diver negligence or a mishandling of the situation, which then leads to panic.* Open water divers going into caves and getting lost (see Question 33) and drowning was once more prevalent. Recently, there has been a better effort to keep those divers from diving in established cave systems, as well as warning novice divers.

If you are not trained or equipped for cave and cavern diving then stay alive by staying out. Your life is worth more than a few minutes' excitement in the exploration of a cave. Wrecks have taken their toll of divers also. Again, do not make deep penetration dives in wrecks unless trained and equipped. It is not worth it!

In 1997, DAN reports two diver fatalities classified as drowning/entrapment.[C] One fatality was a certified Master Diver who became entangled in guide wire he was using to try a penetration dive on a wreck. There were at least two problems here. The diver had no dive buddy and was using wire, which he could not cut when he became entangled. Lesson: never use rope, string, or wire you are not prepared to cut.

The other fatality was a diver making his open-water checkout dives for initial certification. His regulator apparently became entangled in the ascent line and his buddy had already ascended without him. As the dive was only to 33 fsw (feet saltwater), the diver could have removed his BC (buoyancy compensator) and easily have ascended. He could have also cut the ascent line, or his buddy could have helped him untangle himself. Additionally, the diver apparently did not try to use his safe second (see Question 97). These two fatalities might have been avoided if a buddy was around to help or they had used common sense once faced with the situation (see Question 45). *Your greatest enemy is potentially yourself. You must keep your wits about you in order to get out of entrapments.*

I may be going to extremes, but I always dive with at least two knives (and in kelp dives with a third knife), a pair of scissors, and a sickle-like razor-blade line cutter (Z-knife). The knives are placed on the BC shoulder strap, BC belt, and lower leg so I can reach them even if I have limited movement of my arms. The best thing is to just stay away from lines that can entangle you, particularly if you have no means of cutting them. Stay away from fishing nets. Practice doffing (removing) and donning (putting on) your BC underwater (you will practice this in your training for open water certification).

Then there are the rare cases where the diver is sucked into an intake pipe or spillway orifice. One actual case was where a non-diving boy was sucked into a spillway orifice. Then, several hours later, a rescue diver repeated the error. As several hours had already passed from the initial accident, there was no emergency to remove the boy's body. The rescue diver should have waited until the suction could be turned off.

In another case, a diver near Los Angeles, CA died when sucked partially into an intake pipe used for power plant cooling. Even though the site was marked on the surface with a warning of the intake, he dove anyway. Stay away from entrapments and stay alive!

30. Won't I get run over by some drunk in a boat?

Being struck by a boat or a PWC (Personal Water Craft) is a potential danger to the diver on the surface, the surfacing diver, and the diver swimming just below the surface. *Of the 82 SCUBA related fatalities occurring in 1997, DAN reported that three were divers killed by boats.[C]* One of the divers died when his head contacted the bottom of the dive boat in rough seas and he drowned (his buddy was back on the boat), one diver apparently ascended into the churning propeller of the dive boat, and one was surfacing far from his floating dive flag when hit by a passing boat.

According to the USCG (U.S. Coast Guard) Auxiliary Department of Boating and Consumer Affairs, there is an average of 46 swimming and diving accidents per year that involve boats.[P] About 10 percent of those accidents are fatal. A further downside of the report is the USCG estimates that they receive only 10 percent of the non-fatal accident reports. Boating accidents are certainly a concern for the diver.

In rough seas, the dive boat becomes a hammer and the diver underneath it, the nail. To avoid getting countersunk, once you are in the water and have signaled OK, then get away from the boat by either swimming away on the surface or by diving with your buddy. While ascending and making your safety stop, be sure to practice what you were taught in your open water class regarding safe surfacing.

Even though diver fatalities caused by being struck by a boat or PWC are relatively low (3.7 percent of the fatalities), the wise diver will follow the suggestions in Listing L.

Listing L. Suggestions for Avoiding Undesirable Contact with Boats.

- *Display a dive flag* on the boat and/or on a float in the water,
- *stay in the vicinity of the dive flag* (some states have fairly severe financial penalties, so be sure to know what the law reads in the state in which you dive),
- ensure there is *enough air* for an extended safety stop so you can *wait out a boat's passing,*

- *listen for boat traffic* while conducting your safety stop,
- *surface cautiously* (with upraised hand) near your dive flag or where the dive started, e.g., shore,
- upon surfacing, *immediately do a 360° scan* of the area for approaching traffic,
- have *neutral buoyancy* upon surfacing so you can exhale and dive immediately if necessary,
- upon surfacing, rather than trying to wave an approaching boat away, *submerge immediately and hold at about 15 feet until the boat passes,*
- if you have to *traverse an area of boat traffic, then do it at least 15 feet underwater,* or in the worse case (low on air) inflate your orange, surface signal wienie (you do carry one don't you?) before cautiously surfacing, and
- *surface a safe distance from the dive boat (not underneath it) and approach the dive platform/ladder with caution.*

31. What happens if I cannot see underwater?

Being visual animals, our sight is very important to us (though some individuals who are blind do dive). As you can imagine, some people just cannot adjust to looking through a mask. If that is you, then it is better not to SCUBA dive until you are comfortable underwater with a mask on. *If being in turbid water is a problem, then do not dive in sight-impaired areas until you are more comfortable doing so. One way to become more comfortable is to dive in clear water. After you gain confidence there, then a progression to turbid water will not be as uncomfortable.*

Some advanced divers actually seek out dives with limited visibility. They generally train for such dives by taking night diving classes, doing blacked-out mask exercises, diving with more experienced buddies, and by studying literature on the subject. These divers might be equipped with compass, dive lights (see Question 106), buddy line, tender line, tether harness, descent line, helmet, leather gloves, and line cutting instruments.

Factors that can produce limited visibility are storms, surf, rough weather, rain, run-off, riverheads, pollution, sewage outfalls, plankton, algae, upwellings, currents, and tidal changes. Yet even for those who do not seek it, poor visibility is occasionally a fact of life for divers (and sometimes the norm). But you will generally realize it before you make the dive. Night or turbid water diving may entail holding your buddy's hand or holding on to a short rope with your buddy at one end (buddy line). If it makes you feel too anxious, then abort the dive and get additional training and wait for another night, or move to another dive site (see Question 115).

Even though a relatively rare event, Listing M, delineates some potential causes and solutions to a diver's loss or decrease in visibility.

Listing M. Potential Causes with Solutions to Loss of Visibility.

- Cause: a diver stirs up the area with their fins or by their careless thrashing around, causes a 'silt-out' (the stirring up of bottom sediment, causing impairment of visibility).

Solution: *if the silt-out occurs in open water (which is where the basic open water diver should be) then ascend slightly off the bottom or swim horizontally out of the muck. Then get training on how to swim close to the bottom without stirring it up.* Stay off the soft bottom when fixing problems. While obtaining my ice diving certification, I stirred up the muck at the bottom of the lake while trying to put my right fin back on. My fin strap had come undone and the fin was kicked loose. My buddy helped replace the fin and strap, but to avoid mucking up the visibility for the other divers I should have moved off the bottom. Another time I finned up muck, was during one of open water training dives (in a Pennsylvania quarry). Upon returning on the reciprocal of the course taken out (returning by the same direction I swam out), I swam though clouds of sediment stirred up on my initial passage. A slight course adjustment to either side or rising a few feet brought clear water.

Cause: penetration diving (diving in a cave, wreck or under ice) and there is a collapse of the roof and/or walls due to currents, earthquake, or most likely, a diver's carelessness.
Solution: In 1995 and 1996, five divers each year lost their lives in caves. In 1997, one diver died. *Unless you are trained in and have the equipment for cave, wreck, or ice diving, stay out of those areas. Problem solved.*

Cause: a diver is in an underwater cave and mucks it up, or is downstream of a severe run-off due to rain, mud slide, and an inflow of water with tannic acid.
Solution: *stay out of caves unless trained.* Certified cave divers are trained in and practice following a line back to the cave's entrance sans (without) sight. It does not appear to be the best idea to swim downstream of a potential run-off, though this may be difficult to predict if there is a large watershed draining into the diving area. Consult divers familiar with the area and get proper advanced training before venturing forth during questionable weather.

Cause: swimming into an area of poor visibility from an area of good visibility, e.g., swimming into the turbid flow of a river from a crystal clear spring.
Solution: *knowing the direction of the current, you can, in coordination with your compass, do a 180-degree turn and return to clear water.* Be sure to take into account the

distance the current has already carried you. Do not dive in strong currents unless trained in current diving procedures.

◉ Cause: diver descends into or through an opaque thermocline or halocline.
Solution: A thermocline is the intersection between two layers of water of decidedly different temperatures. Because of this temperature difference, light is refracted making for poor visibility in the thermocline and possibly below it as well. *Either ascend or descend out of the thermocline. If you decide to descend, then you may want to utilize your flashlight.* The same procedure would be followed passing through a halocline, or the intersection of layers of saltwater and freshwater.

◉ Cause: the facemask floods or is removed.
Solution: one of the necessary skills you will need to master to become certified is clearing your mask when flooded. Thus a flooded mask should not be a problem. Losing a mask is possible. You should always check your mask for a damaged strap before putting it on. When you put your mask on you may want to place the strap of the mask underneath your hood. Thus, even if it is kicked loose you will likely not lose it. I now carry a spare mask (already fitted to size) in a pocket of my BC so that if my primary mask is lost, it is relatively easy to replace it with the spare. Even if you lose your mask entirely, you can still make a safe return to the surface by just breathing as you slowly ascend at 30 feet per minute (preferably with your buddy monitoring the ascent rate) (see Question 98). If you lose your mask, remember not to panic (you can still breathe without a mask!). Find the mask, replace and clear it, get your buddy involved, and/or use your spare mask.

◉ Cause: some pathological problem, e.g., stroke or coronary (heart attack) occurs while diving.
Solution: S*trokes and heart attacks can occur suddenly and unexpectedly even if a diver is given a clean bill of health. Yet it is the wise diver that stacks the deck in their favor by being physically fit for diving.* Do otherwise, and they may be stacking the diver on the deck.

Most of the above can be resolved by following four basic steps: stop, breathe, think, then act. You must not panic! Stay calm, hold hands with your buddy {yes, it is OK}, breathe, do not panic (take deep breaths and slow your heart down). Know that sudden lack of visibility can be stressful. Just remember you will not drown or sink into the abyss if you keep your wits about you.

Experience will bring confidence. Ask your instructor to give you a little extra training if necessary. If you get into low visibility you can break out the buddy line with Velcro® cuffs and connect wrists with your buddy. Velcro®, or similar hook and loop material, is necessary so you can break away if necessary.

Note that most of the above sight challenged problems can be solved with training, being prepared, not diving under certain conditions, remaining calm, and solving the problem at hand. As you become more comfortable in the water, you may even seek out lower visibility dives. Night diving (see Question 32) can be very exhilarating! Unless very experienced, do not combine low visibility diving with difficult environmental conditions, e.g., strong current, high risk of entanglement, very cold water, and overhead structures. If fear of low visibility is an incurable problem for you, then never dive in low vis situations. To a great extent, you can control that {clear water can be fun too}.

32. Why would anyone in their right mind dive at night?

Diving at night is both exciting and beautiful. *Your regular day dive site (see Question 115) literally comes alive with nocturnal underwater life.* It can be a bit intimidating at first, but once familiar landmarks come into view, you will get your bearings. Because of the general lack of visual stimulation (except where your light shines), it really makes the illuminated things stand out. Often, the lack of recreational traffic (particularly in lakes and bays) makes for a more peaceful dive.

Starting a dive with a full moon skimming the surface of the water, diving in phosphorescent waters, viewing otherwise seldom-seen underwater creatures, and surfacing with the sky ablaze with stars makes for a most memorable dive.

Before doing a night dive, you should first go through additional training. A night dive under good conditions is an excellent method to gain experience for diving in turbid waters. Do not attempt night dives in strange areas or under poor conditions. Diving at night in rough or turbid water is hazardous. Seek ideal conditions when you first dive at night.

Your primary concern at night is dive site conditions. At night, you will rely more on your compass and navigation skills. As a minimum, your additional equipment should include at least two dive lights (see Question 106), a tank light, a compass, and a whistle. You should review light signals and procedures with your buddy before your start your dive.

Night diving is a good way to get in more diving and still keep your day job {sorry}. Night diving is an inexpensive way to make your usual dive site seem totally different, but still familiar. As you gain confidence, you will move further afield.

33. I am lucky to know down from up; won't I get lost?

That is actually two questions. One portion of the question deals with disorientation and the other with knowing where you are and how to get back to the boat or shore. Let's deal with disorientation first.

Disorientation means you do not know where you are in relation to the surface, the bottom, your buddy, or anything else and you literally cannot distinguish up from down. If you are disoriented, you may experience *vertigo,* where the whole world appears to be spinning. Causes of vertigo include pressure or temperature differences in one ear compared to the other, sensory deprivation (including poor visibility), carbon monoxide toxicity, nitrogen narcosis (see Question 83), and body positioning.

The good news is that most cases of vertigo are temporary. *The best course of action is to grab hold of something stationary and stay put until it passes.* In mid-water you can hug yourself and get some relief from the vertigo. After the vertigo passes, you can regain orientation by using the direction of the pull of gravity on your weights, the angle of water inside your mask, exhaust bubble direction, and your direction of movement when you increase buoyancy.

Getting disoriented while diving is certainly possible, but getting lost is more difficult and generally the result of carelessness or inattention. As you know, water is much more dense than air and you generally cannot travel far (unless carried by the current or you have an underwater scooter) from your entry area or boat. Further, in open water diving, no matter how far you travel, the surface is always just above you.

Confusion as to direction is not uncommon at various times during a dive. For example: At the start of a dive you are busy adjusting equipment and checking on your buddy and you may become confused as to direction. Descending down the anchor line (being careful if it is whipping up and down due to wave action) may be one way to remain or gain your orientation. Descending feet-first is recommended. *When you reach the bottom, stop and get your bearings before you leave the area.* Remembering the slope of the bottom, wave action, current direction, angle of the sunlight, and prominent landmarks will help in obtaining and retaining your sense of direction (you will learn more about this in your open water course).

Another circumstance that can produce confusion as to direction is when two separate dive groups meet underwater, particularly at night. It is sometimes difficult to know which group to continue with (particularly if you are lagging behind the dive leader or Divemaster). The confusion of all the lights and divers taking off here and there makes for a moment of confusion. Ways to avoid unnecessary confusion in these situations are delineated in Listing N.

Listing N. How to Avoid Directional Confusion at Night When Meeting Another Dive Group.

← Know the dive plan before actually diving (including general compass headings). Make sure the dive leader or Divemaster gives an orientation of the area and discusses the dive plan.

↗ Stay reasonably close to the dive leader and encourage your buddy to do the same (discuss this before the dive). It is particularly frustrating to be pulled in one direction by the dive leader and another by your buddy. Stay with your buddy unless other arrangements are agreed upon. As the dive leader should know the area, they will show you the points of interest that you might not see if you lag too far behind.

↓ Know the fin, BC (buoyancy compensator), and exposure suit coloring and configuration of your partner, the dive leader and at least a couple in your dive group.

→ Consult your compass periodically so you will know which direction to proceed in order to catch up with your group if you should fall behind. You can write compass headings and approximate distances on your dive slate in case you need to refer to them later.

↙ If possible, have a general idea where the other group's dive boat is anchored and its name, markings, or general configuration. One of the more humorous incidents in diving is when a diver (with hopefully their buddy) gets back on the wrong boat and they cannot find their dive bags. Everyone gets a good laugh, but it could be a serious matter if the Captain or Divemaster on your original boat does not realize your mistake in a timely fashion. If it happens to you, immediately have the Captain call your original boat to avoid unnecessary searches ... and then laugh (see Question 27) along with everyone else. It can happen to anyone, just do not let it be you.

↑ Stay with your buddy and if you get completely turned around and cannot retrace your outbound route then, if appropriate (if you are not in a boat traffic lane, etc.), surface together and determine your course of action and heading.

To avoid directional confusion, one reasonable dive plan is for you and your buddy to begin swimming against the current (noting the direction on your compass) and simply returning on a reciprocal compass heading (your outbound heading + or − 180 degrees). Ultrasonic homing beacons and flashing lights (above and below water) may be able to help direct you back to your entry point, even in darkness.

During your open water certification course, you will learn other procedures to retain your bearings. If you and your buddy surface too far from the boat to swim back (which usually indicates poor or no dive planning), then you can always use that signaling device (whistle) on your BC or inflate that long orange wienie. The stories of lost divers at sea make for intriguing reading and have happened, but the fact is that lost divers are rare, particularly in U.S. waters (see Question 110 regarding a 'possibles' kit).

You should always dive with a compass. In very clear water in familiar terrain you may not use it, but you should otherwise know how. In your open water course, you will be taught the use of the compass and be asked to demonstrate its usage underwater.

Some desirable features of an underwater compass are:
1. a movable bezel with index marks,
2. luminous markings on the needle,

3. luminous index marks, and
4. large easy to read markings.

Ask your local dive shop to help you select one that will give you years of trouble-free use.

Have a dive plan that you and your buddy have agreed to before hand and then dive that plan. Be constantly aware of your position, rate of travel, and distance traveled and you should not have to make any trips to the surface to see where you are.

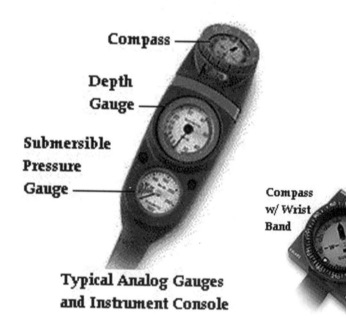

Compass

Depth
Gauge

Submersible
Pressure
Gauge

Compass
w/ Wrist
Band

**Typical Analog Gauges
and Instrument Console**

34. What happens if I cannot breathe?

You are about as likely to run out of air while diving as you are to run out of gas in your auto while driving. If you pay attention to your pressure gauge and the length of time of your dive and surface with a margin of safety, then the probability of running out of air is rather remote. Additionally, the total failure of your breathing equipment, if properly maintained, is highly unlikely (see the 'You Are Well Suited for SCUBA' section for equipment info).

In 1997, DAN (Divers Alert Network) reports eight diver fatalities directly attributable to running out of air.[C] Even so, it appears to me that running low or out-of-air puts the diver at much greater risk of panic, thus possibly contributing to other fatalities. Most certifying agencies recommend that a diver be back on board the dive boat with 300-500 psi of air left in the tank. If you have to hold underwater for a passing boat, swim against a current, share air with your buddy, swim ashore in rough surf, or deal with an entanglement, then you will likely need more than just your usual amount of air to make it back. Give yourself air to spare!

During pool sessions, you will practice several scenarios of sharing air. In most of them the, low-on-air buddy calmly approaches you, calmly gives the "share air" signal, and calmly takes your proffered second stage. In real life, what usually happens is your buddy (or someone else) will frantically swim to you, grab the second stage from your mouth, and possibly cause you to lose balance. That is why to be truly prepared to share air, you must be ready to find and use your own alternate air source and be ready to take control of a diver who may be experiencing panic. You cannot share air for long if that diver is a hoover (consumes mass quantities of air) and you both run out of air. Always maintain a margin of safety.

Divers who try to extend their bottom time by sucking that last draught of air put themselves and others at significant risk. Divers who do not monitor their gauges risk potential tragedy. It is not worth it. If you just have to dive longer (not exceeding the dive tables of course), then get a bigger tank or use your air more efficiently.

The regulator (the second stage regulator is what you breathe from - see Question 90) is simple, sturdy, and usually designed (see Question 97) so that if it does fail, it delivers more air (free flows), not less. During your open water class, you will be taught how to breathe from a free flowing regulator, a procedure you should practice periodically. Besides the reliability of your regulator, you have an extra second stage regulator (your octopus or safe second - see Question 90) and your buddy's octopus. In addition, many divers carry a completely redundant air system with its own regulators (see Question 99). The chance of all them failing is miniscule.

Low-on-air or out-of-air (OOA) emergencies occur primarily because the diver does not monitor their air. Yet, even running low on air with an unbalanced regulator (see Question 97) is not real easy because when the pressure in the tank gets lower you have to suck harder and harder on the regulator to obtain the air. Additionally, there are audible devices (including dive computers) that can be set to signal you when you are running low on air. Regardless, do not depend solely on an (in)audible alarm or a harder breathing regulator to warn you of low air. Monitor your and your buddy's gauges.

Even if all of a sudden you run out of air and you are no deeper than 60 feet you almost certainly have enough air to reach the surface safely (remember to keep letting air out of your lungs as you ascend). As you ascend, water pressure on your body decreases allowing the air in your lungs to expand (see Question 49). Additionally, it is likely that you will have another breath or two you can take from your regulator as you ascend. So stay above 60 feet and out of caves and wrecks until you are comfortable at depth and there is no reason to fear (nor should you) running out of air underwater. *You can further minimize OOA problems if you get your equipment serviced regularly, always dive with a buddy, watch yours and your buddy's gauges, and stay above 60 feet.*

Then there is the condition of over-breathing your regulator. Over-breathing your regulator occurs when a diver over-exerts themselves while under-ventilating (breaths are not frequent or large enough and you feel like you cannot catch your breath). This overexertion (caused by exercise or panic), with the feeling of suffocation, hits suddenly and generally without warning. You should never experience a shortness of breath while diving underwater. *At the first signs of overexertion you should cease all activity, breathe deeply, and recover fully before continuing. Loosening your exposure suit and BC (buoyancy compensator) in the chest area can be helpful. If at the surface, on shore, or aboard the dive boat, then removing the weight belt is also helpful (do not remove at depth to avoid dropping the belt!).*

I experienced 'over-breathing' my regulator while training for the Rescue Diver Certification because of too enthusiastically swimming against a current. Fortunately, I was on the surface and near the boat's dive platform. To resolve the problem I loosened my exposure suit and rested. My brother experienced the same sensation when fighting surf during a shore dive in restrictive dive equipment and a weight belt that was tightly cinched. He eventually had to return to shore to 'catch his breath' by removing the belt and loosening and removing equipment. It is not a pleasant sensation. Do not let it happen to you. Do not exert yourself beyond your capacity to obtain air from your regulator.

Some people worry about the potential of their high-pressure hose (connects the first stage regulator to the pressure gauge - see Question 90) rupturing and thus losing all of their air. *In reality, the high pressure orifice is very small (about .005 inches) so, if the high pressure hose does rupture, the amount of air escaping should not be catastrophic for the open water diver.* If it does happen, the diver should notify their buddy and begin a normal ascent immediately (see Question 98). You should have no problem reaching the surface with a controlled ascent unless in very deep water and low on air to begin with. Yet, even then you still have your buddy and/or redundant air source, don't you?

35. How long does a tank of air last?

Asking how long a tank of air will last is like asking how many miles can you travel with gasoline. It depends. Dives differ in depth, water temperature, and physical exertion. An individual's air use will differ from day to day based on the diver's physical condition, state of mind, environmental conditions, etc. Women typically use less air than men. Additionally, tanks come in a number of sizes and can be filled to different pressures.

The "it depends", is one reason divers, rather than diving with just a watch (see Question 104), have a submersible pressure gauge (SPG) connected to the SCUBA tank. The pressure gauge shows the pressure of the air (see Question 17) in the tank and is an estimate of the amount of air remaining. However, the diver must remember that the pressure gauge is least accurate in the 0-500 psi range. A half-way reading between 500 psi and 0 psi does not necessarily mean the tank pressure is 250 psi.[G] A digital (computerized) pressure gauge is more accurate than analog gauges, but you normally should not be down around 250 psi anyway.

The amount of air in a tank is dependent upon its size and filling pressure. Aluminum 80s (80 cubic feet of air) are the most prevalent SCUBA cylinder in the U.S. and are typically filled to approximately 3000 pounds per square inch (psi). An Al80 at 3000 psi holds about as much air as does a 3.4 feet x 3.4 feet x 7 feet phone booth at sea level and 70° F. Since a cubic foot of air weighs 0.0834 pounds the air in an Al80 weighs 6.7 pounds.

With an Al80, an experienced diver can safely remain underwater anywhere from a few minutes to over two hours depending on depth and other factors. As an approximation, an experienced, physically fit, male diver contentedly sightseeing in calm, warm water in the 15 to 30 foot range can expect the average aluminum 80 tank to last a little more than an hour. *The typical (if there is such a thing) SCUBA dive lasts between twenty and fifty five minutes.*

You can increase your bottom time by diving relaxed, minimizing your effort, and breathing in slow, deep, continuous breaths. One way of reducing the energy required when swimming is to reduce your frontal area (head, chest, tank, BC, arms, etc.) with neutral trim (being nearly horizontal in the water) and secure dangling paraphernalia. A second way of reducing energy expenditure is to slow down in the water. As the drag force is proportional to the square of your relative speed; slowing down enables you to dive more efficiently (from an energy expended standpoint) and thus longer.

36. What happens if I need a bio-break (wee wee)?

OK, you have taken your Instructor's advice and drank plenty of water pre-dive to stay hydrated. Now you have been down here in this cold water for 30 minutes with lots of air left and you just have to take a bio-break. What do you do? It appears that you have two choices: 1) surface now and rush to the facilities on the boat or shore or 2) increase the concentration of salts in the body of water you are diving in. *Mictrating in your personal wet suit is not poor form, but if you do so in a rental suit then please be sure to* rinse it thoroughly (just as you would if it belonged to you.)

For dry suit wearers, the problem is a teeny weenie bit more involved. A dry suit primarily uses the air trapped between the diver and the suit, in addition to the undergarments, as insulation from the cold water vs. the suit material and water in wet suits. As the diver does not have water between them and the suit, any dampness introduced will likely cut down on the insulating factor of the air and generally make a bit of a mess. Rather than suffer with having to hold it (ever try dancing around on the bottom of the ocean with a puckered face?) *I suggest using Depends® or other absorbent material.* Upon surfacing and unsuiting, the diver just places the used pad in a plastic sack and the job is taken care of.

You can also reduce the urge to go by avoiding diuretics like caffeine before you dive. Regardless, be absolutely sure you do not dehydrate yourself (see Question 42 regarding dehydration). If you are properly hydrated, your urine will be clear and minimally offensive to the nose anyway. If you have a big, young bladder then maybe this won't be a problem, for awhile.

37. Won't I drown if I upchuck, sneeze, or cough underwater?

Sometime during your diving adventures you may have to throw-up when down under. *If you do get sick underwater and have to heave then most divers recommend keeping (holding) the regulator in your mouth and just upchucking through it.* Taking the regulator out of your mouth to throw up introduces the possibility of aspirating or choking on water which might subsequently be inhaled. Additionally, in the confusion it is possible to lose contact with your regulator. *Simply hold the regulator in your mouth, throw up, then remove the regulator and purge it to avoid aspirating the vomitus.* After throwing up, it is not a bad idea to cleanse the regulator by taking it out of your mouth and swirling it around in the water or use your octopus (your spare regulator) instead of your primary (the regulator you were breathing from).

Alternately, some divers claim that the regulator will be obstructed with vomitus if you just throw up through it. They recommend placing the regulator in the corner of your mouth with half of it out and depressing the purge button while hurling. This way you will not obstruct the regulator, as little vomitus goes through it, and you can still inhale after vomiting due to the constant stream of air. Note that in very cold water this procedure could potentially cause a regulator freeze up. Consult your Instructor for their advice.

According to the divers I have talked to, you would be surprised at the size of the chunks that you can hurl out your regulator (I have never had the opportunity to throw up underwater). Regardless, it may be wise to thoroughly chew your food before diving, particularly if your dive buddy is your Mom and you do not want to hear about it all the way home. By the way, the fish will love you and it is a good method for seeing more underwater life up close ... say cheese.

For sneezing and coughing underwater I would just hold the regulator in my mouth with a hand and sneeze or cough through the regulator. There should be no problems with either underwater. *The bottom line is you want that regulator there when you first inhale after throwing up, sneezing, or coughing.*

38. I just ate. Won't I get cramps and drown?

From my experience, and that of other divers with whom I have talked, there does not seem to be an increased incidence of cramping if you eat and immediately dive. I am not recommending that you eat and run (off the dive plank) because of other affects (adequate surface interval, blood shunting to the GI tract, etc.). However, it is clear that eating and immediately diving does not cause cramps.

In reality, leg cramps are usually caused by over-exerting the muscle group to such an extent that the oxygen is used up faster than the blood can replace it. This changes the muscle metabolism and causes a buildup of lactic acid in the muscle tissue. Then you get a cramp.

With more blood shunted to the digestive system (right after eating), it might take longer to replace leg muscle oxygen thus theoretically, cramping would be more likely. Additionally, as more blood is shunted to the GI tract, then less circulates to remove nitrogen in other tissue, thus there may be a slight increase in the likelihood of a DCS (decompression sickness). Now I have no data to support these two contentions and they appear to not have a measurable effect but they do logically follow based on information in Question 39.

The most important thing to remember when you have a cramp, whether in the legs, stomach or any other muscle, is to stop, breathe, think, and then act. Cramping is not a life-threatening situation, so do not make it into one.

If the cramps are in your calves, you can help resolve the problem by grabbing the fin tip on the affected leg. Then straighten your leg while pulling on your fin to stretch the cramping muscles (you will be taught this maneuver in your open water class). To prevent leg cramps in the first place, you may find it helpful to switch kicking styles when engaged in lengthy or strenuous kicking. Alternating between a flutter kick, frog kick, and shuffle kick is helpful because different muscles are used. Another way to help prevent cramps is to eat foods such as bananas and oranges prior to diving. These foods are rich in potassium and make good snack food too.

Cramps in the stomach or other muscles will pass in a few minutes if you remain calm, breathe deeply, and stretch the muscle by extension of the affected area.

The best way to prevent cramps is to maintain good physical condition as the better your condition, the longer it will take for lactic acid to build up (see Question 55). You can never predict when you might have to call upon your muscles to give 110 percent, so get and stay in good shape and you will minimize cramping problems.

Alleviating an abdominal muscle cramp.

39. I have heard a lot about the bends. What's the skinny?
To the general public, the 'bends' is the decompression illness (DCI) most associated with diving. Fortunately, a DCI 'hit' is rare and, for the most part, preventable. Treatment usually includes hyperbaric recompression (see Question 40). Most divers get 'bent' by going too deep and coming up too quickly or by making repeated short and deep dives.

As you dive deeper, the pressure on your body increases. This increases the amount of nitrogen that is pressed into your blood and tissues. Going too deep for too long and returning to the surface suddenly can make the nitrogen in your blood and tissues form bubbles. This bubble formation is somewhat like taking the cap off a bottle of soda after you shake it. In fact, the current thinking is that each time a diver surfaces from 100 feet, some bubbles may form. *These 'silent bubbles' may not produce symptoms following one or two ascents, but may collect and cause the 'bends' during repeated ascents.[H]*

A little explanation of terminology is needed here (also see the 'Off-Gassing' or 'Glossary' section). A decompression illness (DCI) as defined by Diver's Alert Network (DAN)[B] is, "...a general term used to describe a broad spectrum of signs and symptoms of diseases caused by excess inert gas {usually nitrogen}, or dysbaric injuries, related to SCUBA diving. Arterial gas embolism (AGE) and decompression sickness (DCS) are the conventional terms used to describe two different and specific types of DCI injuries."[B]

An AGE is caused by the inert gas forming bubbles, which then pass into the arterial vessels and travel to the lung, heart, and brain. This usually happens from voluntary breath-holding while ascending and by pathological conditions in the lung which trap air. The trapped air in the lung then expands upon the diver's ascent and forms a bubble, which goes into the arterial vessels. The greatest risk of an AGE is near the surface as that is where the greatest differences in pressure per incremental depth occur.

As mentioned above, a DCS is caused by bubbles of inert gas forming in the divers' tissues during and/or after ascent from a dive. The two major forms of DCS are: 1) Type I DCS, which involves muscle and joint pain, fatigue and/or skin symptoms of itching or a rash and 2) Type II DCS, which involves symptoms of the respiratory, circulatory, and/or central nervous system. These symptoms include: paralysis, shock, weakness, dizziness, numbness, tingling, difficulty breathing, and varying degrees of joint and limb pain.

Fortunately, the incidence rate for DCS ('bends') is estimated by DAN to be only about 4 divers (not dives) in 10,000. Unfortunately, divers with fewer than 40 lifetime dives or who have been diving for less than two years account for some 40 percent of the DCIs. Paradoxically, divers with over 100 lifetime dives account for 44 percent!

A DCS hit can cripple you. Three months post treatment some thirteen percent of the divers treated continue to experience residual impairment.[II] Minimize your susceptibility to DCI as it can happen to the inexperienced, the complacent experienced diver, and to those pushing the dive envelope.

Looking again at DAN's report, the data strongly suggests that the likelihood of a DCS hit increases significantly when the depth of repetitive dives exceeds 80 feet. For their reporting purposes, a repetitive dive is any dive that occurs within 10 minutes to 6 hours of a previous dive.

DCI will be discussed thoroughly when you take your open water SCUBA certification course. Suffice it to say here, you can minimize your susceptibility to DCI if you follow the recommendations in Listing O.

Listing O. Recommendations for Avoiding DCI.
* *Stay within the safe diving bounds of the dive tables or your computer,*
* *stay hydrated, avoid strenuous exercise, and activities that increase circulation,*
* *slowly ascend to the surface (no faster than 30 feet/minute),*
* *always do a safety stop at about 15 feet for 3 minutes (take into account swells, avoid full inhalations, and breathe continuously (the greatest pressure change occurs in the top 15 feet of water),*
* *ascend slowly from your safety stop,*

❖ *the more repetitive dives you do in a day, the more likely you are to get a DCS hit,*

❖ *do not make repetitive dives (dives within 12 hours) that exceed 80 feet* (some agencies recommend 100 feet),

❖ *extend the minimum time between dives to 60 minutes,*

❖ *stay in shape* (particularly if over 40), and

❖ *take a diving break* (a day off mid-week) if you are doing a week's worth of diving.

A diver literally decompresses (off-gases nitrogen) as they ascend from every dive. Just because a staged decompression (see Question 84) is not required does not mean you do not decompress. Remain cognizant of what causes a DCI, dive accordingly, and you should have not have a problem. I have not experienced a DCI hit nor do I personally know anyone who has.

A hyperbaric chamber.

40. What is a hyperbaric chamber and how is it used?

Hyperbaric or recompression chambers are cylindrical, thick walled chambers with single or double doors (locks) at one end, in which one or more patients are placed (see image in Question 39). These chambers are usually in or near medical facilities located near popular dive sites or larger population centers (see Question 115). If you are a DAN (Divers Alert Network) member (see Question 89) and have DAN insurance, then your hyperbaric chamber costs are covered. Otherwise the cost is location, facility, and treatment-dependent and varies from about $500 to more than $5,500 plus Physician and other fees including transportation and hospital stay, if necessary.

Small, single lock, single-person (monoplace) chambers can be pressurized to a depth equivalent of 60 feet. Double-lock chambers are generally larger and capable of pressures up to at least six atmospheres, or about 165 feet. Oxygen within the double-lock chamber is usually supplied via demand masks or an oxygen hood.

The initial depth equivalent for bends (DCS or decompression sickness) treatment is about three atmospheres (66 feet). For air embolisms (obstructions to blood flow in blood vessels due to a bubble of air), the chamber is initially pressurized to 165 feet. If the diver is unconscious, then ear and sinus squeezes (unequal exterior vs. inner pressure between air spaces) could be a problem even with an open airway. In some cases, a medical professional will 'ride' along to monitor and deliver medical assistance to the patient.

Hyperbaric recompression generally follows a table or schedule of treatment varying from 90 minutes to 5.5 hours or more. Commonly-used tables are Table 5 (2.5 hours of varying compression), Table 6 (5 hours), and Table 6A (5.5 hours). The application of pressure and the breathing of oxygen reduces the size of circulatory nitrogen bubbles. That is why in DCI emergencies, 100 percent oxygen should be given as part of the first aid treatment. Chambers are also used in the treatment of non-dive related problems like carbon monoxide poisoning and gangrene. If possible, try and get a 'ride' in a chamber just to see what it is like.

41. Why don't whales get the bends?

Whales do not get the bends because there is no hyperbaric chamber big enough to accommodate them. OK, actually it is *because they do not breathe compressed air at depth. Additionally, their small lung capacity compared to humans does not enable them to inhale enough nitrogen to saturate much of their huge body mass.* According to the Guinness Book of Records a sperm whale is on record of diving to 8,202 feet! Talk about a diver feeling insignificant with maximum recreational SCUBA depths of 130 feet and that for only a few minutes.

While I am talking about free-diving whales and SCUBA, let me express a warning about mixing the two, i.e., free-diving and SCUBA (not whales and SCUBA). In 1997, there was a fatality from a young man free-diving then breathing off his father's SCUBA unit at depth (about 20 feet) then rising to the surface with an AGE (arterial gas embolism).

When you free-dive, you take a breath at the surface then dive and generally hold it on ascent. This is not a problem (unless you experience shallow-water blackout (see next paragraph)). However, if you free-dive, descend, take a breath off a SCUBA unit at depth and hold it upon ascent, then the gas (air) in your lungs will expand and potentially cause an AGE (arterial gas embolism) or rupture your lung. Of course, you can vent the air upon ascending, but are you going to remember that sometimes you have to vent and sometimes you do not? *Do not mix free-diving and SCUBA! Do one or the other, but not both at the same time.*

Now about shallow-water blackout when free-diving. The sensation of needing to breathe is triggered in the brain by the buildup of carbon dioxide in the body, not because of a lack of oxygen. If you hyperventilate (take breaths in quick succession) at the surface, then you can generally hold your breath a little longer because you have eliminated more carbon dioxide from your body. The problem occurs when the diver hyperventilates so much that the build up of carbon dioxide does not trigger the desire to breathe until the diver is hypoxic (insufficient oxygen) to such an extent that they pass out before reaching the surface (shallow-water blackout). This hypoxia occurs because at depth, the increased pressure of the air in the lungs enables the body to consume oxygen at levels that would leave the diver unconscious on or near the surface. *To avoid shallow-water blackout do not hyperventilate more than three breaths before free-diving.*

A Gray Whale diving .. without SCUBA.

42. I'm all wet. How can I become dehydrated when diving?

One of the interesting paradoxes in diving, is the tendency for the diver to become dehydrated (lose water or body fluids). Dehydration related to diving is important because it can sneak up on the diver. Dehydration is connected with increased stress on the heart and the decreased ability of the body to regulate its temperature properly. Additionally, dehydration increases a diver's propensity toward decompression sickness (DCS).

As a diver becomes dehydrated, the volume of blood in the body decreases, which causes the heart to work harder and pump faster. This leads to a decrease in endurance. Additionally, as your blood supply is being shunted to your vital organs and away from skin and muscle (see Question 38), your ability to adequately regulate your extremity temperature is decreased. Thus, dehydration increases because of that shunting. Further, the lower blood volume impedes your body's ability to eliminate wastes, e.g., nitrogen. Thus the diver can not off-gas (remove nitrogen via the lungs) as efficiently or as completely. This higher nitrogen level remaining in the body increases the risk of DCS (decompression sickness or 'bends').

As a diver, you will need to be aware of the mechanisms that increase your loss of water and body fluids. See Listing P for a list of some of those processes.

Listing P. Mechanisms Causing Dehydration in the Diver.

✿ *Increased physical activity* associated with diving and non-replacement of the fluids lost,

✿ *heavy perspiration and loss by heavy breathing* due to exertion and effects of sun and wind in a warm climate,

✿ *loss through breathing low humidity air, e.g., airline air, air conditioned motel rooms,* etc.,

✿ your body, upon entering the water, tends to constrict the blood vessels in the skin to minimize heat loss, which serves to *push more blood to the center of the body thus increasing urine output,*

✿ *SCUBA tanks have extremely dry air* in them, causing increased amounts of water to be lost from the body by breathing (your exhaled breath has a humidity of 100 percent) {check out some Apollo and Sherwood regulators that have metal fins or sponges which add moisture to the air you breathe},

☼ *immersion diuresis* (kidneys excreting an increased quantity of fluid or urine) is seen in divers, snorkelers and swimmers because of the negative pressure breathing (sucking air), which causes a fluid loss of some 350 cc/hour from the circulating blood volume,

☼ *cold inhibits the anti-diuretic hormone,*

☼ *hypercarbia (increased CO_2 levels) with diving decreases antidiuretic hormone* (see above),

☼ *diuretics such as alcohol, coffee, tea contribute to fluid loss,*

☼ *the state of chronic hypovolemia (reduced amount of liquids in the body) and hypokalemia (abnormal decrease in blood potassium concentration) caused by oral diuretics* (medicines),

☼ *traveler's diarrhea* can result in dehydration in a very short time, and

☼ *menstruation* is important, as some women can become slightly dehydrated during their menses.

With all the above mechanisms causing dehydration and the negative affects of becoming dehydrated, its prevention cannot be over-stated. To avoid becoming dehydrated, you should hydrate with regular ingestion of non-diuretic fluids (water, dilute juice, sports drinks, etc.) several hours before, 15-20 minutes before, and between dives. Particularly if multiple dives are to be made each day. As a means of monitoring hydration, Dr. Jeff Davis proposes that the urine of an adequately hydrated diver should be "clear and copious".

One way to fight dehydration while on an extended saltwater dive is to carry a half-liter Platypus® (or similar) with a bite valve, obtainable from a sports outfitter. These bags can be filled with fresh water or dilute juice and placed in a BC pocket. The tube can then be routed up the BC shoulder strap and secured at the shoulder. To get a swig, hold your regulator in one hand and the tube in the other and bite on the bite valve. I have heard that some divers take a container of Capri Sun fruit juice to depth and drink it via the attached straw.

For further information on dehydration and diving please see www.scubadiving.com/training/medicine/dangersdehydration. shtml, www.gulftel.com/~scubadoc/dehyd.htm and the diving medicine references in the 'Diving Deeper into SCUBA' section.

A diver not watching his level of dehydration!

43. Won't my ears hurt when I dive?

As you descend, the increased pressure of the water pushing on your eardrums can cause pain (ear squeeze) unless the internal and external pressures are equalized. To avoid ear squeeze you should equalize before you begin feeling the pain and equalize often. If you are having problems equalizing, then you will want to ascend a little and equalization should become easier. Adequate equalization depends on air flowing through the Eustachian tubes from the throat to the middle ear, so do not dive if they are blocked. By the way, never ever dive with earplugs!

During your open water course you will be taught several methods to equalize and thus avoid the pain associated with an ear squeeze. Four methods are: the Frenzel maneuver (thrusting the jaw and tongue forward while keeping your throat closed), the Toynbee maneuver (swallowing with the mouth and nose closed), swallowing and jaw wiggling work for some, and the Valsalva maneuver (attempting to blow or exhale against a closed nose and mouth).

As the Valsalva maneuver is the most forceful, the other techniques should be used instead, if possible. Again, it is critical to apply these techniques often enough and properly so as to avoid potentially serious problems with your ears. See Listing Q for measures to take to avoid ear squeezes.

Listing Q. Measures to Take to Avoid or Minimize Ear Squeezes.
- *Always test to be sure you can equalize before you dive,*
- *do not dive with a cold* even if you can equalize since nasal congestion can get worse during a dive, making equalization difficult, which could lead to ear injury and cessation of your diving for life,
- *if possible, equalize using the least forceful equalization techniques,*
- *equalize before you feel ear discomfort,*
- *if you cannot equalize then abort your dive,* and
- *descend slowly while equalizing often.*

Dr. Ernest S. Campbell at www.gulftel.com/~scubadoc/ fitear.htm states, "Ear problems are the most common medical problems in diving. The ears, including the ear drums, must be healthy in order to dive safely. Fitness evaluation requires a thorough evaluation of the ears. Aural barotrauma (ear squeeze) occurs in all divers, and can be avoided by careful attention to ear clearing during descent, and the maintenance of open air passages in the ears and throat. A perforated ear drum, chronic ear infections, and unilateral hearing loss should make a candidate unfit to dive."

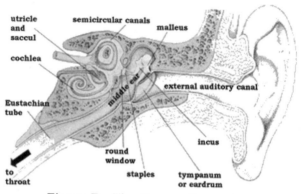

Figure B. The Human Ear

My Father was SCUBA certified many years ago. After a time, he stopped diving because of pressure trauma to the middle ear and bleeding from the middle ear so that blood came down the Eustachian tube (see Figure B). Whether the problem was congenital (we have genetic problems with our ears) or brought on by diving, it is critical to take proper care of the ears or your diving years could be cut short.

44. My boat just sunk. How do I go about recovering it?

For some, one of the neatest things about becoming SCUBA certified is the ability to search for and recover lost items underwater. *One of the specialties offered by most of the certifying agencies, see Question 12, is in fact, 'Search and Recovery'.* To help in the search, an underwater metal detector can be used (see http://www.detectorpro.com for one company of several offering such devices.)

However, before you get carried away trying to raise your yacht, there are a few things you should know. Be aware that the recommended maximum capacity of a recreational lift bag is 50 pounds and you should not attempt to carry anything by hand to the surface greater than 10 pounds. If the object weights more than 50 pounds then attach a line from it to the surface and pull it up from within the boat.

Getting the specialized training for search and recovery is necessary to avoid injury to yourself and others. Using a large lift bag to lift a small object is unwise because of the potential for a runaway ascent (faster than 60 feet per minute). Lift bags must be controllable and professionals often attach multiple lower capacity bags than one large one. The most important safety feature of a lift bag is a means to vent the air that expands during ascent.

There will be numerous pleasure dives during which you will come across something you would like to bring back to the boat. Carry a 'bailout bottle' (not your redundant air source) and a lift bag with marker-buoy for retrieving weight belts and heavier items (to 50 pounds) lost from boats. Freeing an object embedded in the mud can be dangerous. You will be taught the proper methods in the specialty, but one thing is a no-no. Never use the lift bag to free the object from the mud. This is because as it becomes free of the mud's suction it could very well rocket uncontrolled to the surface.

In the Search and Recovery specialty, you will be taught how to rig the lift bag to support the object, attach the item securely, attach the item so it will not flip over, and attach your treasure so it is easily untied. The most important thing to remember is to keep everyone clear of the area below the lift. When possible, secure the item to the surface via the boat, float, or a surface support station.

Raising heavy and bulky objects (like your yacht) should be left to the professional and experienced recovery (salvage) diver.

45. I have no friends. How important is buddy diving?
Unless you are a sociopath (which if you are, please take up writing a book on diving instead of diving), SCUBA is a great way to meet some nice people and make some long term friends.

According to DAN (Divers Alert Network), in 1996 8.2 percent of the fatalities occurred while diving without a buddy, and in 1997 it was 12 percent. Every open water certification agency I know emphasizes the importance of buddy diving. All those making solo dives can be considered in 'violation' of accepted safe-diving procedures for recreational SCUBA divers (RSD) and thus theoretically making a technical dive.

According to DAN, buddy separation (at sometime during the accident) is reported in nearly 61 percent of the fatalities reported each year.[C] Thus, not only must you start your dive with a buddy, you must also stay close to each other. DAN's opinion is, "While diving with a buddy may range from keeping close contact throughout the dive, to being in the same general area, having another diver available to offer assistance may mean the difference between life and death. Buddy separation eliminates the availability of immediate assistance and significantly increases the chance that a diver in distress will drown before reaching the surface." That is a strong statement and certainly a word to the wise open water certificated diver.

Not only is a buddy someone with whom you can share air and who provides other assistance during the dive, but you should also assist each other in your pre-dive equipment donning and checks. Ideally, buddies should have similar training, skill levels, and dive goals. It is not buddy diving when a buddy dives deeper or stays down longer than you do or takes 20 minutes to photograph a rock when you want to explore. Buddies should stay close together and always be aware of each other's location.

On the other hand, Robert Von Maier makes the point in his book Solo Diving, The Art of Underwater Self-Sufficiency[JJ] that there certainly are solo divers (and of course DAN's statistics bear that fact out). Von Maier cautions that solo divers should be experienced divers that are physically and mentally fit, well-trained, and capable of self-sufficiency (including self-rescue). They should also be self-evaluative (there may be times one should not dive solo), practice effective air management, always conduct safe dive planning (see Question 48), and carry a redundant air supply (see Question 99).

Von Maier has two primary rules for solo diving. The first rule is to never dive solo deeper than twice the depth to which you can free-dive. The second rule is that a fully equipped, solo diver's underwater maximum distance from the point of exit should not exceed the distance that they can comfortably and easily swim on the surface.

Probably the most likely cause of an accident for an experienced diver, diving solo is becoming unconscious due to any number of causes {full-facemasks may mitigate this problem}.[F]   Yet many agree that it is better to dive solo than with an incompetent or dangerous (careless, untrained, or unfit) buddy.

It can be argued that the professional underwater macro photographer and spear fisherman often dive solo. Diving solo is certainly done, but the fact that 61 percent of DAN's diver fatalities were separated from their buddy (including diving with no buddy) and that most divers do not dive solo makes for some pretty substantial rational for diving with a reliable buddy with similar dive goals.

If you do agree to be a buddy, then you take on moral, if not legal, obligations during a dive. Some of those obligations are listed in Listing R.

Listing R. Buddy Obligations.
- ✓   Stay *within visual or physical contact* with your buddy,
- ✓   *communicate with your buddy as to their well-being and monitor each other's air,*
- ✓   *have a plan to reunite if separated and implement it if necessary* (generally look around for a minute then surface but it is situation-dependent, just agree before the dive),
- ✓   *provide help or assistance to your buddy as needed,*
- ✓   *if needed, perform a rescue to the best of your ability* (this does not include sacrificing your life), and
- ✓   upon surfacing, *review what a great dive you two just had!*

One last thought on buddy diving: *Do not get into diving situations or conditions that you know are too advanced or dangerous for you with the expectation that your buddy is going to save your bacon.* Never dive above your abilities for self-rescue, as you might be the buddy called on for assistance. Giving that assistance to your buddy would be difficult to do if you are also in trouble or do not know what to do.

46. I have lots of friends. How do I converse underwater?
Communicate means "to transmit information, thought, or
feeling so that it is satisfactorily received or understood".[O]
There are numerous ways that divers can communicate
amongst themselves underwater. *The three primary means of
communication include visual (seeing), tactile (feeling), and
audible (hearing).*

On land, a good portion of close-proximity human
communication is done using our vocal cords and ears {though
with the advent of the Internet the fingers and eyes are
becoming more important}. Yet, for humans, water is a poor
medium in which to converse, particularly with our unaided
vocal chords {though great for whales, dolphins, etc.}. As the
majority of recreational diving is done in water where there is
adequate to excellent visibility, *the majority of diver
communication is probably visual* {this may change with the
increased use of full-face masks and electronic inter-personal
communication}.

*Common visual communications used by divers are hand signals,
written messages, and the use of light.* You will be taught the
common hand signals used in SCUBA diving in your open water
course. Some divers go so far as to learn a modified form of
American Sign Language (ASL). This modified version attempts
to restrict signing to the use of only one hand thus freeing the
other hand for diving tasks. SeaSigns has a video and flash
card training program that uses ASL (they can be contacted via
http://www.seasigns.com.) You should also always carry at
least a small underwater slate for more complex
communications or to record headings, time, and distance. A
flashlight should also always be carried.

*Tactile communication is mostly used in water with limited
visibility or in restricted areas where divers cannot easily make
visual contact.* Examples would include cave and wreck diving
(neither of which should the open water diver participate in
without additional training). In caves and wrecks, divers may
have to proceed in single file thus tactile communication
becomes important (though light is also used extensively). If
you choose to take additional training in wreck and cave diving,

you will be taught appropriate tactile communication (line pulls and hand squeezes).

As mentioned in Question 108, sounds travels well in water, but it is difficult for humans to determine from whence the sound came. *As of this printing, sound is used primarily as a means of attention getting, as a distress signal, and a means of recalling divers to the dive boat* (though I suspect Morse code could be used?) Typically, the sound produced by the diver is via tank tapping (using the metal cap on the handle of a dive knife (see Question 105)), whistle attached to BC (above water), compressed air 'horn' (above and below water models), and clicking devices.

The use of underwater communication (comm) units (think of it as underwater CB) by recreational SCUBA divers is in its infancy and no doubt will improve with time. Comm units work best with full-face masks, but are expensive at around $900 for mask, comm unit, and regulator.

Use of the standard SCUBA mask makes your communications more difficult to understand and the equipment tends to be bulky. These comm units have a range of some 300 feet (depending on intervening underwater structure), thus are more than adequate for most recreational SCUBA uses. An Ocean Technology Buddy Phone XT 100H will set you back about $425 and a Divelink UC01-120 is around $750.

Personally, unless there were good reasons to wear a comm unit, i.e., safety considerations, assist in meeting the dive objectives (search and rescue), etc., I would not invest in them. For me, part of the recreational SCUBA diving experience is the absence of human vocalizations and being able to hear the background noises in the ocean (sense of solitude). To go diving and have a CB like unit constantly going off in my ears would not be relaxing. However, they do have their uses and when needed are certainly better than two tin cans and a string.

47. Will future advances make SCUBA diving even safer?

There are quite a few enhancements to recreation SCUBA diving which are being implemented and others that are undergoing continued development. These improvements will continue to make SCUBA one of the safest and enjoyable avocations. Some of the implemented and under-development improvements can be viewed in Listing S.

Listing S. Future Enhancements to SCUBA for Increased Safety.

- The *increase in the number of hyperbaric chambers* throughout the world,

- the *increased posting of underwater signs and educational efforts to keep untrained open water SCUBA divers out of caves,*

- the *increased usage of dive computers,*

- use of *full-face masks* that can remain covering the diver's face if they become unconscious, thus helping to protect against immediate drowning,

- increased perfection of *underwater voice communication and homing systems,*

- *longer lasting, more reliable, and brighter underwater lights,*

- use of *"heads up" displays* in divers' masks enabling the ready viewing of pertinent dive related information, and

- *continuous monitoring of nitrogen concentrations in the diver by the dive computer* via transducers attached to the diver.

48. I drive a Volvo. Can I be safe diving?

Recreational SCUBA diving (RSD) is a relatively safe avocation, but it is not risk free {what is?}. Ultimately, you dive at your own risk. *Looking at diving's safety record over the past 15 years (1983 to 1997), DAN (Divers Alert Network) estimates that there have been on the average only 89 fatalities per year.* There are some 8,500,000 certified divers in the U.S. with some 2,500,000 of them making an estimated 19,000,000 dives a year (see Question 21). *Over the past 15 years that is only one fatality for every 215,000 dives* {estimated, as no one knows for sure how many dives are made each year}. The RSD accident rate is well below that of snow skiing or mountain biking and even lower than American football, baseball, water skiing, soccer, volleyball, and racquetball.[S]

Please note that the fatality rate of 1 in every 215,000 dives relates to all types of recreational SCUBA dives. If you dive more cautiously, with well-maintained equipment, are in good physical condition, and well-trained, then you can dramatically reduce that rate as it applies to you {remember that old bell curve from dreaded statistics?}

The reader should also note that of those 89 fatalities per year, roughly 40 percent of them {36} were fatalities in which coincidental medical events occurred while diving. This reinforces the concept that the wise diver is a healthy and fit diver who gets regular checkups. Do that and you have drastically reduced the likelihood that you will end up in DAN's report. {Caveat: a vascular incident while diving is not always foreseeable, even with a medical checkup.}

Looking further into the causes of the remaining 53 fatalities, it was found that approximately 25 percent of the yearly fatalities were due to environmental causes. These environmental causes include cave dives, rough surf entries, rough seas, and strong currents. Thus the importance of knowing your physical limits, being adequately trained and equipped, and knowing the dive conditions. If divers would abstain from diving under questionable environmental conditions and be physically fit, it would bring the fatalities down closer to 31 a year.

Fatalities caused by denizens of the deep are relatively rare. The concern over shark attacks on divers is grossly overstated. We must be far more concerned about running out of air, being over-weighted, and diving with poorly maintained equipment. *In fact, about 15 percent of the fatal accidents are due to equipment problems.* Thus, maintaining our equipment and monitoring our air, not diving in questionable environmental conditions, and being physically fit would bring the yearly fatalities nearer to 18.

The remaining some 18 fatalities are generally due to panic, exhaustion, AGE (arterial gas embolism), bad air (see Question 17), collisions with boats, etc.

The good part of all this is that the diver generally has some control over about 80 percent of the causes of diving fatalities (Dr. Samuel Shelanski in Question 24 argues for 100 percent). The bad part is that there will always be those divers who stretch the limits. Additionally, Murphy lives, we do not always make the right decisions {in hindsight}, there will be physical conditions that cannot be foreseen, and even following the recommended procedures will not guarantee absolute safety.

The lowest numbers of yearly RSD fatalities in the past 28 years were 66 in 1988 and 67 in 1991. So you can see that RSD is relatively safe, but we can do better. We can do better by following as many of the suggestions in Listing T as reasonably possible.

Listing T. Suggestions for Safer Diving.

- *Never hold your breath underwater.*
- When faced with a problem: *stop, breathe, think, then act.*
- *Get adequately trained for the diving* you intend to do.
- *Apply and augment your training on every dive.*
- Realize *there will be dives that are beyond your capabilities* and do not do them.
- *Recognize your limitations* and correct them before proceeding with that riskier dive.
- *Adhere to an exercise program* and be physically fit.

➤ *If you must drink, do so in moderation* and stop at least 12 hours before a dive. *If you do drugs* (even some over-the-counter and prescription drugs), *then do not dive.*

➤ *Get regular checkups* and seek additional medical advice for changes in physical condition between checkups.

➤ *Give your equipment regular checkups.* Bring all the equipment you will need on a dive so you will not have to 'make do' with unfamiliar equipment. Put together an equipment list and check it before leaving home (see Question 93).

➤ *Do an introspective check on mental, emotional, and physical well being* before each dive. Do not dive if you do not feel well (do not deny potential DCI symptoms). Do not be pressured into diving. Be rested and reasonably unstressed.

➤ *Practice boat safety*, including donning, doffing, and storage of equipment while on board.

➤ *Be knowledgeable concerning the dive you are about to make.* Know what to avoid and what to look for. What are the environmental issues. If you have questions, ask the Divemaster or crew.

➤ *Do equipment checks and dive planning* (including depths and bottom time) before each dive.

➤ *Dive with a competent and responsible buddy.*

➤ *Dive with reliable, safe, and friendly dive operators.*

➤ *On descent, clear ears, etc. before you feel any pain.*

➤ *Monitor your air supply.*

➤ *Monitor your buddy's air supply.*

➤ *Try to resolve problems at depth* rather than resorting to panic (see Question 22) and rapid ascents {easy to say, much harder to adhere to}. If all else fails, then get positively buoyant on the surface (DROP THE WEIGHTS!) (see Question 101).

➤ *Do not become hypothermic or dehydrated.*

➤ *Be fanatical about slow ascent rates (rates of 30-45 feet per minute) (see Question 98) and completing a full safety stop* on every dive. Be sure the surface is clear (as much as possible) before ascending to the surface.

- *Know what to do if faced with different accident or problem scenarios.* Review and practice techniques. *Become CPR, Medic/First Aid, Rescue diver, and Oxygen Provider certified.*
- *Read everything you can on recreational SCUBA diving and related.*
- *Know and respect the physical laws which govern SCUBA diving.*
- *Be alert and have fun diving.*

As a certified open water SCUBA diver, it is you who are responsible for the safety of your dives. Practice safe diving. Sell that Volvo, get a sports car, SUV, or 4x4 and live a little. Life goes by way too fast. Ok, Ok, then get a sporty Volvo C 70 convertible coupe.

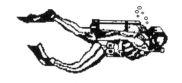

sc**U**ba

The U in SCUBA ..
Personal Considerations

49. Can I dive with my rubber ducky?

Hey, if you feel more comfortable having your bathtub rubber ducky along with you, then place him/her/it in a pocket of your BC and go diving together. Note that rubber duckies do NOT count as dive buddies and it does not matter if it is a diving duck. When I rode my Goldwing motorcycle, I always had a stuffed Alf go along on the handle bar {Alf's real name was Gordon Shumway, so I figured we must be related somehow}.

Do be aware, though, that the deeper you go the more pressure that will be applied to your rubber friend. At 130 feet an originally hollow ducky will be pretty flat {this is a neat thing to see with a tennis or racket ball if you do not have a rubber ducky}. One warning though: Do not inflate ducky at depth or you could have a very distended if not exploded ducky at or near the surface. This would not be good because a bloated ducky does not float up right very well {I suspect}.

50. Do I have to be a good swimmer to get my C-card?
You do not need to be a Johnny Weismuller {shows my age} or a Mark Spitz to be SCUBA certified, but you should be a reasonably proficient swimmer who is comfortable and able to relax in the water. If you do not currently know how to swim, it is an easy thing to learn. Take lessons from your local YMCA, college, independent instructor, or similar.

The swimming requirements to begin your certification work are generally a 200-yard nonstop swim with no time constraints or specific strokes required, and diving to pick an item off the pool bottom. You will also need to be able to tread water or float for at least 10 minutes unassisted. Finally, you should be able to submerge and open your eyes underwater and swim 15 yards underwater without pushing off or using gear. None of these requirements are difficult if you know how to swim and are in reasonable shape.

Some people argue that knowing how to swim is not necessary for SCUBA as you always have a BC for flotation and fins for propulsion. However, it is the opinion of many that *the primary key to being successful with SCUBA, is being comfortable in the water.* Knowing how to swim just increases that comfort level. Your swimming abilities will likely improve during the pool sessions by virtue of practice, repetition, and your increased self-confidence. Swimming is great exercise, too.

51. Won't I get claustrophobic or agoraphobic when I dive?
SCUBA diving can produce some symptoms of claustrophobia (fear of closed spaces) and even agoraphobia (fear of open spaces) in otherwise 'normal' people. If you tend to be more than normally claustrophobic or agoraphobic, then you should certainly seek medical advice as to how severe your condition is and whether you should be involved in diving.

Diving is a little claustrophobic for some because you dive with a mask that covers your eyes and nose. Having anything on our face is unnatural for us terrestrials and may take a little getting used to. Possibly getting a high volume mask with side panels would help. You will be a little busier clearing mask squeezes, but your peripheral vision will be increased.

Additionally, dives among kelp and other underwater structures may be a little intimidating at first, but when you see all the life these structures harbor, you will become enchanted and likely end up enjoying the dive. I was initially apprehensive of ocean and kelp diving as I was trained in Pennsylvania quarries. So on my first dive off Catalina Island, California (famous for its kelp) I paid for a Divemaster to buddy up with my brother (who has dived for years) and myself. The kelp dive turned out to be fantastic and I now thread my way through the stuff with relish, always wondering what is around the next frond.

Another way to minimize your claustrophobia is to get used to diving in warm water with minimal underwater structures and good visibility before venturing into colder waters with minimal visibility.

Open water can seem to go on and on and on when you are looking down into it, particularly when there is great visibility and the suns' rays are jutting toward the edge of your visibility. We humans have been subjected to the forces of gravity since birth and it is believed that the only innate fear we have is that of falling. *Certainly, floating effortlessly over a seemingly bottomless water column is a new experience for some.* Because of our experiences with gravity, we may think we are going to fall or sink into the abyss.

Buoyancy control is the key that makes SCUBA work for us. In fact, most of us have to add weight to achieve neutral buoyancy. However, if initially you feel intimidated, then start with relatively shallow water dives with OK visibility. Most of the marine life and light is above 80 feet or so anyway. If you feel more comfortable at 80 or 50 or 15 feet, then you need not go deeper to enjoy SCUBA diving.

The primary thing you must keep in mind is that RECREATIONAL SCUBA diving is supposed to be just that: recreational, which means enjoyable. If you are not comfortable with a dive, then do not do it (but of course do not leave your buddy at risk or in the dark about your desire to abort the dive; abort the dive together). Anyone so insensitive and ignorant as to chastise you about your choice is not a good dive buddy for you. You both should choose different dive partners.

52. I am pretty lazy. Is SCUBA strenuous?

Depending on the type of diving, SCUBA diving can be strenuous or relaxing, with all gradations in between. As SCUBA diving is a fairly equipment intensive avocation, it means that somebody will have to get the equipment to the dive site. After that, you will have to don all that equipment. Then you will have to get into the water and deal with the environmental conditions you find there. When you have completed the dive(s), you will have to do everything in reverse. I will go through three dive scenarios, two extremes, and something in the middle. You can decide which suits you.

One example of a strenuous dive could be some shore dives (dives such as cave, deep, and ice diving can be even more strenuous but they are beyond the scope of 'SCUBA Scoop'). It can be strenuous if you have to make a long walk from the parking lot to water's edge over sand while carrying or rolling your gear (yet for some shore dives you obviously can park at water's edge).

Donning the equipment in extreme temperature will also increase the effort and discomfort involved (do not let your self get over-heated!). Upon entering the water, you might find strong surf and currents in which it could be difficult to maneuver. Know the area and surf ingress/egress techniques before diving. Cold water temperatures, lack of visibility, rocks and other hazards can make the dive more strenuous. When the dive objectives have been met, you will have to turn around and do everything in reverse. This type of diving appeals to some but as the question includes the statement "I am pretty lazy", let's assume this type of dive is not for you.

Something between the extremes is a day boat dive not far from home. Pile all the gear into the car, pick up your buddy, and drive to the dock. As your dive bag has wheels, it is relatively easy to wheel your gear along the dock to the boat. In this scenario, the tanks and weights are part of the package so you do not have to lug them around. The weather is good and you will be diving in good visibility in reasonably temperate water with minimal current.

Don your gear without breaking much of a sweat and after the pre-dive stuff you just plop over the side. Ease on down and make a relaxing dive. This is probably a more typical recreational SCUBA diving scenario. Not too strenuous, but you will have to work harder than sitting in your easy chair typing on your computer while in a chat room.

Probably one of the least strenuous ways to dive is diving from a live aboard. Select a week-long live aboard which cruises warm, clear, low current waters, has great food, warm showers, comfortable beds, lots of elbow room, knowledgeable and helpful staff, and the hardest thing you will have to do will be to go back home.

Of course, this question is somewhat tongue-in-cheek. A truly lazy person would (should) not become a SCUBA diver. Getting trained, maintaining fitness to dive, and actual diving all involve an activity level which a truly 'lazy' person would avoid. On the other hand, we do participate in recreational SCUBA diving, so keep it enjoyable.

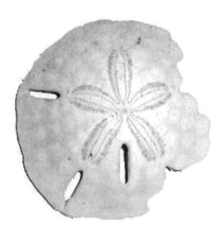

53. I am overweight. Can I SCUBA dive?

Yes.

Now the long answer. As with most things in life, there are gradations of being overweight. Of course, to know if you are overweight, you have to know your ideal weight. There are many ways of determining your ideal weight. Insurance companies use actuarial data on life expectancy based on the correlation of weight-for-height to life span. Many doctors use a Body-Mass Index (BMI) measurement or a person's weight divided by height. Some clinicians use the percent-total-body-fat measurement for determining level of obesity. Total body fat of less than 22 percent in males and less than 28 percent in females is recommended.

A simple, though not extremely accurate, rule of thumb for determining if you are overweight for men is to start with 106 pounds for the first 5 feet of height and add 6 pounds for each additional inch. For women it is 100 pounds for the first 5 feet of height and 5 pounds for every additional inch {yeah, I know, men must have made up this rule}. Of course, the majority of Americans come in overweight and some of these rules do not take into account body composition, but that is beyond the scope of 'SCUBA Scoop'.

Since a goodly number of Americans are overweight, it is conceivable that there will be overweight SCUBA divers. In fact there certainly are some very experienced and adroit divers who are overweight. Yet being overweight increases health risks. These health risks involve the musculoskeletal system (neck and back problems due to heavy lifting, climbing, exaggerated movements, etc.), cardiovascular system (coronary artery disease, hypertension, etc.), and general stamina.

Some of the problems encountered by those who are grossly overweight or obese are listed in Listing U. These problems alone should encourage the obese diver to shed those extra pounds.

Listing U. Problems Encountered by the Obese Diver.

♥ *Increased risk of DCS* (decompression sickness) because nitrogen (the gas most responsible for DCS) is five times more soluble in fat than in muscle tissue. This means that the obese diver will accumulate more nitrogen on any given dive than a thinner diver. This predisposition to increased nitrogen solubility was not factored into the original Navy dive tables because they were created for young, fit, male divers. The obese diver should therefore follow a more conservative dive profile (older, obese, female divers should really be conservative in their dive profiles).

♥ *Increased risk of heart attack* because the overweight diver is less prepared to deal with the increased exertion that a long surface swim or long swims against current necessitate. Having a mild heart attack on land is not a wonderful experience, but in water the diver who could have survived the mild attack might not because they drowned.

♥ *Increased air consumption is common in obese divers* because of cellular need, decreased physiological efficiencies, and increased drag while swimming. Significant currents can pose a very real danger to the obese diver. On one of my earlier dives, I was paired as a buddy with a diver who must have weighed in excess of 350 pounds. He was a tall, big man and turned out to be a good guy. We had an interesting time diving among kelp of Catalina Island, California and I was surprised by his ability to match my air consumption (least as we compared pressure gauges during the dive). Upon getting back aboard the dive boat I commented on his great air consumption and was chagrinned to learn he was diving with an over-pressurized steel 120 compared to my Al 80 (see Question 96). All else being equal, larger divers do consume more air and must compensate with larger and heavier tanks for equal bottom time.

♥ *Given the increased air consumption, there may be an increased propensity to panic because of regulator over-breathing during over-exertion.* Regulator over-breathing could lead to a rapid ascent, which would further increase the likelihood of DCS in obese divers.

♥ *Obese divers tend to have more problems with buoyancy control.* They have to carry more weight to counter the increased buoyancy of fat as compared to muscle. Not only is the increased weight potentially hard on the back and hips but, if it is not well distributed it can lead to difficulties in balance.

♥ *Poorly fitting equipment is also a problem.* Most of the manufactures make equipment based on what sells. Obese divers may have difficulty in finding BCs (buoyancy compensators) that fit well and are thus constricting or hinder movement. Exposure suits have to be custom made in order to fit. Obese divers should make sure their suit fits or it could lead to constriction of the chest, inability to breathe properly, and carbon dioxide buildup. Finding a weight belt long enough could also be a problem. Linking two belts together could create a safety problem. If you are using weight harnesses, be sure your buddy knows how to remove it quickly {and that it can be removed from under a BC}. One recent SCUBA fatality involved a problem that occurred at depth. The diver could not get his weight harness off and he was too heavy to be lifted by his buddy. If you wear a harness, make sure it can be removed easily and that your buddy knows how to do it too.

Recreational SCUBA divers need to have a reasonable level of physical fitness because of the stresses of the underwater environment and the pre- and post-dive exertion required. The initial medical clearance to dive does not absolve the diver from getting regular checkups and keeping reasonably fit. Getting in shape for active diving is a great incentive for a regular exercise program, good dietary habits, and adequate sleep.

54. What are the physical benefits of SCUBA?
Being a conscientious and frequent recreational SCUBA diver encourages you to be more health-conscious and physically fit, gets you outdoors, and keeps you physically active. As can be seen in Question 24, it is the wise diver who minimizes their risk of panic, DCS (decompression sickness), being incapacitated underwater with a physical problem, and increases their ability to deal with emergencies by being physically fit (see Question 53).

The principled recreational diver will minimize their drinking, refrain from taking illegal substances that negatively impact body or mind, be careful about mixing medications and diving, stay hydrated, be physically fit, get regular checkups, and not smoke (see Question 18).

Not only does all of the above encourage a healthy life style, but it is certainly worth the effort (see Question 7).

55. What exercises are most beneficial for training to dive?
Fitness improves circulation, slows your heart rate, increases stamina, and provides a feeling of well-being. It takes six to eight weeks to develop fitness for an activity but only one week of inactivity to notice a decrease {doesn't that figure}.[M] A training program in which each workout produces slight incremental improvements is recommended.

The effectiveness of your training for diving depends upon the similarity between the training and diving. Therefore you would be best served by increasing your heart and lung capacity and flexibility. Consider exercises that increase flexibility, strength, and aerobic abilities. As the legs are the main means of propulsion, you should strengthen them. Swimming is a great exercise, particularly leg kicks.

Additionally, the more skilled an individual is at a certain activity, the more efficient will be their movements, thus saving energy and increasing stamina. Knowledge increases proficiency, so combine your study with physical exercise (skill practice).

Obviously, you expect me to tell you to consult your Physician before beginning an exercise program, so I just did.

56. I have a physical disability. Can I still SCUBA dive?
Recreational SCUBA diving offers those with disabilities an escape from the restrictions imposed upon them by gravity. Most disabled divers have learned that there is no one right way to accomplish a task (other than safely). The experts do not always have all the answers thus the disabled diver should be innovative and resourceful and seek assistance from one or more of the organizations in Listing V. As with most things in life, if you never really try, you will never know what you can accomplish.

NAUI, PADI, and most, if not all, of the certifying agencies, are in compliance with the Americans With Disabilities Act (ADA), and offer open water training for the disabled. Generally, their policy is that all possible and reasonable accommodations should be made to train and certify those individuals with disabilities, as long as it can be done safely and the student meets the minimum requirements for certification (see Question 80).

For more information regarding SCUBA diving for those with disabilities, you might contact one or more of the organizations and clubs in Listing V.

Listing V. Associations and Clubs for Disabled Divers.

  ♿ *Alpha One/Open Waters*, 127 Main St., So. Portland, ME 04106, (800) 640-7200, open_waters@alpha-one.org, http://www.alpha-one.org

  ♿ *American Association of Challenged Divers*, 8862 Sparren Way, San Diego, CA 92129; John Ellerbrock, (619) 538-3483, (619) 738-5204 fax, pinnacle@cts.com

  ♿ *Club Challenge*, 3108 Woodland Park Dr., Burlington, Ontario L7N 1L2, Canada, (905) 634-8234

  ♿ *Dis-A-Dive*, 3530 Warrensville Center Road, Suite 200, Shaker Heights, OH 44122 Bart Schassoort, (216)752-DIVE

  ♿ *Diving With Disabilities*, 14960 Penitencia Creek Road, San Jose, CA 95132, Bruce Van Hoorn (408) 258-9789

  ♿ *Eels on Wheels Adaptive Scuba Club*, 4020 Travis Country Circle, Austin, TX 78735, Tim Skelly, (512) 892-0863, tskelley@sig.net, http://www.eels.org

   ♿ *Handicapped Scuba Association International,* 1104 E. Prado, San Clemente, CA 92672-4637, Jim Gatacre, (949) 498-6128, hsahdq@compuserv.com www.ourworld.compuserve.com/homepages/hsahdq

   ♿ *Houston Disabled Scuba Divers Association,* 403 East Nasa Road 1, Suite 325, Webster TX 77598-5314, (713) 477-5556, swa@neosoft.com

   ♿ *Japan Underwater Leaders & Instructors Association (JULIA),* Let's Building, First Floor 2-18-6, Kohama-Nishi, Suminoe-Ku Osaka 449, Japan, +81-6-675-1228, Julia@maido.ne.jp, www.ryukyu.ne.jp/~annou/julia.html

   ♿ *Moray Wheels: Adpative Scuba Association,* P.O. Box 1660 GMF, Boston, MA 02205, Rusty Murray, Karen Clark, (603) 598-4292, info@moraywheels.org, www.moraywheels.org

   ♿ *National Instructors Association for Divers with Disabilities (NIADD),* Dorothy Shrout, P.O. Box 112223, Campbell; CA 95011-2223; (408) 379-6536, (408) 244- 8652 fax , stonely@pacbell.net

   ♿ *Pacific Northwest Scuba Challenge Association,* 14286 72nd Ave., Surey, BC V3W 2R1, Canada, Ron Stead, (604) 525-7149, ken_nore@sympatico.ca

   ♿ *Persephone Scuba Diving Club,* 188 St. Charles Rd., Beaconsfield, Quebec H9W 2X4, Canada, Dr. Louis Jankowski, (514) 848-3320, janoslu@vax2.concordia.ca

   ♿ *Southern Wheelchair Adventurers Association of Galveston-Houston,* P.O. Box 58118, Webster TX 77598-9118, (713) 477-5556, (Lytle Seibert); swa@neosoft.com, http://www.neosoft.com/~swa

   ♿ *Zero Gravity Diving Center,* P.O. Box 2893, South Portland, ME 04116 or 103 Ocean St., South Portland, ME 04106, Bill Demmons, (207)741-2110, (207)741-2881 fax, (800) 437-1220 (TTY), zerog @ ime.net, http://www.ime.net/zerogravity.org

57. I danced to Buddy Holly. Am I too old to dive?

Buddy who?

There is no set chronological age at which a diver should cease SCUBA diving {skin diving could still be an option} or that their certification is revoked. *Most of the issues dealing with senior divers deal with the diver's ability to physically and mentally do what is required during a dive.* Some recommend that the pre- and post-dive issues can be minimized by a senior diver having a personal dive guide who helps with donning and doffing of equipment, helps with water ingress and egress, and accompanies the senior on a minimally-demanding dive profile. This is true, but personally I would be hesitant to dive if I was unable to control most, if not all, aspects of the actual dive myself.

The Author

The reason for not having a set age for "hanging it up" is because a diver's chronological age is not the same as their physiological age {you are as young as you feel}. Yet senior divers do have a higher incidence of chronic diseases, e.g., cardiovascular and chronic lung diseases. Atherosclerosis decreases the blood flow to vital organs (heart and lungs) and the muscles, thus decreasing their functionality. Senior divers should unfailingly get yearly checkups and periodic exercise testing.[U]

Accident data indicates that as divers get older, their risk of DCS (decompression sickness) increases. This may be due, in part, to a decreased blood flow to the tissues. This decreased blood flow would decrease the body's ability to off-gas (eliminate excess nitrogen). Air Force data on altitude {not dive} DCS shows that even 28 year-olds are twice as likely as 18 year-olds in getting DCS.

Data collected from 1987 through 1996 by DAN (Divers Alert Network) shows that approximately 15 percent of the DCI (decompression illness) accidents were attributed to divers 45 and older.[C] PADI estimates that about 19 percent of the divers certified are 45 or better.[AA] Even though no one knows how many seniors are still diving, it does appear that the older diver might be more susceptible to DCS. Yet, because seniors generally dive more conservatively (and maybe do fewer dives per year) their DCS hits are not out of proportion. As we baby boomers age it would an interesting study to further investigate DCS in senior divers.

According to DAN data, cardiovascular disease is thought to contribute to some 20 percent of the recreational SCUBA diving fatalities. In a study done in Australia and New Zealand in 1989, it was found that the majority of diving fatalities (from all causes) occurred in the 21 to 35 age group, with the second most in the 45 and older group. Yet, as most of the fatalities in the 45 and older group were attributed to cardiac causes[CC], it appears obvious that senior divers should pay particular attention to cardiovascular risk factors. Those factors include smoking, hypertension, high cholesterol levels, and obesity.

Some recommendations to extend your years of active diving are listed in Listing W.

Listing W. Recommendations to Extend Your Diving Years.

1 Institute a program of *aerobic exercise, strength, and flexibility training* and consistently follow it.

1 *Get yearly physicals* and watch for risks of coronary artery disease, impaired pulmonary function, hypertension, high cholesterol, and obesity.

1 *Do not smoke.*

1 Pay close attention to *cautions on drugs being taken.* Be sure they are not contraindicated at depth or that there is not a dangerous interaction between two or more drugs.

1 Consider *dietary supplements* of vitamin C, E, and beta carotene if unsure of their intake in your diet.

1 Seniors can benefit more from a *lower fat, higher carbohydrate diet* than younger whippersnappers.

1 Keep the *mind active.* Get additional training and certification. Read up on and explore new dive sites (see Question 115).

1 Seniors generally have a harder time dealing with the *thermal stress* of exertion in warmer water, so stay hydrated.

[1] Be careful of *stressing your back.* If necessary get help hefting that BC and putting on and taking off your exposure suit.

[1] You can afford it, so minimize your hassles and *buy the best equipment* for the job.

[1] *Get nitrox certified* and it is likely you will feel less fatigued and as a bonus, have a lower risk of DCS. Nitrox is also known as the old wheezing geezer's gas.

[1] *Slow down a little.* Acclimate. You can afford the biggest boat in the bay and you have proved yourself in other ways. Let those still needing to, do so.

In summation, the best advice for seniors appears to be to:

[1] get regular physical exams (paying particular attention to the cardiovascular system),

[1] maintain a regular physical training program with an emphasis on cardiovascular fitness, flexibility and endurance,

[1] select dives that minimize the need for a lot of heavy equipment or exposure protection,

[1] follow conservative dive profiles, and

[1] if all is go ... then go divin' with Peggy Sue!

58. Am I old enough to become SCUBA certified?

During gestation, we all essentially used SSA (Surface Supplied Air) and a hookah (see Question 2) to our belly. After birth, if we were fortunate enough to be reintroduced to the water world at an early age and took swimming lessons, then we should feel right at home. Taking up SCUBA diving would be a natural 'progression'.

The problem with determining if one is old enough is due to the variability in psychological, intellectual, and physical factors in humans. Regardless of age, some of the traits of a mature person who would be a good candidate for SCUBA certification include: exhibiting responsible behavior, the ability and desire to be a good buddy, attention to detail, good judgement under duress, and the respect for guidelines established for everyone's safety. (Also see Questions 2 and 3, who should and should not be SCUBA certified.)

A person would likely be too immature or undisciplined for safe diving, if they did not have the strong desire to dive or they could not remain responsibly focused on necessary tasks. The maturity of a person's intellectual capacities should be such that they have the ability to understand the physics and biological principles of diving and how to apply them for safe diving.

As to physiological appropriateness, Dr. Campbell at http://www.gulftel.com/~scubadoc/fityouth.htm states, "Physically, the young diver should be near 45 kg. (108 lb.) and 150 cm. tall (60 inches). He/she should be able to handle the bulky diving equipment and should be able to enter and exit the water without difficulty. Cold stress and buoyancy control pose special problems for the person of smaller statue, particularly on the surface in a suit. Gear size can be reduced and smaller tanks utilized. I strongly recommend that children take lessons with other teens-not in a mixed class with adults; and, that the instructor be knowledgeable about teens, and have a supportive style without the "macho" attitude that some instructors exhibit, often humiliating members of the class. Finally, there is nothing worse than being "dragooned" into diving. For those who are too small to use diving equipment comfortably, or who are too young intellectually there are alternatives to diving which will prepare them for diving later, i.e., swimming in waves and currents, underwater swimming, swimming with fins or kickboard and snorkeling offers a great transition to diving for youngsters. My youngest son was 11 when he became certified--and was the best diver in the family!"

Another physiological factor is brought up by Dr. Samuel Shelanski at www.scubadiving.com/training/medicine/ age&dive.shtml. Dr. Samuel Shelanski states, "It is believed that diving prior to reaching full bone maturity can lead to bone defects or adversely affect growth. The epiphyseal plates near the ends of long bones are the major sites of new bone growth during development, and are very susceptible to injury or damage. The destructive effects that diving and DCS can have upon bone are well documented in commercial divers, but have not been described in recreational divers. Despite the lack of direct evidence, Dr. Carl Edmonds, author of Diving and Subaquatic Medicine and an expert on hyperbaric medicine, recommends that children not dive below 30 feet until their epiphyseal plates have fused--during puberty--in order to minimize the risk of bony deformities. There is little hard data to support this recommendation, but it is a reasonable extrapolation of what is known. Because only x-rays can show if a child's epiphyseal plates have fused, diver wannabes should have a radiologic check-out before enrolling in a junior diver class."

For the protection of all, the certifying diving organizations in the U.S. have set the minimum age for full certification to be 15 years old. Individuals between the age of 12 (has been lowered to 10 by some agencies) and 15 can, with adequate training, receive Junior or conditional certification. This conditional certification enables the adolescent to dive with a fully certified adult present. When the individual turns 15, they can upgrade the Junior certification to the basic open water diver certification. As recommended by Dr. Samuel Shelanski, younger divers should use conservative dive profiles in order to minimize the risk for decompression sickness and its affect on growing tissues. Additionally, be sure that equipment is properly fitted for the young diver, as an ill fitting BC (buoyancy compensator), mask, fins, etc. can be annoying, if not unsafe.

Dr. Samuel Shelanski at http://www.scubadiving.com/training/medicine/age&dive.shtml concludes that, "Parents must be realistic in deciding when their children are ready to start diving. As divers, many of us are fanatical about our sport, and cannot understand how the rest of the world survives without breathing compressed air. Make sure that little Billy wants to dive before signing him up for a class. A child may be reluctant to express fears in the face of a parent's enthusiasm, and an unwilling participant is substantially more likely to wind up in trouble while diving."

59. I am (or trying to get) pregnant. Should I SCUBA dive?

No. For the long answer let's see what the medical professionals say.

Dr. Ernest S. Campbell at http://www.gulftel.com/~scubadoc/prgdiv.htm states: "One of the most frequent questions people ask is regarding scuba diving while pregnant. The quick answer is "Please don't dive" while you're pregnant. We don't have very good data showing that hyperbaric pressure harms the fetus, and in fact, there are case records of HBO {hyperbaric oxygenation} treatment of pregnant mothers with carbon monoxide poisoning without adverse effect on the fetus. However, the fetus does not have the protection of the lungs in filtering out the bubbles as does an adult.

Studies on pregnant sheep in hyperbaric chambers are particularly telling, as the sheep's placenta is very similar to that of a human's. These sheep studies of DCS (decompression sickness) all showed high rates of fetal death, particularly in the fetuses that had been instrumented {operated upon}. This increase rate is probably due to the bubbling that crossed into the arterial circulation via the patent foramen ovale (a hole in the heart between the left and right atrials).

"The same woman who will not drink coffee or smoke during her pregnancy will want to know why she should not dive. In this litigous society there is only one answer "no diving while pregnant or even trying to conceive".(Dr. Maida Taylor). No major studies prove it unsafe but the hazards are there.

Presently, every HBO treatment chamber does not allow female personnel who are pregnant to act as tenders. Since diving is an entirely elective activity for 99% of all women divers, the obvious choice would seem to be not to dive. If one has been inadvertently diving while early in her gestation, there is no good data which would justify an abortion."

Dr. Ernest S. Campbell in http://www.gulftel.com/~scubadoc/rskwomdiv.htm further states: "Dr. Caroline Fife, after considering all the experimental

and survey data, had the following comments to make at a course given in 1993.
There is no conclusive data linking human birth defects to maternal diving. The human fetus may be at greater risk of injury than the diving mother. The potential risk primarily consists of DCS, but hyperoxia and CO2 retention may also be problems. There is insufficient experimental evidence to establish safe depth and time profiles for the pregnant woman. Pregnant women who choose to dive should be informed that potential fetal risk probably increases as the no-decompression limits are approached. Women who discover they are pregnant after performing multi-day or deep diving should not be counseled to terminate their pregnancy. The odds are still in their favor. Until further data are available, women who know that they are pregnant should not dive, just as they are advised against alcohol intake, radiation exposure, smoking and other environmental factors which may increase the risk of fetal injury."

Dr. Fred Bove in http://scubamed.com/qapage.htm states:
"General advice is to avoid diving while pregnant. The concern is that a bubble could form in the fetus even though the mother has no evidence of decompression sickness. A strategically located bubble in the fetus could retard development of an organ or tissue. The data on diving while pregnant indicate that there may be a slightly increased rate of spontaneous abortion from diving while pregnant. Even though your pregnancy may only be in the first one or two weeks during your holiday, this is a critical time for initial growth and development. Without solid data to support a recommendation, I would still recommend that you plan to get pregnant after you have completed your diving."

At http://www.diverlink.com/pregnancy.htm we find the following: "Women sometimes ask "is it safe to dive if I'm pregnant?" The short answer is "probably not". It would be unethical to ask pregnant women to dive and risk damage to the fetus, so conclusive studies with humans have not been conducted. However, two studies in humans that surveyed pregnant women after they went diving have been done. One study showed no increased risk of birth defects or fetal loss. The other suggested a higher incidence of low birth weight, birth defects, neonatal respiratory difficulties, and other problems in the group that continued diving perinatally, although a statistical analysis was not done. The more severe (heart) abnormalities were associated with deeper diving (120-160 feet, about 36-48 meters).

Dr. Maida Taylor wrote a chapter in Bove and Davis' Diving Medicine that includes a discussion on Diving, Hyperbarics, and Pregnancy. She lists several reasons why women should not dive while pregnant. While a fetus seems to be at no increased risk for developing DCS (decompression sickness) than the mother, (and may even be at decreased risk) the risk to the fetus if it does develop DCS may be significant. Animal studies in sheep show a high risk of fetal death if DCS is induced in the fetus (but studies in dogs and rats do not.)

Since the fetal blood is oxygenated by the placenta, there are shunts around the fetus' lungs (patent foramen ovale and ductus arteriosus.) Because of these shunts, fetuses lack the filtering qualities of the lungs for bubbles. If bubbles do form in DCS the bubbles are more likely in a fetus to reach a vital organ. Most animal studies are done at depths that far exceed recreational diving limits (6.4-7.1 ata.)

Although there are no known studies on Arterial Gas Embolism (AGE) in diving, the literature shows a very high rate of death in both mother and fetus in cases of AGE in non-diving incidents.

The end result is that the effects of diving on the human fetus cannot be stated conclusively. The risk is probably low in typical recreational diving not associated with DCS or AGE, although the potential injuries could be severe. All available evidence strongly indicates that pregnant women should not dive.

Swimming and snorkeling are good exercise for most. The near weightless condition, relieving the strain of the additional weight, and the lack of deep bending found in many other exercises, makes these activities ideal for most pregnant women in most any stage of pregnancy. Naturally, they should consult with their doctors in order to rule out any possible consequences due to unforeseen medical complications."

60. Can I dive during my 'period'?

The medical diving community concurs, that in most cases, a woman can dive during her menstrual period. Yet they also recommend conservative dive profiles to be on the safe side. Specifically:

Dr. Ernest S. Campbell in http://www.gulftel.com/~scubadoc/rskwomdiv.htm states: "Dr. Caroline Fife, after considering all the experimental and survey data, had the following comments to make at a course given in 1993. Normal, healthy females are at no greater risk for diving DCS than their male counterparts. Menstruating women are at no greater risk for diving DCS than non-menstruating women. (This may not be true for altitude or saturation diving)."

Dr. Maida Taylor in http://www.ismax.com/cgi-bin/cgiwrap/ismax/htmlos.cgi/00308.1.4.45597890870 states: "Sharks are not an issue {see Question 25} -- there is no evidence of increased attacks on menstruating female divers. Heavy flow and menorrhagia may be different than light flow. This may be an increasing concern as the female diving population ages. Most women with very heavy flow probably would skip diving on those days.

Issues of hygiene, privacy and convenience may also be a factor. If flow is very heavy with superimposed anemia, chronic or acute, that would limit potential O2 delivery, and impair circulatory dynamics.

There is some suggestion from aerospace literature and from dry chamber dives for medical hyperbaric therapy that women may be at increased risk for DCS during the first week of their cycle, that is during the menstrual week. This phenomenon has not been studied in open water divers. It might, however, suggest that due to changes in hormones, electrolytes, vasomotor reactivity and peripheral vasoconstriction, and other unknown variables, women might handle a gas load differently during the menstrual phase of their cycles. One might caution women who dive while menstruating to dive more conservatively, doing shallower dives, and prolonging safety stops."

Dr. Samuel Shelanski writing for Rodale's Scuba Diving magazine at http://www.scubadiving.com/training/medicine/menstruation.shtml states regarding the question, is it safe to dive during menstruation? "As with many diving-related health issues, the answer is "yes, but ..."

Over the course of their periods, most women lose between 50 to 150 ml (one-quarter to three-quarters cup) of blood and tissue. While this is not a physiologically significant amount, many women fear that this discharge may attract sharks. The truth is that women divers are attacked by sharks less often than men are. In his book Diving and Subaquatic Medicine, Dr. Carl Edmonds suggests that this may in part be due to a repellent effect of some component of the menstrual blood that is released. While this has not been formally tested, it is fair to say that the danger of shark attack from diving during one's period is substantially less than what results from other activities, such as spear fishing.

There is currently no direct evidence linking menstruating divers to a higher incidence of DCS than nonmenstruating divers. A U.S. Air Force study found women to have a 4.3 times higher incidence of altitude DCS than men. All of the afflicted women were menstruating but none had been diving. Another study, conducted by the Hyperbaric Medicine Department at Virginia Mason Medical Center, found that hyperbaric chamber attendants who were menstruating showed a sevenfold higher risk of DCS than male attendants and nonmenstruating female attendants. Again, there is no research to show that this risk applies to divers, though much research remains to be done on this subject.

The reason that women may be more susceptible to DCS during or close to their periods is not known, but it may be related to the bloating many women experience with the onset of their menstrual cycle. This bloating, or edema, is caused by fluid moving from the blood vessels of the body into the body's tissues, resulting in less volume in the bloodstream. The resulting state is similar to dehydration, a risk factor for DCS.

Some over-the-counter medicines, such as Midol PMS and Premsyn PMS, contain diuretics. Diuretics are drugs that help the body eliminate water and relieve the feeling of bloating. Use of these medications, or any type of "water pill," can lead to dehydration; therefore, they should not be taken while diving.

Some women complain that they have difficulty equalizing their ears and sinuses when menstruating. Edema may also be responsible for this. The fluid that moves into the tissues from the blood vessels causes puffiness, much in the way that putting a sponge into water makes it swell. If this swelling affects the lining of the sinuses and Eustachian tube, it can make equalizing these spaces more difficult.

Many women report feeling increasingly anxious around the time of their period. For a woman experiencing anxiety, making the decision to dive should depend on whether or not that anxiety impairs her ability to respond appropriately in an emergency situation. A smart diver recognizes her limitations, and avoids endangering herself or a buddy. One thing experts do agree on: Sex plays no role in determining successful scuba divers. Most women will find that they are able to dive without difficulty throughout their menstrual cycles. The main consideration for a menstruating woman is to avoid pushing herself. And if unsure, consult a doctor about whether or not you should dive."

61. What other female-specific issues are there in diving?

As about a third of recreational SCUBA divers are female (see Question 10), it would be appropriate to address some of the questions that pertain specifically to females interested in diving. The topics addressed below include: safety, contraceptives, breast feeding, menarche, menopause and osteoporosis, premenstrual syndrome, postpartum diving, and breast implants.

{Note: The information presented herein is not specific for any particular individual. It is presented only to encourage you to seek your diving Physician's medical opinion specifically for your condition. Do not base your diving solely on the information presented below.}

Safety
Dr. Ernest S. Campbell in http://www.gulftel.com/~scubadoc/rsk womdiv.htm states, "It appears that from the best information and experience *that it is as safe for women to dive as it is for men*, using the diving safety guidelines which are standard for all national certifying agencies and the federal government."

Women on average have some 10 percent more body fat than men. As fatty tissue holds much more nitrogen than muscle there is the hypothesis that women are more susceptible to decompression illness. However, the few studies in this area are inconclusive and based on current wisdom there is no differences.[EE]

Contraceptives
There appears to be little or no data that indicates that taking oral contraceptives increases a woman's propensity to have a diving accident. *If the oral contraceptive is not contraindicated for a woman on land then there should be no problems if she dives.*[EE]

Breast Feeding
Dr. Ernest S. Campbell in http://www.gulftel.com/~scubadoc/womdiv.html#Breast Feeding states: "There is some concern among divers who are

nursing that their infants might be harmed by 'nitrogen bubbles' in breast milk. This of no concern as nitrogen does not seem to form bubbles in the milk located in the breast glands. Even if the *nitrogen were in bubbles, it would do the infant no harm.* Ingesting bubbles, even if microscopic, would in no way be harmful to the child, as it would reside in the gastrointestinal tract where gas is a prominent feature already. *Breast engorgement* can occur during the dive excursion since the infant will be away from the breast for several hours. This engorgement can be uncomfortable due to snug dive suits and gear straps. Some accommodation should be made for this eventuality. The changes in pressure of diving would not effect the engorged breasts in any way. Thought should be directed toward possible use of a breast pump, saving the milk in refrigeration for the infant.

There are some further concerns about *possibility of transmission of marine pathogens from the nipple to the infant,* with the production of a particularly stubborn infectious diarrhea. These same bacteria are fully capable of causing a severe mastitis if the exposed nipple ducts and skin have any irritations or skin breaks.

Finally, Dr. Maida Taylor has stated (Medical Seminars, 1998), that there are some concerns about the *combined energy expenditure of nursing and diving, and the associated dehydration related to immersion causing a decrease in the amount of breast milk.* Should this happen, the mother should be prepared to supplement with some formula approved by the Pediatrician. In this regard, it might be wise to consider postponing diving until the infant is weaned, which is usually around the sixth month in Western culture."

Menarche (beginning of the menstrual function)
Dr. Ernest S. Campbell in www.gulftel.com/~scubadoc/ womdiv.html#Menarche states: "At menarche the girl usually has reached 95% of her terminal height, most often reaching full adult size and stature within 1-2 years. *There is a phase of rapid fat deposition in this 13-15 year old period, sometimes with a significant decrease in power and aerobic capacity.* Performance measures peak at age 13 and then level off and decline. For some, this becomes a problem in the management

of heavy scuba gear. Minimum size for comfort with conventional scuba gear is 45 kg (105-108 lb.) and 150 cm (60 inches). There is ossification of long bones in this period and concerns directed to the possibility of nitrogen bubble localization in the growth plates. This ossification (closure of growth plates) takes place one to three years sooner in girls than in boys, varying with the bone involved.

Young divers have several metabolic disadvantages. They become hypovolemic much more rapidly than adults, generate more metabolic heat and burn more energy from a larger surface area to body mass ratio. Girls get colder more quickly than older women under similar environmental conditions, there being a 20 fold increase of conductivity into water. Greater thermal protection is needed for the young diver and the importance of a properly fitted wet suit is stressed." Also see Question 60.

Menopause and Osteoporosis
Dr. Ernest S. Campbell in www.gulftel.com/~scubadoc/ womdiv.html#Menopause, Osteoporosis states: *"There is no pool of diving data to indicate that women are at any more or less risk of DCS or osteonecrosis when perimenopausal or post menopausal.* Average menopausal age is 50, osteoporosis usually starts between ages 60-65 and fractures average at 70-75. Osteonecrosis and osteoporosis have differing pathophysiologic mechanisms; osteonecrosis resulting from blockage of the small blood vessels of the bone, while osteoporosis comes from changes in cellular activity. Diving does not seem to have any effect on the changes in the osteoblasts and osteoclasts that occur with aging and diminished estrogen. *Good advice would be for the elderly female diver to dive conservatively* so as to not add the risk of bubble damage to a porous bone from osteoporosis."

Premenstrual Syndrome (PMS)
Dr. Ernest S. Campbell in
http://www.gulftel.com/~scubadoc/womdiv.html#PMS states: "PMS is an ill-defined group of symptoms that are associated with the hormonal changes that occur in the week or so prior to menses. *When severe, the personality and anti-social behavior associated with PMS could be a definite problem in diver*

interaction on a dive-boat and with a buddy. If the PMS is severe, there seems to be an association with underlying psychiatric disorders. *It also worsens as the diver ages, associated with the widening range of estrogen swings.* Hormonal replacement works well with PMS. SSRI's {Selective Serotonin Re-uptake Inhibiters} have been found beneficial."

Postpartum Diving
Dr. Ernest S. Campbell in
http://www.gulftel.com/~scubadoc/womdiv.html#Postpartum states: *"After vaginal delivery, diving can be resumed after being released by the obstetrician.* This is usually after the cervix closes, about 21 days. In another week, most muscle tone has returned, depending upon the level of activity of the mother. Barring any pregnancy related complications, such as anemia and poorly healed episiotomy return to diving is usually permitted at 4 weeks.

Most obstetricians advise a wait of 4-6 weeks before returning to full activity after caesarian delivery. Couple this with the need for conditioning, complete wound healing and the possibility of need for blood regeneration - a period of 8 weeks would be advised before diving. A postpartum hemoglobin determination should be performed and anything below 10 Gm Hgb should be corrected before diving.

Multiple births, medically complicated pregnancies with underlying medical conditions, complications of both vaginal and caesarian births all have to be individually assessed in the decision as to approval for return to diving."

Breast Implants
Dr. Samuel Shelanski in
http://www.scubadiving.com/training/medicine/diveyorn.shtm l states: *"Assuming that you have recovered fully from your surgery, there is no reason a breast implant should keep you from diving.* The implants are constructed of a tough, flexible shell filled with saline. They are very durable and can easily withstand the pressures associated with even the deepest recreational dives.

Although the outer layer of most implants is gas-permeable and will absorb small amounts of extra gas from the surrounding tissues while diving, this amount is too small to cause any noticeable increase in the size of the implant on ascent, let alone enough stress on the shell to cause rupture on ascent. This is true of the older silicone implants as well. Any rupture while diving would be due to a defect in the implant itself."

Dr. Ernest S. Campbell in http://www.gulftel.com/~scubadoc/womdiv.html states: "There has been one study done with implants placed in a hyperbaric chamber. This study included silicone, saline and silicone/saline filled at various depth/time profiles that would be seen during recreational diving. The study indicated a 1-4% increase in size of bubbles during the study. Saline implants absorbed less nitrogen, N_2 being more soluble in the silicone. The amount of volume increase was not enough to cause rupture and the bubbles resolved over time. This study did not answer the question of implants in situ in in vivo conditions (Implanted in the living human).

Silicone implants are heavier than water and possibly can alter buoyancy and attitude in the water, particularly if large. Diving should not be attempted until completely released by the surgeon and some thought should be directed toward change in body configuration, wet suits, gear straps and appropriate weighting so as to avoid undue pressure over the implant bag and buoyancy problems."

Dr. Studin in http://www.webbreast.com/askdoc/_askdoc/00000046.htm states: "Saline is nothing more than water and salt, and is therefore not compressible by surrounding water pressure. Therefore, scuba diving should have no effect whatsoever on breast implants. Silicone, has a similar density to water. While it is minutely compressible, this is not enough to {cause} any problems with these types of implants either."

62. I get seasick easily. Can I still go SCUBA diving?

Motion sickness (seasickness) is apparently caused by the erratic and conflicting stimulation of the brain from the various sensory receptors. This conflicting stimulation is due to the fluid in the ear's semicircular canals moving with the motion of the head, the inconsistent visual information gathered by the eyes, and the propriocepters (nerve endings) in the muscles, skin, and tendons (see Figure B of The Human Ear in Question 43). It is much easier to avoid seasickness than treat it once it occurs.

The best ways to avoid becoming seasick include minimization of motion, natural remedies and trinkets, medications, and just staying off a pitching boat, i.e., go shore or freshwater diving or just wait for a calmer day. There is hardly anything worse than a bad case of seasickness but on the bright side, after you throw up you will likely feel better and probably attract fish.

If you choose to combat seasickness without drugs and such, then you should position yourself amid ship and as close to the water line as possible. This is where the motion of the boat is the least. Getting a constant flow of fresh air (see Question 17) is also very helpful. Avoid strong odors such as diesel fumes! As seasickness has to do with sensory input to the brain, another thing to do is put that brain of yours to sleep during the ride out and back and take a nap mid-day. You might also try bracing your head against something if you are sitting up.

Some divers get relief from motion sickness when in the water, but it is probably unwise to rush to dive if you are feeling really bad. It is far better to be sick on the ship than throwing up in your regulator (see Question 37), not to mention the lapse of diving safety that might occur by the stampede to water. Of course, if you are not that bad off, then be the first in the water by having your gear ready to go. If you get your gear ready at the dock, then you will not have to fuss with it as much on a rocking boat. You might also consider taking the biggest boat you can, as they should furnish more stable platforms. Lastly, it is best to focus your eyes on a stationary distant object and definitely do not read {I once lost a tin of mustard sardines because of reading}.

For more natural remedies and prevention, you might try taking ginseng root starting the day before diving. Some people swear by Sea Bands®, bracelets that have beads that touch the acupuncture points on your wrist. The ReliefBand® NST device works for some in the treatment of nausea and vomiting due to chemotherapy, motion sickness and pregnancy. A tablespoon or two of Italian Fernet Branca bitters in a half-glass of water is said to work well and quickly.[W] You might also try taking Pepto-Bismol.

For those wishing to use medications, Dr. Ernest S. Campbell at http://www.ismax.com/cgi-bin/cgiwrap/ismax/htmlos.cgi/-00852.1.39955371641 states, "The scop {scopolamine} patch is the best thing going for seasickness. Of course, all medications vary with the individual and it would be a good idea to try it out several days before you go diving. If you have too strong a reaction, then cut the patch in half or thirds and find your level needed. Unless you are especially sensitive to scopolamine the patch should work just fine relieving your motion sickness. I have not recommended the tablet due to the lack of slow release of the drug. There is no danger diving with the patch if you do not have any of the side effects of blurred vision and confusion. Your dive instructor is correct in warning about diving with any of the motion sickness medications -- but the scop patch is the safest and most effective."

Over-the-counter medications may be comparable in effectiveness to prescription drugs for some divers. Over-the-counter meds include Dramamine® (dimenhydrinate), Bonine® (meclizine), Tigrazine®, Marazine® (cyclizine), Benadryl® (diphenhydramine) etc. (ask your pharmacist if unsure). If one of them works better for you than another, then use that one. Take the pills early (at least three hours before the boat ride) to build up levels of the medication. After you start feeling queasy, it is too late for the pills.

Your pre-dive diet can contribute to seasickness. Stay away from fats, acidic foods and other foods that you know to cause your digestive system problems. Hangovers (you are not drinking heavily the night before diving are you?), stress, anxiety, and fatigue tend to exacerbate seasickness. Keep yourself well hydrated with non-alcoholic and non-acidic beverages. Light meals of carbohydrates and proteins are thought to minimize seasickness. Some have found oatmeal, bagels, crusty bread or any food that forms a bolus {a wad of stuff} in the stomach to be helpful.

A few interesting tidbits regarding seasickness are that our propensity toward seasickness tends to decrease with age (except babies, who do not get seasick), women tend to be more susceptible to it than men, and increased experience on the water tends to decrease seasickness.[N]

One last thing: if you feel the urge, then go to the downwind (lee) side of boat and let fly. If you use the toilet or a wastebasket, you just may be forced to walk the plank. *The bottom line is, do not let seasickness stop you from diving. It does not have to. There are ways to combat it and there are types of diving that will not subject you to seasickness.*

63. Can I keep a non-diving spouse & kids happy while I dive?

For a few guys, this might be difficult because they will have to actually talk to their spouse and kids. Then they will have to understand what it is the family likes to do and find a dive site (see Question 114) that they can enjoy too. Being rather goal-driven it is hard for me to fathom my significant other just hangin' out on the beach while I am having a great time diving. Yet she tells me it can happen.

One of my brothers has been actively diving for years. He and his wife (who could not clear her ears and is thus not certified) work their vacations so they both enjoy them. He gets up early and goes diving while she leisurely gets up and going. When the dive boat returns in the late morning or early afternoon, he has had a couple of great dives and she has caught some rays on the sand. They are then ready to spend the rest of the day and evening together doing what vacationers do.

Your dive vacations can range from do-it-yourself minimalist extremes to live aboards and very fancy resorts in developed countries. It is probably difficult to get the non-diving spouse and kids enthused about a week long live aboard with minimal amenities, diving in remote locations. Yet there are hundreds (if not thousands) of other dive sites that offer a full range of activities, sun tanning, shopping, sight seeing, etc. for the non-diver. There are times for an all divers excursion (particularly if it is Alaskan ice diving) and other times for Bonaire, Maui, and Curaçao.

Think about it. Would you rather be sitting at home with six-foot snowdrifts outside the window and a -40° F chill factor or on a white, sandy beach with the smell of the ocean and tropical flowers, warm water, gentle breezes, twittering birds and beachside service? Hmmm ... maybe there is life after diving.

64. I need vision correction to see. Is this a problem?

If your visual acuity is such that you cannot drive a car or function well on the surface then you might be best advised to seek additional information from disabled diver groups (see Question 56) and a dive Physician before training. Otherwise, *if your vision is correctable with contacts or glasses then SCUBA diving should not be a problem.* Generally, if you need correction lenses you have four choices; *1) wear contacts, 2) have prescription lenses put into your facemask, 3) if your vision is not too bad then there are relatively inexpensive lenses that can be affixed to your existing mask's lens, or 4) Radial Keratotomy or similar corrective procedure.*

If you choose to wear contacts underwater, then be sure you can dive safely if you lose them. If your mask is knocked off and you open your eyes or, if enough water gets into your mask, you may lose a contact or two. One way to handle lost contacts is to dive with a spare mask (which, in my opinion, is a good idea anyway) with or without corrective lenses (depending on your eyesight). That way you can lose both contacts and your mask and still dive safely by donning your spare mask. Wearing soft contact lenses is recommended, but hard lenses are ok if they are gas-permeable. If you wear non-gas-permeable contacts then bubbles may get under them unless holes are drilled in them.

The down side of soft contacts is that there may be an increased risk of eye infection in certain situations. Be sure you discuss the current medical thinking with your Opthalmologist regarding soft contacts and swimming or diving.

Many SCUBA divers use contact lenses and do not seem to have an inordinate number of problems. One of my brothers wears soft contacts while diving and surfing and has not lost any over the years, but he does not open his eyes underwater. Being a minimalist, he considers carrying a spare facemask over-doing it ... but hey, I would let him use my spare mask at depth anyway. His sons surf quite a lot and wear contacts. They have only lost a couple over the past several years, and then, only from one eye at a time. Regardless, it would seem wise to carry an extra set of contacts in your possibles kit (see Question 110), just in case.

At about $100 per mask, having custom lenses placed in your mask is not exceedingly expensive and they are available for many masks (contact your dive shop or mask manufacturer.) However, custom lenses are not available for all masks. You also may have a minor problem when you are topside (without mask or glasses) or when you take your mask off when returning from a dive. Having glasses readily available may mitigate the problem. Another option is to ask your dive shop if they stock relatively inexpensive lenses that can be affixed to your stock mask lens.

Radial Keratotomy (RK) is a procedure that corrects nearsightedness or myopia. This correction is accomplished by making radial incisions in the cornea of the eye. Additionally, there are newer laser surgeries, e.g., Photorefractive Keratectomy, that also correct a diver's vision. According to DAN (Divers Alert Network) in 'The Best of Alert Diver', Physicians performing RK generally recommend up 10 months healing time before the patient dives again. Most of the divers having this procedure done are happy with the results and do not experience any problems.

Whatever solution you choose, needing correction lenses should not keep you from diving.

Fire Coral – A good reason to be able to see where you're going.

65. I have a medical condition. Is it safe for me to dive?

Recreational SCUBA diving, depending upon the dive's profile, can be demanding. Even though the wise diver 'plans the dive and dives the plan', things like unexpected currents, water temperature variations, equipment failure, entanglement, buddy problems, deterioration in visibility, disorientation, etc. can occur. *The diver should be physically, mentally, and emotionally fit (and trained) to handle those events. Succinctly stated, any condition or substance that could incapacitate you due to a seizure, unconsciousness, debilitation, produce irresponsible behavior, or inhibit the normal progression of physical laws, could place you, your buddy, and resulting rescue personnel at grave risk {and risk of the grave}.*

This is serious business. Situations occurring on land can be annoying, but underwater, those same situations could easily be fatal. Dangerous situations can be precipitated at depth by anxiety, exertion, cold, darkness (see Question 51), or the increased pressure. Also, conditions not thoroughly known and not always avoidable in the water, may cause or contribute to a problem. Get a physical exam before becoming involved in recreational SCUBA diving. Do not endanger yourself and others by not reporting and dealing with medical or psychological conditions you may have now or those that may develop after you become certified.

The experience I had with a recent traumatic pneumothorax is illustrative of some of the issues a diver might have to deal with and where a basic knowledge of physiology and the gas laws related to diving are important. I suffered the pneumothorax when the motorcycle I was riding on the freeway had a flat rear tire. My significant other and I were thrown off and she came away with lacerations and shoulder separation, while I broke four ribs and a scapula, had contusions to the pelvis, and experienced a badly sprained ankle. Either the rapid chest compression on contact with the curb "blew out" a portion of my air-filled lungs or the broken ribs punctured the peritoneum (sack like tissue surrounding the lungs) or possibly the lungs, thus causing the pneumothorax.

After 5 months of recovery (8 days in the hospital with a drainage tube attached to a pump), reading the medical diving literature, and talking to Physicians, I decided to get the ventilation portion of a VQ (perfusion-ventilation) scan and a chest x-ray. During my discussions with various Physicians, it became clear that unless the doctor was familiar with dive medicine, a diver could be cleared to dive and yet still be at inordinate risk {word to the wise here!}. Fortunately for me, both tests turned out negative and after getting back into shape I have continued my diving.

My concern regarding the traumatic pneumothorax is that if the lung is sufficiently damaged and/or if there is scar tissue which inhibits the expiration of air breathed in at depth, then I could get an AGE (arterial gas embolism) upon ascending. This could lend itself to a new vocation for myself, pushing up daisies.

Interestingly, during my literature search, I found that Jacques Cousteau also had a traumatic pneumothorax due to a car accident early in his diving career. Of course as they say, the rest is history and he continued diving after a year of healing. The iffy part is, back then they did not know as much about DCS (decompression sickness), AGE, or have the tests they do today. SCUBA diving may have turned out differently if Cousteau had not been around to advance regulator development and sales and also produce the books and films we associate with him and diving.

In any event, before taking diving instruction you will likely be asked to complete a personal physical history or medical checklist. Some of the questions you are likely to be asked are similar to those asked on the PADI (Professional Association of Diving Instructors) Medical Checklist (product 10065). Any affirmative response to a question on the list should require a Physician's OK before you get on with your SCUBA training (see Question 79) and diving. A checklist, such as that in Listing X, would be a good list to peruse during each of your future physicals to ensure your continued ability to dive safely.

Listing X. Medical Checklist Questions Needing a Physician's OK.

🚑 Could you be pregnant or are you attempting to become pregnant (see Question 59)?

- Do you regularly take prescription or non-prescription medications? (with the exception of birth control)
- Are you over 45 years of age and have or do one or more of the following: smoke a pipe, cigars or cigarettes? high cholesterol level? have a family history of heart attacks or strokes?
- Asthma, wheezing with breathing, or wheezing with exercise?
- Frequent or severe attacks of hay fever or allergy?
- Frequent colds, sinusitis or bronchitis?
- Any form of lung disease?
- Pneumothorax (collapsed lung)?
- Chest surgery?
- Claustrophobia or agoraphobia (fear of closed or open spaces)?
- Behavioral health problems?
- Epilepsy, seizures, convulsions or do you take medications to prevent them?
- Recurring migraine headaches or do you take medications to prevent them?
- Blackouts or fainting?
- Frequently suffer from motion sickness?
- Is there a history of diving accidents or decompression sickness?
- Have a history of recurrent back problems or surgery?
- Diabetes not controlled by diet?
- History of back, arm or leg problems following surgery, injury or fracture?
- Inability to perform moderate exercise, e.g., walking one mile in 12 minutes?
- High blood pressure or taking medication to control blood pressure?
- Heart disease?
- Heart attacks?
- Angina or heart surgery or blood vessel surgery?
- Ear or sinus surgery?
- History of ear disease, hearing loss or problems with balance including recurring vertigo?

- Problems equalizing ears with airplane or mountain travel?
- History of bleeding or other blood disorders?
- Any type of hernia?
- History of ulcers or ulcer surgery?
- Colostomy?
- History of drug or alcohol abuse?

It is generally recommended by dive Physicians, that in addition to your pre-certification physical, divers under 40 should get physicals every two years and annual physicals for those 40 or over. If you have any question as to your fitness for a dive, then you should absolutely see a Physician, preferably one knowledgeable in dive medicine.

Such a list of such Physicians can be found by searching the URL http://www.gulftel.com/~scubadoc by the key word 'physician'. You can also consult your HMO (Health Maintenance Organization), your local medical society, nearby university hospital, local dive shops, your instructor, your certifying agency, or yellow pages for the dive Physicians in your area.

As with much in life, there are absolutes and there are relatives {some of whom you do not want to claim}. Dive medicine is no different, as there are absolute and relative contraindications. Contraindications that are absolute permanently place a diver, his diving buddy, and rescuers at increased risk for injury or death. Relative contraindications to diving may be resolved with time, exercise, diet (see Question 53), and proper medical intervention or contraindications may be intermittent.

Listing Y of absolute contraindications to diving is presented to the reader as a guideline to the conditions that are generally considered absolute contraindications to diving. Some of the contraindications are very rare, so do not let the length of the list frighten you away from SCUBA. You should seek medical advice relative to your specific condition(s), if any. As stated previously, I am not medically trained, I am not representing myself to be so, and I am not offering any medical advice {except that the reader should seek some before diving}.

Listing Y. Absolute Contraindications to Diving.
Note: This table should only be used as a starting point in determining your fitness to dive. **Just because your medical condition is not included here does not mean you should dive.** You should seek medical advice specific for you and your condition. The absolute contraindications compiled herein are those presented by the sources at the time of 'SCUBA Scoop's publication and are obviously subject to change. The sources abstracted for this compilation are:
http://www.gulftel.com/~scubadoc/ftnss.htm (Dr. Ernest Campbell)
http://www.naui.org/index-side.html (NAUI Medical Evaluation Form)
(note: the NAUI Medical Evaluation Form is based on Drs. Bove and Davis' book, <u>Diving Medicine</u>, 2nd Ed., W.B. Saunders, Philadelphia; 1990.)

<u>OTOLARYNGOLOGICAL (EAR, NOSE, and THROAT)</u>
+ inability to equalize pressure in the middle ear by auto-inflation
+ perforation of the tympanic membrane (TM) until healed with good eustachian tube function
+ open, non-healed perforation of the TM
+ uncorrected upper airway obstruction
+ history of round window rupture (see Figure B of the ear)
+ inner ear disease other than presbycusis
+ monomeric TM
+ tympanoplasty other than myringoplasty (Type 1)
+ tube myringotomy
+ stapedectomy
+ ossicular chain surgery
+ history of inner ear surgery
+ status post laryngectomy or partial laryngectomy
+ history of vestibular decompression sickness
+ radical mastoidectomy (posterior) involving the external canal (closed childhood OK)
+ meniere's disease
+ labyrinthitis
+ perilymphatic fistula
+ cholesteatoma
+ cerumen impactions - remove before diving
+ stenosis or atresia of ear canal
+ facial nerve paralysis secondary to barotrauma
+ tracheostomy, tracheostoma
+ incompetent larynx due to surgery (cannot close for valsalva maneuver)

+ uncorrected laryngocoele

NEUROLOGICAL (NERVOUS SYSTEM)
+ history of seizure disorder (other than childhood febrile seizures)
+ intracranial tumor or aneurysm
+ history of TIA (transient ischemic attacks) or CVA (cerebral vascular accidents)
+ history of spinal cord injury, disease or surgery with residual
+ Type II DCS (decompression sickness) with permanent neurologic deficit
+ history of unexplained syncopal episodes (cardiovascular or neurogenic)
+ peripheral neuropathies

CARDIOVASCULAR (HEART and VESSELS)
+ coronary artery disease (unusual cases of exceptional rehabilitation after dilations and revascularization procedures)
+ intracardia shunts (particularly large right to left shunts), PFO (Patent Foremen Ovale)
+ asymmetric septal hypertrophy
+ congestive heart failure
+ hypertension (controlled can dive, but drugs that limit exercise response (beta blockers) need to be evaluated. OK if person can reach 13 METS on the treadmill)
+ angina controlled with medications
+ coronary spasm (can be cold or exercise induced)
+ silent ischemia on Holter
+ status post-op CAB {cardiac artery bypass} with no symptoms and negative treadmil OK to dive if can reach 13 METS (8-9 METS = 100 ft/min swimming)
+ valvular lesions
+ mitral regurgitation (aortic insufficiency with no left ventricular dysfunction can dive)
+ aortic and mitral stenosis
+ mitral valve prolapse with symptoms of chest pain, syncope, dyspnea
+ intracardiac defects
+ Wolf-Parkinson-White syndrome
+ supraventricular tachycardia within six months of cause

+ acute heart dysrhythmias

PULMONARY (LUNGS)
+ spontaneous pneumothorax
+ traumatic or surgical pneumothoraces if not cleared with diving Physician, chest surgeon, or pulmonary disease specialist
+ significant obstructive pulmonary disease
+ air-containing pulmonary cysts or blebs which can trap air
+ asthma in the active phases (mid-expiratory flow needs to return to baseline)

GASTROINTESTINAL (DIGESTIVE SYSTEM)
+ high-grade gastric outlet obstruction
+ chronic or recurrent small bowel obstruction
+ entrocutaneous fistulae that do not drain freely
+ esophageal diverticula
+ severe gastroesophageal reflux
+ achalasia
+ unrepaired hernias of the abdominal wall potentially containing bowel

METABOLIC and ENDOCRINOLOGICAL
+ diabetics on insulin therapy or oral anti-hypoglcemia medication (adult-onset diabetes controlled by diet and exercise is OK)

HEMATOLOGICAL (BLOOD)
+ sickle cell disease
+ polycythemia
+ leukemia

DENTAL
+ major oral surgery with prosthetic devices
+ osteomyelitis of the mandible
+ osteoradionecrosis of the jaw

PSYCHIATRIC and BEHAVIORAL
+ persons with a history of uncontrollable panic attacks
+ claustrophobia and agoraphobia
+ reluctant diver with a definite fear of diving or of a particular dive.

- "macho" buccaneer
- counter-phobe (diving to get over the fear of same)
- truly psychotic disorders or while receiving psychotropic medications
- chronic substance abuse including drugs and alcohol

WOMEN
- pregnancy or intention to become pregnant (venous gas emboli formed during decompression may result in fetal malformations)

As stated above, relative contraindications to diving may be resolved with time and proper medical intervention or they may intermittently be absolute contraindications to diving. Both NAUI and Dr. Campbell offer listings of relative contraindications that can be reviewed in Listing Z.

Listing Z. Relative Contraindications to Diving.
Note: This table should only be used as a starting point in determining your fitness to dive. **Just because your medical condition is not included here does not mean you should dive.** You should seek medical advice specific for you and your condition. The relative contraindications compiled herein are those presented by the sources at the time of 'SCUBA Scoop's publication and are obviously subject to change. The sources abstracted for this compilation are:
http://www.gulftel.com/~scubadoc/ftnss.htm (Dr. Ernest Campbell)
http://www.naui.org/index-side.html (NAUI Medical Evaluation Form)

OTOLARYNGOLOGICAL (EAR, NOSE, and THROAT)
- history of significant cold injury to pinna
- perforation of tympanic membrane (TM)
- history of tympanoplasty
- mastoidectomy
- fractures to the mid-face
- history of head and/or neck therapeutic radiation
- temporomandibular joint dysfunction
- recurrent otitis externa
- significant obstruction of the external auditory canal
- Eustachian Tube dysfunction
- recurrent otitis media or sinusitis
- significant conductive or sensorineural hearing impairment particularly if unilaterally
- facial nerve paralysis not associated with barotrauma

+ full prosthodontic devices
+ unhealed oral surgery sites
+ congenital or acquired hearing loss

OPHTHALMIC (EYE)
+ lens implants can dive when completely healed (6 weeks)
+ radial keratotomy can dive when healed (3 months)
+ individuals with glaucoma can dive if vision is not affected

NEUROLOGICAL (NERVOUS SYSTEM)
+ history of head injury with sequelae other than seizure
+ spinal cord or brain injury without residual neurologic deficit
+ history of cerebral gas embolism without residual, pulmonary air trapping has been excluded
+ migraine headaches whose symptoms or severity impair motor or cognitive function, cause nausea and vomiting, impairment of one of the senses, or photophobia
+ individuals with head injuries causing intracranial hemorrhaging, brain contusion
+ individuals with a history of amnesia, unconsciousness, brain surgery, CNS (central nervous system) decompression sickness, and cerebral gas embolism please review the URLs listed above and see a dive Physician before diving
+ herniated nucleus pulposus
+ peripheral neuropathy
+ trigeminal neuralgia
+ cerebral palsy in the absence of seizure activity

CARDIOVASCULAR (HEART and VESSELS)
+ suggested minimum criteria for stress testing is 13 METS.
+ history of CABG (Coronary Artery Bypass Grafting) or PCTA (Percutaneous Transluminal Coronary Angioplasty) for CAD (Coronary Artery Disease)
+ myocardial infarction
+ dysrhythmia requiring medication for suppression
+ hypertension
+ valvular regurgitation
+ asymptomatic mitral valve prolapse
+ pacemakers (must be depth/pressure certified by the manufacturer to at least 130 feet of sea water)

PULMONARY (LUNGS)

+ asthma (reactive airway disease), COPD (Chronic Obstructive Pulmonary Disease), cystic or cavitating lung diseases all may lead to air trapping
+ prior asthma or reactive airway disease (RAD) (air trapping must be excluded)
+ patients with a thoracotomy can be certified for diving after thorough evaluation by a dive-savvy thoracic surgeon
+ divers with pulmonary barotrauma may return to diving after no less than a three month diving hiatus and certification from a diving Physician re: no air trapping
+ history of exercise/cold induced bronchospasm ((EIB Exercise-Induced Bronchoconstriction))
+ history of solid, cystic or cavitating lesion
+ pneumothorax secondary to: thoracic surgery, trauma or pleural penetration, previous over-inflation injury (air trapping must be excluded)
+ restrictive disease (exercise testing necessary)

GASTROINTESTINAL (DIGESTIVE SYSTEM)

+ peptic ulcer disease
+ inflammatory bowel disease
+ malabsorption states
+ functional bowel disorders
+ post gastrectomy dumping syndrome
+ paraesophageal or hiatal hernia
+ reflux disease and gastric outlet obstruction need to be evaluated prior to qualification
+ history of bowel obstruction and corrective surgery within past six months
+ esophageal diverticulae, severe reflux, achalasia, and gas bloat syndrome

METABOLIC and ENDOCRINOLOGICAL

+ hormonal excess or deficiency
+ obesity
+ renal insufficiency

HEMATOLOGICAL (BLOOD)

+ sickle cell trait
+ acute anemia

ORTHOPEDIC (MUSCULOSKELETAL SYSTEM)
+ chronic back pain
+ amputation (obviously relative, as many amputees dive)
+ scoliosis - assess impact on pulmonary function
+ aseptic osteonecrosis
+ do not dive while fractures are healing and until acute inflammatory conditions of bone and joints subside

DENTAL
+ carious teeth

PSYCHIATRIC and BEHAVIORAL
+ history of drug or alcohol abuse
+ previous psychotic episodes
+ developmental delay

Additional information regarding specific conditions can be found by asking your dive Physician, calling the Diver's Alert Network (DAN) at (919) 684-2948, calling the Undersea and Hyperbaric Medical Society (UHMS) at (301) 942-2980, contacting your certifying agency, and reviewing the following:

Via the Internet:
+ http://scubamed.com
+ http://www.diabetesmonitor.com/diving.htm
+ http://www.diversalertnetwork.org
+ http://www.scubadiving.com/training/medicine
+ http://www.thebody.com/cdc/facts
+ http://www.uhms.org

Other medically-related publications:
+ Bennett, P., Elliott, D., editors, The Physiology and Medicine of Diving, 4th ed., W.B. Saunders Co., Philadelphia, Copyright 1993.
+ Bove, A.A., Davis, J.C., editors, Diving Medicine, 2nd Ed., W.B .Saunders., Philadelphia, Copyright 1990.
+ Davis, Medical Examination of Sport Scuba Divers, 2nd Ed., Medical Seminars Inc., Copyright 1986.
+ Edmonds, C., Lowry, L., and Pennefather, J., Diving and Subaquatic Medicine, Butterworth Heinemann, Oxford, Copyright 1992.

+ Edmonds, McKenzie, and Thomas, Diving Medicine for Scuba Divers, 2nd Ed., JL Publications, Copyright 1997.
+ Hornsby, A., Brylske, A., Shreeves, K., Averill, H., and Seaborn, C., Encyclopedia of Recreational Diving, PADI, Inc., Santa Ana, Copyright 1989.
+ Martin, Lawrence, M.D., Scuba Diving Explained, Questions & Answers on Physiology and Medical Aspects, Best Publishing Co., Flagstaff, Copyright 1997.
+ NOAA Diving Manual, 3rd Edition. U.S. Department of Commerce, National Oceanic and Atmospheric Administration, Washington, D.C., Copyright 1991.
+ U.S. Navy Diving Manual, Vol. 1 (Air Diving) and Vol 2 (Mixed Gas Diving), Best Publishing Co., Box 30100, Flagstaff, AZ, Copyright 1993.

After reading the above, you are not alone if you are totally confused as to whether you are healthy enough to dive. Let me remind you that it is estimated that some 500,000 people in the U.S. get certified every year.[FF] Obviously, in part because of the sorry litigious society in which we live, Physicians and authors are very careful to err on the side of caution.

As indicated by the number of individuals certified yearly, the average healthy person is certainly fit enough to dive. You should get a physical, talk to several dive Physicians if there are any questions as to your fitness, and then make a determination as to whether you should dive. Believe me, if you are or can become healthy enough to dive, then getting SCUBA certified is certainly worth the effort.

66. How do I start the SCUBA certification process?

The first thing you need in order to get open water SCUBA certified is the desire and commitment (see Question 9). SCUBA training is not all fun and games, but it is not difficult if you have the desire and commitment. It is important that you take your training seriously. Your life and that of your buddy's may hang in the balance. That said, once you get certified, you will wonder why it took you so long to take the plunge. Recreational SCUBA is a fantastic avocation which is essentially without limits in expanding your knowledge and enjoyment of life.

You may want to consider several options for certification (see Question 20). *If you opt to get trained in your hometown, then probably just stopping by several dive shops close to home to gather information would be sufficient.* Be sure to get information on the training process (not just cost) and class schedules (see Question 76). Going by several shops is recommended so that you can choose the one that best meets your needs.

To find dive shops in your area, *you can contact the certifying agencies (see Figure D in Question 72) and get the phone numbers for the local dive shops associated with that agency.* You can also get on the Internet and surf for dive shops until you find a few that meet your needs and give them a call. You can call the Diving Equipment and Marketing Association (DEMA) at (800) TM2-DIVE or access their web site via http://www.dema.org for a list of dive centers in your area. Then, if all else fails, there is always your local phone directory.

If you wish to get trained out of town, then there are many dive shops that will accommodate you. An address CD that I recently purchased lists some 2,170 dive shops and training facilities in the U.S. If you want to be trained while on vacation, then check with your local dive shops, travel agencies, and review ads and recommendations in the various SCUBA periodicals (see 'SCUBA Periodicals' section).

67. Is getting certified physically or mentally difficult?

Getting your open water certification card (C-card) is not physically or mentally demanding for anyone in reasonably good shape with the ability, desire, and commitment to assimilate the material presented. Certification is even easier if you are already comfortable in the water.

The notion that certification is a strenuous test of physical and mental abilities is simply wrong (join the military if you are looking for that - see Question 52). Recreational SCUBA diving should be approached as a fun and stimulating avocation. If the training becomes difficult for you, then let your Instructor know so (s)he can help you. See Question 56 if you have physical disabilities. Even individuals who are quadriplegic or blind have been certified. Do not let a physical disability hold you back if you have the desire and can be certified to dive safely.

As for physical abilities, you do need to be in good general health and you may be required to obtain a doctor's OK that you are, if anything on the agency's medical questionnaire indicates something to be cautious about (see Question 65). A Physician familiar with dive medicine is your best bet for a pre-course checkup. If you cannot find a doctor in your area by asking your instructor or dive shop, then you can request such information on Physicians from the Undersea and Hyperbaric Medical Society at (301) 571-1818 and the Divers Alert Network (DAN) at Duke University (919) 684-2948.

Remember, every year hundreds of thousands of people get certified. You can do it, too.

68. How long does it take to get certified?

Some of the factors that determine the amount of time required to obtain your open water SCUBA certificate are listed in Listing AA.

Listing AA. Factors Determining Time Necessary for Certification.

- The *requirements of the certifying agency* you choose (see Question 80),
- the *frequency (scheduling) of class meetings and pool sessions,*
- *the ability of the instructor to convey the material and the students to assimilate it,*
- the *amount of additional material added* at the instructors prerogative,
- the *scheduling of your open water dives (note that the weather does not always follow class schedules so be upset with the weather forecaster not your instructor for having to wait out foul weather),* and
- your *individual progress.*

Your instruction will consist of classroom meetings (which include take-home reading assignments and written examinations), pool sessions, and finally, your open water dives. Typically, two to three hour classes are offered one or two nights a week, with the pool and classroom sessions extending over three to six or more weeks. Some instructors also offer intensive weekend courses, with classes meeting eight hours per day. However, as a general rule, expect your open water SCUBA certification to take about four weeks to complete.

'Executive courses' are also offered, where the student progresses at their own rate and time available. I used this concept and received my open water SCUBA certification in two weeks (see Question 76). On learn-to-dive vacations, you can use videos or CDs at home for the classroom work, then complete the testing and water skills (pool and open water) training in just a few days while on vacation. Regardless, your open water dives must be done over a period of at least two days.

With the amount of material to be covered, be sure you do not rush yourself. It is much more important to understand and apply the material in a conscientious manner than to be the first one into the water. Someday, you or your buddy's life may depend upon your diligence during your certification.

69. Is SCUBA certification training safe?

The student is relatively safe while undergoing open water certification with a certified SCUBA professional Instructor. Yet SCUBA diving is not without risk, whether you are under instruction or otherwise. In 1997, according to DAN, there were 4 fatalities during open water certification training, or 4.9 percent of all SCUBA fatalities for that year in the U.S. That seems like a large number, but looking at the numbers a different way, if there are *some 500,000 individuals getting certified each year (high side estimate) and there were 4 fatalities, then that is a fatality rate of 0.0008 percent, or one in 125,000 students.*

You must remember that some of those fatalities were caused by the student's personal physical factors, such as cardiovascular disease. Additionally, a student may exhibit behaviors that an Instructor may not be able to prevent, e.g., rapid ascents (greater than 60 feet per minute) due to panic with a resulting AGE (arterial gas embolism (see Question 39)).

SCUBA instruction is relatively safe, but it is important to select a good instructor (most of them are), pay attention, be able to do the underwater tasks with minimum apprehension, be physically fit, and know when you need more help to safely and effectively do the tasks required. Doing those things will decrease your instructional risk dramatically.

Double OK!

70. Will I be required to buy equipment to get certified?

When you begin your pool training, you will need some equipment. Depending upon the dive center, location, and/or instructor you may or may not be required to buy that equipment. *In most cases you will be required to buy your basic equipment such as a mask, snorkel, fins, probably booties (depending on fin type and water temperature). You may also want to purchase a good pair of gloves if you will be training in cold water. A few agencies are now also requiring the purchase of a dive computer rather than teach using dive tables.*

The above equipment (except dive computer) are personal items and should be fitted so you are comfortable using them. Even if you decided not to get certified or are unable to be certified, then you could use them to snorkel. Be aware that some dive shops may require you to buy equipment only through them for your certification course (see Question 94). This may or may not be a good deal. Shop around and explore your options.

As for equipment pricing, the cost of a mask is $40 to $80, snorkel $20 to $60, fins $40 to $100, booties $20 to $60, and gloves $30 to $50. *Thus the cost of the basic equipment would run (in aggregate) approximately $150 to $350* (see Question 91). Dive computers, if required, are about $225 on up (see Question 103). As this is the equipment you will use on every dive, be sure you do not scrimp and buy cheap or ill-fitting equipment. See Question 90 for more detailed info regarding the equipment required.

The two schools of thought on the purchase of additional equipment are: 1) wait and buy most of it after certification and 2) buy most, if not all, of your equipment during certification. By additional equipment, I am referring to regulators, BCs, exposure suit, weights, dive computers, tanks, etc.

Those that argue for post-certification equipment purchase contend that you will have a better idea of what diving is all about, what types of diving you prefer, and what your individual needs might be after you garner additional diving experience. Additionally, as you will likely be renting equipment from time to time, it is better not to become too dependent upon a single configuration of equipment.

The other school of thought contends that you should buy all of your equipment during the certification process so that you become very familiar with it, thus making its use second nature. They also contend that most of the above equipment is general enough in function so that it can be used in most of the diving you will be doing.

Which school of thought you adopt (or some hybrid of both) may ultimately be dependent upon the thickness of your wallet and the amount of research you do into the equipment you need (and want). If having to buy most of the equipment up front, including a dive computer, stops you from diving then buy as you go along. If you are well-heeled (rich) then you can buy the best equipment that fits the widest range of applications up front and buy the additional specialized equipment as needed.

If you ask experienced divers (including your instructor), read equipment evaluations, shop around for prices, and know what you want, then buying equipment up front might be a good choice. Yet if you realistically plan on diving just a few times a year {that is unfortunate!}, then renting most of your equipment may be your best course of action financially, but you may potentially have a problem with logistics and/or with equipment fit. See the Equipment Exposés section for further equipment discussion.

In addition to the above equipment, you will also need to purchase classroom material such as books (CDs), dive tables, etc. These are usually included in the course cost but you should verify this with the dive shop or instructor so that there are no surprises. If bought separately, the above classroom materials would set you back approximately $40 to $70.

71. How much does SCUBA certification cost?

This is often the first question asked by the prospective diver because it is relatively easy to quantify (though variable) and because cost is a factor for most of us who are not independently wealthy. However, your first question should be, "how good is the training for the money I will be spending". See Question 74 and others in this section to help answer that question. In short, money should not be your primary determinant of which course to take.

Continuing with your question though, the cost of becoming certified will depend on the equipment purchased, class size, location, duration, instructor(s), checkout dive destination, and materials included. *Courses tend to range in price from $100 to $350+ dollars with about $225 being average.* Included in this cost is usually the use of a regulator, buoyancy compensator (BC), weights, tank, etc. during the pool sessions. The rental of the exposure suit and other equipment may be additional for the open water dives. Depending upon where you take the course, you may have additional expenses for the open water training dives such as travel, motel, boat, exposure suit, miscellaneous equipment, etc.

Because of the variety of training options, it is difficult to give a total cost for certification, but you probably are looking at about $600 for basic equipment, course costs, and a few bucks for miscellaneous. You no doubt can get your C-card for less, but the one over-riding consideration is the quality of both the instruction and equipment. In the final analysis, your comfort and life are worth a few more bucks, are they not? A certification cost checklist for comparing several different open water certification options (courses) is presented in Figure C.

After certification, the ongoing costs of SCUBA diving (exclusive of equipment) will approximate that of snow skiing (see Question 113).

193

Figure C. Certification Cost Checklist.
(Remember, cost should not be the primary course determinant of which course to take – see the other
questions in this section.)

	Course Option #1	Course Option #2	Course Option #3
Equipment:			
mask	____	____	____
snorkel	____	____	____
fins	____	____	____
booties	____	____	____
gloves	____	____	____
other required	____	____	____
misc. (slate/knife flashlight/watch)	____	____	____
Course Materials:			
manual/CD	____	____	____
dive tables	____	____	____
other	____	____	____
Open Water Dives:			
equipment rental	____	____	____
boat/dive charges	____	____	____
transportation	____	____	____
motel	____	____	____
other	____	____	____
Course Cost:			
instruction	____	____	____
equip. rental (pool)	____	____	____
certif. processing	____	____	____
photo(s)	____	____	____
other	____	____	____
Totals Costs:	____	____	____

Notes:
Option #1 from: _____

Option #2 from: _____

Option #3 from: _____

Note that the cost of a physical examination was not included in the certification cost, as you should be getting those on a regular basis anyway and they vary depending upon location, medical insurance plan, extent of physical findings necessitating further exploration, etc. Please get a physical and let your Physician know you will be diving. You will be completing a medical history in order to begin instruction (see Listing X in Question 65).

72. Who will certify me and which agency is the best?

When you decide to get SCUBA certified you may ask yourself, "Who is going to certify me?" *The answer to that question depends on with which agency your instructor is affiliated.* Your instructor trains you and vouches for your satisfactory completion of the open water SCUBA certification requirements (see Question 80). However, you are actually issued your C (certification) card by the authority of the instructor's agency. Though it is relatively rare, an instructor may be certified to and does instruct through more than one agency. You will also notice that your local dive shop, through which an instructor usually works, is typically affiliated with one or more of the agencies.

There is a plethora of open water SCUBA certifying agencies worldwide. At last, count there were at least twelve based in the U.S. alone. A partial, alphabetical listing of those in the U.S. include: IANTD, IDEA, MDEA, NASDS, NASE, NAUI, PADI, PDIC, SDI, SSI, WASI, and YMCA (see Figure D). Note that in 1999, SSI and NASDS merged and could eventually form one organization. Additional certifying agencies that offer advanced, specialized, or foreign (to U.S.) SCUBA training would include (list provided in part by Dr. Larry "Harris" Taylor):

ANDI .... http://www.andihq.com
BSAC .... http://www.bsac.com
CMAS .... http://www.cmas.org
DAN .... http://www.diversalertnetwork.org
Dive Rescue .... http://www.diverescueintl.com
Diver Unlimbited .... http://www.diversunlimbited.org
Global Underwater Explorers .... http://www.gue.com
IAHD .... http://www.iahd.org
Lifeguard Systems .... http://www.teamlgs.com
NACD .... http://www.afn.org/~nacd
NAPSD .... http://www.napsd.com
NASAR .... http://www.nasar.org
Norges Dykkeforbund .... http://home.sn.no/~dykke
NSS-CDS .... http://www.caves.org/section/cds
PSI .... http://www.marinestudio.com/sunpacific/psi
SAA .... http://www.saa.org.uk
SUF .... http://www.asian-diver.com/suf.html
TDI .... http://www.tdisdi.com
Universal Referral Program .. http://www.universalreferral.com

Figure D. Requirements* for Open Water Certification by Agency.

(*Minimum standards when data was compiled and subject to change.)

Agency Acronym, Phone, & URL (www._)	Agency Name (began business)	Classroom Hours or Sessions Required	# of Pool / Confined Water Dives Required	# of Open Water Dives Required	Additional Information
IANTD 305-751-4873 .iantd.com	International Association of Nitrox and Technical Divers(1985)	12 hours minimum for classroom and pool combined (see also ->)	pass 34 water skills test + 4 additional skills set (<-see also)	minimum four dives over at least 90 minutes	
IDEA 904-744-5554 .scuba-idea.com	International Diving Educators Association (1952)	up to instructor with a minimum of 24 hours	up to instructor with a minimum of five	six	
MDEA 615-352-8890	The Multi-national Diving Educators Association (1984)	generally 4 sessions lasting 2.5 to 3 hours each	generally 4 sessions lasting 2.5 to 3 hours each	four	student must pass a final written exam
NASDS 901-767-7265 .divesafe.com	National Association of Scuba Diving Schools (1961)	10 modules at 60-90 minutes each	10 modules 60 to 90 minutes each	four	
NASE 904-264-4104 .nasrescuba.com	National Academy of Scuba Educators (1982)	five classroom sessions minimum	five sessions minimum	four dives minimum	students may home study classroom material, instructor gives exams
NAUI 800-553-6284 .naui.org	National Association of Underwater Instructors (1960)	minimum of 14 hours	10 hours minimum (17 hours typical) in pool and open water	five open water dives (one can be skin diving)	
PADI 800-729-7234 .padi.com	Professional Association of Diving Instructors (1966)	five modules	five minimum	four minimum	
PDIC 717-342-1480 .pdic-intl.com	Professional Diving Instructors Corporation (1975)	minimum of six	minimum of six	one skin and four SCUBA	
SDI 207-729-4201 .tdisdi.com	International Training Inc. (Scuba Diving International 1999)	suggested minimum of 20 total training hours and pass all written exams	pass water skills proficiency test (20 hours minimum includes pool)	four minimum	age range for restricted scuba diver certification is 10 to 14 years old
SSI 800-892-2702 .ssiusa.com	Scuba Schools International (1970)	six	six	one skin and five SCUBA recommended	16 to 32 total course hours recommended, depending if home study or classroom
WASI 801-836-9274 .divewasi.com	World Association of Scuba Instructors (1997)	four units, instructor determines time required	minimum of four sessions	four	
YMCA Scuba 770-662-5172 www.ymcascuba.org	Young Men's Christian Association (1959)	approximately 12 hours	12 hours	one skin and four SCUBA	pool & lecture must total at least 24 hours, minimum 12 hours in the pool

OK then, which certifying agency is the best? One good way to start a fight is go into an X affiliated dive shop and defiantly proclaim, "X certified divers are well-trained if they know in which orifice to insert their snorkel, let alone what a snorkel is. Z agency trains much better divers." Try that on the Internet at the rec.scuba newsgroup and you will be flamed (severely chastised) as a troll (someone just asking to start something).

My open water certification was issued by PADI. Why? Because, at the time I began my training, I did not know the difference between PADI and a rice field. It just happened that the dive shop nearest to my apartment was affiliated with PADI and they offered an 'Executive Course' (a 1:1 student-to-instructor ratio geared to meet based on my time constraints (see Question 68)).

It is my opinion that for your open water SCUBA certification, the specific certifying agency is not critical {and now I will get flack from all the agencies}. All the certifying agencies in the U.S. exceed the minimum standards for entry level SCUBA instruction. The minimum certification standards were originally written by the Recreational Scuba Diving Council (RSTC). RSTC was composed of representatives from IDEA, NASDS, PADI, PDIC, SSI, and the YMCA. Those ANSI (American National Standards Institute) X-86.3 and Z-375.1 standards specify the minimum course work, student age, water skills, health requirements, and the completion of at least four open water dives for certification.

Now, it is true that some of the agencies require a bit more work or an extra open water dive for certification. Yet I have not seen any objective literature documenting that being certified by one agency over another puts the student at less risk. Additionally, they all monitor (to various degrees) their instructor's teaching and have formal grievance procedures if problems arise. Further, it is my opinion that the wise diver will not stop training with just the basic open water certification. The additional training you hopefully avail yourself (see Questions 11 and 12) and your own diving experiences would soon level the field as to one agency being slightly 'better' than another.

It has been said that a larger percentage of divers that become injured are PADI divers. It has therefore been argued by some that PADI divers are not as well trained as divers trained by other agencies. It may be true that more PADI divers are injured, but it is also true that PADI issues the majority of the C-cards in the U.S. There simply are more PADI divers to be injured. According to University of Rhode Island National Underwater Accident Data Center figures, from 1974 to 1987 the fatalities per 100,000 divers went down from 12 to 4.5, but PADI's market share went up from 25 percent to 65 percent.[Y] Those figures support the contention that PADI trains as safe an open water diver as any of the other agencies. It really boils down to how well the instructor presents the material and the ability and desire of the student to absorb it, not the agency.

All of the certification agencies mentioned above and in Figure D enable you the same privileges or rights to rent and buy SCUBA equipment, get air refills, and to go basic open water diving. A SSI affiliated dive shop is just as happy to sell you a tank or BC as is a PADI shop if you are certified via NAUI or the YMCA.

That said, there may be several other factors you may want to consider in your selection of a certifying agency, but for most, they will not be a factor. It may be a bit more of a hassle getting advanced certification through an agency other than the one you started with. Yet all the agencies are eager for you to get that advanced training (thus generating more income for the agency). Note though that some of the agencies may want you to demonstrate certain pre-requisite skills if you were not previously trained through them. Additionally, if you ever plan on becoming a Divemaster, Assistant Instructor, or Instructor, that is turn Pro, then you may want to start your certification process with the agency most likely to employ you on that tropical island where you will be relocating.

Finally, you will want to be sure that your C-card will be recognized at that far, far away dive resort. If you get certified through one of the above agencies, then you can be almost positive your card will be accepted. If you have any doubts then contact that dive resort directly, work through your travel agent who will contact the resort, or get certified by all the above agencies. In other words, cover your bases and then do not worry about it, just be sure to bring along your dive log as insurance (see Question 111).

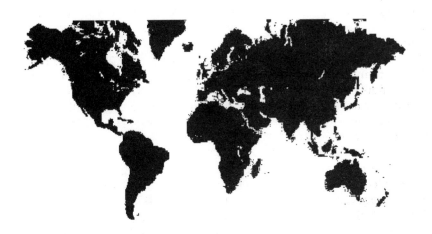

73. What is more important, Instructor, shop, or agency?

The prospective student has a difficult time choosing the best agency, shop, or Instructor, because there are so many different ones to choose from. Further, the larger dive shops generally have more than one Instructor! So you ask, which is more important, the certifying agency, the dive shop, or the Instructor?

For the author's money, *the instructor is of paramount importance.* It is not that the agency is not important, and their training procedures and manuals do differ but *you will be well trained by any of the agencies in Figure D* (and likely by some I have missed). PADI trains the majority of the divers in the U.S., but the other agencies' certification cards are accepted worldwide and their training programs are just as good (see Question 72).

The dive shop is important in that Instructors generally work with specific shops. The dive shop will be helpful to you in selecting equipment, scheduling classes, renting equipment, organizing SCUBA trips, hosting a SCUBA club, and be a place to hang out and tell everyone about the great time you had when you ...

However, in my opinion, *selecting the right open water Instructor is more important than which agency or which dive shop.* Your Instructor teaches basic open water SCUBA under the auspices of one of the (inter)national SCUBA certifying agencies and is the only person trained and qualified to do so. Your Instructor can be assisted by other SCUBA professionals, i.e., Divemaster and Assistant Instructor, but only the Instructor can OK your certification as an open water SCUBA diver.

In selecting an Instructor, you want one that you can work with. It is your Instructor who will be training you regarding safe diving practices. He or she will be the one in the water with you in your pool training and on your open water dives (see Question 69). You want an Instructor you can trust and optimally develop a rapport with.

Instructors are human, no two are the same, and no two teach the same. You might want to read over Question 74 on what to look for in an Instructor. Or, maybe more realistically, like most of us, you found a dive store near your home that had classes when you could take them and you signed up without ever meeting the Instructor. I was fortunate, in that scenario worked for me. Most of the time it will likely work for you, too. Instructors have to love to teach and dive, because no one gets rich just instructing.

Often the store keep is also an Instructor.

74. What should I look for in an Instructor?

I am assuming that you read Question 73 and have decided to check out what I, and others, believe you should look for in an Instructor and how they conduct the course. Do not expect to find all the qualities presented in Listing AB in any one Instructor or course; they are only guidelines. If Instructors were perfect (whatever that means), they would not be teaching SCUBA, they would be teaching inter-island jogging.

Listing AB. Qualities to Consider in Selecting an Instructor and Course.

☺ It is important to *choose an Instructor that you can trust and feel comfortable with.* They should be thorough, patient, and supportive.

☺ Be sure you get *the individual attention* that you will need to become reasonably proficient in your underwater skills. In large classes (7-10 students), it is helpful to have an Assistant Instructor or Divemaster available if you need assistance.

☺ *Verify, by calling your Instructor's certifying agency, that they have a valid and current Instructor's card and are in good standing with the agency.* You may also want to find out how long they have been teaching and how many dives they have done. Be aware though, that some new Instructors are no doubt better than some 'old salts' or 'seasoned' Instructors. Maybe length of time instructing is more indicative of the financing terms they have on their house.

☺ In this sorry litigious society we live in, you may want to *verify your Instructor has liability insurance.* Yet if they are in good standing with their agency, then that is likely a given.

☺ *In your evaluation, focus on your Instructor's teaching ability and style.* An Instructor with good people skills will generally make better communicators. You should feel comfortable asking questions. People learn at different rates and a good Instructor should provide you with the individual attention you need. There may be an additional charge if extra sessions are needed, but most Instructors will bend over backwards to help you succeed.

☺ *Within reason, it is generally best if the course is taught over more, rather than fewer sessions.* Students generally learn better over, say, six sessions rather than three. The repetitive assembly and use of equipment and the shorter, easier to assimilate class and water sessions generally make for better learning sessions. A fair amount of SCUBA diving is learning by doing, so be sure you get *adequate in-water time* to become reasonably proficient in the tasks required.

☙ A *good Instructor understands that it is reasonable for new students to have fears* and will attempt to reassure and work with the student.

☙ Your *Instructor should teach both from experience and via 'the book'*. A good Instructor will keep the class interesting and moving with minimal irrelevant digressions.

☙ Your *Instructor should have a course material presentation plan and implement it.* Your Instructor should be in control of the class.

☙ Your *Instructor should be on time and prepared for each class.* Since you or your classmates may have obligations before and after the class, your Instructor should be punctual and prepared for each class. The class should also end on time.

☙ Your *Instructor should be very diligent in teaching you the skills upon which your life will depend.* A haphazard, slap-happy, good old boy/girl may not be the best Instructor for most SCUBA students.

☙ Though likely not controlled directly by the Instructor, *the class should be offered at a fair price.* Be sure to verify all costs before plunking your money down (see Question 71). Considering that your life is potentially at risk, cost should not be your primary concern, but neither should you be over charged.

Before closing on this question, and lest too much emphasis be placed on the Instructor, it is ultimately you who must learn the material and the skills being presented. *You are paying the Instructor to teach you, but you have the obligation to do your best.* Do not waste yours and other student's time by being disruptive or coming to class unprepared. When at depth, the training you get and your assimilation of same could save your life or that of your buddy's.

75. My Instructor rubs me the wrong way. Suggestions?

Fact: not all students will get along with all Instructors. Further, there may be a few bad apples (Instructors and students) out there. You, as a student, should never feel intimidated nor should there be any form of discrimination or sexual harassment. *If you believe that something is not right then you should, depending on the circumstances and people involved, first try to work it out with the Instructor.*

If it is not possible or appropriate to work it out with the Instructor, then talk to the dive shop management, and as a last resort the Instructor's certifying agency (see Figure D in Question 72 for phone numbers). It is in the best interest of the dive shop to retain you as a satisfied customer and associate with quality Instructors. Additionally, each certifying agency monitors their Instructors and have formal grievance procedures if significant problems arise. If the issue just cannot be resolved, then seek out another Instructor. Most dive shops will let you transfer into another class one of their other Instructors is teaching, or if that is not possible, then they can probably refer you to another shop.

As an aside, if you have special needs or concerns at the outset, then it is best to clear them with the Instructor or shop before starting the course. Sometimes one Instructor will be better prepared or have more experience than another to meet a specific need. It is best to get that taken care of up front.

76. How many students should an Instructor have in a class?

During your open water certification instruction you will want to make sure that you get the individual attention you need. I was trained via an 'Executive Program'. So called because the dates and times for instruction were set by agreement between the student and Instructor. In that type of course, there is usually one student per Instructor and you can progress at the rate convenient for you. The 'Executive Program' costs more, but the training can be completed in a couple of weeks and you get individual attention.

In the more typical class, you should expect one Instructor per six to eight students, and the number of students in a class will vary depending on the time of year and location. If the student ratio is greater than 8:1, then you may receive too little individual attention. A more optimal situation is when there are six to eight students but the Instructor has a certified Assistant Instructor or Divemaster helping out.

The student-to-Instructor ratio should never exceed 10:1. It is not in the classroom or the pool where this ratio is as critical as during your open water certification dives. You will have a buddy, but most likely the buddy will be another student (see Question 77). You do not want your Instructor too busy handling other situations that things get out of control for you. That is the beauty of the 'Executive Program'; your buddy is your Instructor and they will "only have eyes for you".

77. Can my SCUBA certified buddy go to training sessions?

All right! You have decided that you want to get SCUBA certified, but you are wondering if your previously certified spouse, significant other, best friend or family member can take the course with you. The answer is, maybe.

Whether your previously certified buddy can join in the pool and open water sessions generally depends upon the Instructor, and sometimes the dive shop. *If the Instructor allows it, then the certified diver will typically have to do whatever skills (including open water dives) required along with you, not interfere with the instruction, and they pony up some cash. The course cost for the certified diver is generally the cost of a "SCUBA Refresher Course" which is about one-half of an open water course.*

Some Instructors question the potential dependence you may develop upon your 'buddy', and thus discourage their attendance. Additionally, a 'know it all' buddy could be disruptive to the entire class. Finally, it is definitely a problem if the spouse or family member is always looking for approval from the certified diver rather than the Instructor. How can an Instructor teach under those conditions? On the other hand, a good buddy can be helpful in instilling in you the confidence and the desire to learn, as well as providing another pair of eyes in case of trouble (depending on their level of training).

One of my Instructors told me of a time he was instructing a young man and his previously certified father was in the class. On the first open water training dive the son's mask flooded at depth and he bolted for the surface. Fortunately, the Instructor was able to catch the lad by the foot before he was able to get too far thus saving him a possible AGE (arterial gas embolism). There was simply too much pressure on the son to perform. What he needed, and should have asked for, was additional instruction and experience with clearing a flooded mask.

If you are adamant about having your buddy train with you and the Instructor will not allow it, then you might consider getting trained by another Instructor. Yet it is not fair to the Instructor to have your buddy take up a seat in the class, which could go to another student, and the Instructor not compensated.

78. I do not live near the ocean. Can I still get certified?
You do not need an ocean to become certified and to experience some great diving. Other than needing a body of water that is at least 15 feet deep, you certainly can be certified without having an ocean nearby. According to a business address CD I have, there are some 665 U.S. SCUBA dive instruction (SIC code 799924) and diver equipment and supply (SIC code 594137) shops in states that have no ocean shoreline. That is 31.6 percent of the total number of such shops in the U.S. Additionally, of the shops in states with ocean shorelines, there are some that are located a long way from the ocean and conduct their training in fresh water.

However, remember that your certification should be used to dive in situations similar to those in which you were trained. You should get additional instruction or supervision if you are diving in a totally new environment. For example, if you were trained in a freshwater quarry in Pennsylvania then you should get a checkout dive with a Divemaster or Instructor as your first ocean dive.

Be sure to check out the most popular dive sites in the U.S. for the best diving areas in your state (see Question 115). A lot of people think that no ocean means only diving for golf balls, but in reality there are freshwater springs, rivers, lakes, quarries, etc. Also see Question 14 for a comparison of freshwater and saltwater diving.

Try your local lakes and quarries for freshwater diving

79. Where can I get my training?

You can get your training locally, at a vacation dive resort, and most anywhere in between (see Question 66). According to a business address CD I have, there are some 2,170 dive training and equipment centers in the U.S. As of this printing, if you decide you want to be certified via NAUI, you have a choice of some 1,200 NAUI affiliates worldwide. For those considering PADI certification, there are more than 100,000 individual professional members and more than 4,300 dive centers and resorts in at least 175 countries. For those wishing to be trained via YMCA SCUBA there are over 2,200 YMCAs in the U.S. which have access to some 1,200 YMCA pools and aquatic facilities.

Other certifying agencies that you could consider include IANTD, IDEA, MDEA, NASDS, NASE, PDIC, SDI, SSI, and WASI. Check out the agency's web sites or give them a call to find a specific dive center or Instructor near you. The certifying agency's URLs and phone numbers can be found in Figure D in Question 72.

As you can see, finding a training center near you should not be difficult. You can also be SCUBA certified by an Instructor who, though affiliated with a certifying agency, contracts directly with the student. Whatever your choice, you definitely have a lot of them!

Peacock Springs, Florida

80. What are the specific requirements for becoming certified?

Each certifying agency has their own set of requirements for certification, though they all adhere to the same minimal requirements. You can review Figure D in Question 72 for a general idea of the classroom, pool, and open water hours, modules, units, and/or number of dives required. Listing in detail each agency's requirements is overkill, because when you get right down to it, the goal of each agency is to make you a safe and knowledgeable diver, they just go about it a little differently. Additionally, Instructors will emphasize different material and likely add some of their own. Here again, the goal is the same, just different ways of getting you there.

However, the above paragraph does not really tell you very much. Thus I present Listing AC as a means of giving you an idea of some of the things you will likely be required to know or do in order to get your certification. Note that Listing AC is by no means all-inclusive. If you still have questions about the requirements for certification, it would be most appropriate for you to ask those questions of your Instructor, the person you are considering as your Instructor, or dive shop.

Listing AC. Some of the Requirements Likely for Certification.
✓ Be able to *pass the initial swimming test* (see Question 50),
✓ successfully *pass the classroom exams (see Question 81),*
✓ be able to *accurately and consistently use the dive tables,*
✓ be able to *equalize the pressure in your ears,*
✓ be able *to remove, reattach, and clear your facemask,*
✓ *know how the SCUBA equipment works, how to assemble and disassemble it, how to care for and store it, and demonstrate its proper use,*
✓ demonstrate *buoyancy control,*
✓ be able to *doff and don equipment underwater,*
✓ *demonstrate buddy breathing techniques* satisfactorily,
✓ effectively *communicate underwater, and*
✓ be *reasonably at ease in the pool (see Question 86) and during the open water (see Question 87) dives.*

81. What does classroom instruction cover?

Your SCUBA certification classroom instruction covers quite a few topics and they do vary from agency to agency and to a certain extent, from Instructor to Instructor. Yet the primary goal of the classroom instruction is for you to understand the effects of increased pressure on the human body; more to the point, your body. You will also be taught *the master rule of SCUBA diving: never hold your breath underwater, particularly while ascending.* Classroom instruction will likely also include the topics in Listing AD.

Listing AD. Sample of Topics Covered in Classroom Instruction.

- *Buoyancy and buoyancy control,*
- *pressure/volume/density relationships,*
- *equalization techniques,*
- *dive equipment,* e.g., mask, fins, snorkel, BCD, exposure suit, weight systems, alternate air source, low pressure inflator, dive knife (see Question 105), dive instruments,
- *SCUBA systems,* e.g., tank, valves, regulator, SPG,
- *buddy system* and procedures,
- *underwater hearing, vision (see Question 31), heat loss, environment,*
- *breathing techniques, airway control, nitrogen narcosis (see Question 83), and DCS,*
- *underwater communication (see Question 46),*
- *dive planning,*
- *boat diving procedures,*
- *problem recognition and management,*
- *accessory dive equipment,*
- *health and diving,*
- *use of dive tables, safety stops, emergency decompression, multiple repetitive dives, and surface interval, and*
- *compass navigation.*

The required classroom instruction is an effort to keep you safe and out of trouble. In SCUBA diving, the answer to that physics problem at depth is not simply a number, it involves a decision you may have to make and it may affect a life ... yours! Do your homework and take classroom instruction seriously.

82. Why is the maximum recreational SCUBA depth 130 feet?

The 130-foot maximum depth limit used by recreational SCUBA certification agencies was adopted from the early work of the U.S. Navy. There are several schools of thought as to why the 130-foot limit. One school contends that the limit was adopted because it gave navy divers about 10 minutes of bottom time on compressed air. Apparently the Navy believed that there was not much use in a diver going deeper when there was only about 10 minutes bottom time before requiring a decompression stop. Another school of thought is that the limit was set based on the limitations (ability to deliver air at a reasonable resistance) of the double hose regulator and the necessity of setting operational limits based on that equipment. Regardless as to why, as with many diving issues in the early days of SCUBA, e.g., the 'no decompression' limits (see Question 84), the Navy standard was also adopted by the recreational training agencies.

Experienced divers do go deeper than 130 feet and still stay within no decompression limits. However, at 130 feet there is an *increase in the risks of DCS (decompression sickness), problems associated with running out of air at depth, and nitrogen narcosis. Thus the training agencies, believing that some limit must be set for recreational SCUBA diving, have stayed with 130-foot limit.* If you choose to dive deeper than 130 feet, be aware of the risks involved, get additional training, and dive safely.

83. What is this rapture of the deep thing (getting narc'd)?

Nitrogen narcosis, rapture of the deep, getting narc'd, etc. all mean the same thing. When a diver dives deep, generally 100 feet or more, they will experience the affect. The Myer-Overton Theory states that any inert gas (nitrogen in recreational divers) will cause an anesthetic effect if enough of it is dissolved in the fatty tissue of the nervous system. It is thought that the nitrogen absorbed in the fatty tissues interferes with the transmission of nerve impulses and creates an anesthetic or drug-like effect.

Now your initial response may be, "let's strap on the tanks and go do it!" but remember you are 100 feet or more below the surface. Not having full control of your faculties at depth may be the last time you have any control of them.

Most divers do not notice any nitrogen narcosis effects above 70 feet, but most notice some affect at 100 feet. The affect is similar to drinking alcohol, i.e., slowed reactions and thinking. Generally speaking, reasoning and short-term memory are affected before motor coordination. Delayed recognition of and delayed response to stimuli are among the first symptoms of sensory degradation.

The effects of nitrogen narcosis can vary from diver to diver and also from dive to dive. Some divers are able to tolerate it better than others but are still affected. Experienced divers may be able to handle nitrogen narcosis better, partly because they are able to increase their concentration on tasks at depth, thus 'adapt' to narcosis. Yet only a naïve and foolish diver dives deep and discounts the effects, particularly when the onset of narcosis is usually rapid.

Divers having experienced marked narcosis tell tales of either feeling great and whistling as they are merrily swimming along or an exaggerated feeling that something is lurking just out of sight. Divers have been known to acknowledge an ascent signal from their buddy then proceed to descend rather than ascend! Others have thought they were descending when in actuality they were ascending and increased their buoyancy that started them ascending too fast. Narcosis is not something to discount as purely textbook fear mongering. Good buddies, when diving deep, will keep an eye out for inappropriate behavior in each other and call for at least a partial ascent to remedy the problem if it occurs.

One of the tasks you may do during your advanced open water certification or deep diver specialty dives is to perform a timed mathematical problem on the surface then go to depth and try a similar task. You may not be aware of it at depth, but your task completion time will likely increase. The important point here is that if you need to solve safety-related problems at depth you may not be able to resolve them as quickly.

If you feel like you are becoming narc'd, then inform your buddy and ascend together to shallower water. The level and degree of becoming narc'd will vary from dive to dive depending on stresses, your physical condition, number of previous dives, water temperature, etc. *Nitrogen narcosis is not believed to cause any lasting damage to you physically, but does hinder your thinking and reactions in an emergency at depth. Avoid getting narc'd.*

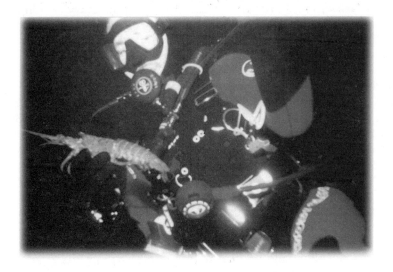

84. Why is mandatory decompression not taught?

In fact, "decompression" always occurs as a diver goes from high to low (relative) ambient pressures. Therefore, all compressed gas diving is actually decompression diving. *When recreational SCUBA diving (RSD) is said to be "no decompression diving", that actually means "no mandatory decompression stop diving". Note that a safety stop (see below) is not the same as a mandatory decompression stop.*

Mandatory decompression is not taught because a decompression stop should never be required if you dive within the guidelines of RSD (see Question 1). It is assumed that diving is made safer for the recreational SCUBA diver by avoiding dives that require decompression stops with their inherent additional calculations, equipment, air, and expertise.

For more advanced/technical/professional dives, an actual decompression stop provides time for some of the excess nitrogen that entered the divers' tissues to "off-gas" (diffuse into the blood stream and be ventilated out of the body by the lungs). This minimizes the risk of the diver having a DCS (decompression sickness) hit. Decompression stops are often necessary in dives that are deeper and/or longer than 'allowed' in RSD.

The "no decompression stop" limits in RSD are based on maximum depth, time, altitude, water composition (fresh or salt), and preceding dive profiles. All these factors, and others (see Question 39) directly affect uptake of nitrogen by body tissues. The "no decompression stop" limits are incorporated into dive computers and the dive tables (see Question 102) used by recreational divers.

The "no-decompression stop" limits are determined by the excess quantities of nitrogen that enter our tissues due to the increased ambient (surrounding) pressure when at depth. A non-repetitive dive (no previous dive within 6-12 hours) to 130 feet has an allowable "actual bottom time" (measured from the time dive commences to start of ascent) of only about 10 minutes. Diving beyond that short time period, increases the divers' risks of developing decompression sickness from a no-decompression stop ascent. In contrast, with a maximum dive depth of 60 feet, on a non-repetitive dive, the 'no-decompression' bottom time is about 55 minutes.

Although RSD is always planned such that no decompression stop is required, you should always make a 3-5 minute "safety stop" at about 15 feet (10-25 feet) before surfacing from any dive deeper than about 40 feet. In theory, if you dive by the recreational diving tables, you should not experience a DCS hit even if you do not make a safety stop. Yet a safety stop helps compensate for ascent rates faster then 60 feet per minute, it gives you a chance to adjust buoyancy, and to ensure the surface area directly above you is clear before surfacing.

In summary, if any dive you make <u>requires</u> a decompression stop for any reason, then you have exceeded the limits of recreational SCUBA diving. Unless you have advanced training in decompression diving, you should not do decompression diving. You should always do a safety stop.

Taking time for a safety stop

85. I have heard about nitrox. What is it and how is it used?

Nitrox is essentially any mixture of nitrogen and oxygen. Divers generally refer to nitrox as air that has a higher concentration of oxygen then the air we normally breathe. The air we breathe is called normoxic nitrox because it contains the 'normal' concentration of oxygen on earth (21 percent). Yet when divers speak of using nitrox, they are generally referring to Nitrox I which is 32 percent oxygen or Nitrox II which is 36 percent oxygen. Other concentrations of oxygen are used, but concentrations greater than 40 percent require additional specialized equipment. Cylinders containing enriched-air nitrox (oxygen concentrations above 21 percent) must be specially cleaned, color coded, and tagged.

Some of the advantages of using nitrox are shown in Listing AE.

Listing AE. Advantages of Using Nitrox.
- The *decreased likelihood of DCS* (decompression sickness),
- *decreased nitrogen narcosis,*
- *reduced residual nitrogen times* (thus shorter surface interval times between dives),
- *if a diver exceeds recreational SCUBA diving (RSD) bottom time limits, then reduced decompression time would be needed* (this should not be an issue for the novice diver as RSD limits should not be exceeded by them),
- *reduced surface intervals* between dives and when it is safe to board a plane and fly,
- *reduced air consumption* while diving, and
- possibly *feeling better* after a dive.

The disadvantages of using Nitrox are listed in Listing AF.

Listing AF. Disadvantages of Using Nitrox.
- The *specialized training* required,
- the requirement for *specialized equipment* (cylinders) just for enriched-air nitrox,
- *increased oxidation of SCUBA cylinders,*
- *possible increased deterioration of equipment parts,*
- *fire hazards,*
- *increased cost,*
- *increased risk of oxygen toxicity,*

- ⚘ *inability to use air-only based computers,* and
- ⚘ *the potential for nitrox mixing and filling problems.*

As to my experience with nitrox, I am PADI nitrox certified and working on an IANTD nitrox certification. I have found Nitrox diving to be a mixed bag. After diving with nitrox, I do seem to feel better than after diving with air. Using nitrox does increase my bottom time a little and I have never had a DCI hit with either air or nitrox. To date, I have not been trained in nor make decompression stop dives. Finally, I tend to be conservative on surface intervals anyway, so being able to decrease them is not a big issue for me.

The nitrox certified tanks (Al80s) and valves are an added expense (about $185 vs. $130 for air). Owning an oxygen analyzer (starting at about $200) is also an added expense, nitrox is about $12 a fill vs. air at $4, and nitrox is not always available. Regardless, my primary concern when using nitrox is oxygen toxicity, so I take the appropriate precautions and have not had a problem to date. In short, nitrox has its place in a diver's bag of tools but I will not be giving up my air cylinders anytime soon.

86. What does the pool/confined water instruction cover?

Your training in the pool is where the real fun begins. There is something incredible about that first breath of air you take from your regulator underwater! I thought, "This is GREAT. It really does work!" The specifics of your pool instruction (see Question 75) and the order in which you will be taught will vary, depending upon certifying agency and Instructor. In general you will be instructed on the items in Listing AG.

Listing AG. Pool Instruction Likely Includes.

- ⚓ The *purpose, inspection, assembly, disassembly, and care of your gear,*
- ⚓ *proper tank handling,*
- ⚓ *how to attach the tank to the BC (buoyancy compensator),*
- ⚓ correct procedures *for attaching the regulators and gauges to the tank,*
- ⚓ how to *don and get comfortable with the BC* including inflation and deflation,
- ⚓ how to *strap on the weights* (see Question 101),
- ⚓ *pre-dive safety check,*
- ⚓ methods of *pool ingress and egress,*
- ⚓ taking that first breath underwater!
- ⚓ *practice equalizing squeezes* in ear and mask,
- ⚓ how to *swim efficiently with fins and correct body orientation,*
- ⚓ *snorkel breathing, clearing, and transfer to regulator,*
- ⚓ how to *clear or flush the water from your mask,*
- ⚓ *no-mask breathing and replacing the mask underwater,*
- ⚓ how to *ascend and descend safely,*
- ⚓ practice *obtaining neutral buoyancy* and determining how much weight you need to be properly weighted,
- ⚓ *obtaining and breathing off your octopus* or safe second regulator,
- ⚓ *regulator recovery, air depletion exercise, buddy breathing,*
- ⚓ *free-flow regulator breathing,*
- ⚓ *controlled emergency swimming ascent,*
- ⚓ *reading of gauges,*
- ⚓ practicing *hand signals,*
- ⚓ *tired diver tow,*

- *surface diving,*
- *hyperventilation,*
- *taking weights on and off underwater,*
- *doffing and donning BC underwater,* and
- generally getting familiar with your equipment.

As a student, you may be concerned about what happens if you are not able to do all the required underwater skills. In a word, relax. You should not be pressured, by your Instructor or fellow students, into doing procedures you are not ready to do. Your Instructor has been trained to not pressure a student to do a task that they indicate verbally or otherwise that they can not or do not want to do it (unless there is a safety issue).

For example, if your Instructor asks you to flood and clear your mask (commonly a tough task for the first few tries) and you are not ready, then so signify by shaking your head. Your Instructor may signal "are you okay?" or repeat the request to make sure you understood and are OK but then should move on to the next student. Your Instructor should come back to you when you are ready to do the task or signal the Assistant Instructor to help you.

The worst that will happen if you refuse to do a requirement for certification (assuming you do not put yourself or someone else at risk) is that your Instructor will not be able to certify you until you can meet all the requirements. You can always get additional help, reschedule your training, or get another Instructor.

There is POSITIVELY NO disgrace in foregoing a dive or a dive activity that you are not feeling comfortable with. There will always be another day and another dive. This attitude should be carried over to all your future diving. It is a mature person who knows their limits and dives within them. Do not let anyone tell you different.

87. What happens during my open water training dives?

After you have successfully completed your pool and classroom sessions, you will make four or five open water dives with your Instructor (and class, if any (see Question 76)). The main difference between the pool or confined water training and the open water training is that open water dives take place {this is a shocker} in open water, e.g., the ocean, a lake, a quarry, a spring, etc.

As in the pool, the open water dives are conducted so your Instructor can determine, if you have mastered the skills you need to be a certified diver. *On the first few open-water dives, you will be asked to demonstrate many of the same skills you already successfully completed in the pool. For example, you will be asked to* flood and clear your mask, remove, replace, and clear your mask, demonstrate buoyancy control, practice 30-45 feet per minute ascents and descents, do buddy breathing at depth and during ascent, and communicate underwater (see Question 86).

The limited amount of new material presented includes: dive environment inspection and considerations, dive planning, descending and ascending a line, underwater compass work, mid-water buoyancy control, underwater tours ("for fun and relaxation"), actual use of dive tables, and properly logging the dives. As with the written test, the purpose of the training dives is not to disqualify you. They are to help the Instructor judge whether you are ready to dive without supervision and to help you feel safe and comfortable in the water. The depth of these training dives differ based on facilities and instructor, but are generally from 15 to 60 feet deep.

Clearing a mask.

88. What will my first open water post-cert dive be like?
Your first open water dive after earning that coveted C-card will be exhilarating! I suggest diving with an experienced buddy under similar conditions (or same dive site) in which you were initially certified. Diving familiar water tends to be less intimidating, making for a great, memorable dive. Good visibility, calm environmental conditions, an interesting dive site, using the same equipment you trained with, and a good dive buddy will maximize your enjoyment.

My experience was a bit atypical and I did not follow the advice I gave above (which is probably why I give you that advice). I obtained my open water certification in a Pennsylvania quarry with 20-foot visibility and a depth no greater than 38 feet. As I wanted to continue my diving education, I opted to go directly into instruction for the Advanced Open Water diver certification. In retrospect, I should have done at least a few "for fun and relaxation" dives first.

So here I am with a new Instructor, at a new dive site (Vepco Lake) in West Virginia that has a depth of 125 feet and I am told to avoid the center channel because at about 120 feet, there is a large power plant intake pipe. I sure was not planning on going that deep but the caution, though advisable, did stir up thoughts of being sucked down (see Question 29) and into the power plant. Anyway, the first dive was to be a deep dive to about 90 feet (remember I had not previously dove deeper than 38 feet).

The dive started OK with the instructor being my buddy and an Advanced Open Water father/son buddy team along for the dive. Visibility was about 15 feet at the surface, then an algae bloom began at about 10 feet. At about 45 feet there was total darkness. We had brought along flashlights and had tank lights so we were able to keep in contact with one another. At 89 feet we stopped, I did a math problem (to show the affects of slight narcosis) and played around with a rather compressed racket ball (which of course I accidentally released but did not ascend after!) After a short, 20 minute bottom time, we ascended and debriefed about the dive on shore.

That fifth dive was not what I would call a dive "for fun and relaxation". The sixth dive was spent at an equivalent depth, swimming around looking for a dive platform in total darkness. All-in-all, a couple of dives I would have enjoyed more had I had some additional dive time before doing them. Regardless, those fifth and sixth dives were exhilarating and they were not unsafe. But you will enjoy yours more if you heed the advice I gave at the beginning of this answer. Now go divin'!

Taking a Giant Stride into a lifetime of adventure!

89. What is DAN (Divers Alert Network) and should I join?
DAN (Divers Alert Network) was founded in 1980 and is a 501(c)(3) non-profit dive safety organization affiliated with Duke University Medical Center in Durham, N.C. DAN was originally funded by government grants, but is now supported by the largest membership association of divers in the world, dive industry sponsors, product sales, and fund raising. DAN is best known for its 24-hour Diving Emergency Hotline, divers insurance, Dive Safety and Medical Information Line, and its dive-related medical research programs.

In my opinion, all divers should be DAN members. DAN members not only support diving's only 24-hour diving emergency hotline, but also get emergency travel assistance, subscription to the Alert Diver magazine, DAN's Dive and Travel Medical Guide, dive and travel discounts, and access to affordable diving insurance.

As of this printing, the basic annual DAN membership is only $29, but for an additional $35 a year you can get dive accident insurance which covers $125,000 worth of decompression illness and in-water injury plus a lot more. Give DAN a call at (919) 684-2948 or check out their web site at http://www.DiversAlertNetwork.org. To be fair, dive insurance can also be purchased from a few other agencies, including PADI (800) 223-9998 for $40 to $80 and DSI (800) 288-4810 for $25 to $60. After calling 911 and when the immediate diving emergency is under control, give DAN a call on their hotline at (919) 684-8111 for added assistance.

I talked to one Divemaster who said when a diver has a DCI (decompression illness) on board a dive boat, there is always the concern of who to contact and where to take the diver. If the stricken diver is a DAN member, with DAN insurance, then things tend to come together a lot quicker. Help yourself while helping your avocation: join DAN. End of unsolicited commercial.

90. What does the well-dressed SCUBA diver wear?

SCUBA diving is an equipment-intensive activity. It is the *equipment you carry which enables you to survive and enjoy the alien underwater environment.* The incredible growth of recreational SCUBA diving as an avocation has depended heavily upon the development of safe, reliable, comfortable, readily available, and competitively priced equipment.

Reviewing the accident reports, it can be seen that the failure of diving equipment is seldom the cause of diving accidents. Yet equipment problems and the diver's inability to manage those problems can contribute to accidents. If you have the right equipment for the dive and if you care for your equipment properly, adjust and inspect it regularly, and can manage problems when they occur, then you minimize your equipment-related risks.

During your open water course you will be instructed on how the equipment works, how to ensure it fits correctly, and how to keep it in good condition. Some of the equipment used in SCUBA diving is shown in Figures E, F, and G. Configuration of your equipment is both standard and personal, so your Instructor may suggest a different configuration.

The Equipment Specialty is one of the specialties you should take after receiving your basic open water SCUBA certification. Keeping your equipment in good repair and knowing how to handle minor problems, enable you to concentrate on enjoying your underwater experience rather than fussing with equipment.

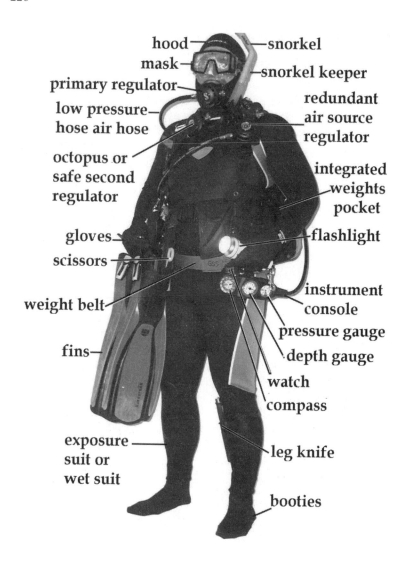

hood — snorkel
mask — snorkel keeper
primary regulator —
low pressure — redundant air source regulator
hose air hose
octopus or safe second regulator
integrated weights pocket
gloves — flashlight
scissors —
weight belt —
instrument console
pressure gauge
fins —
depth gauge
watch
compass
exposure suit or wet suit — leg knife
booties

Figure E. SCUBA Equipment

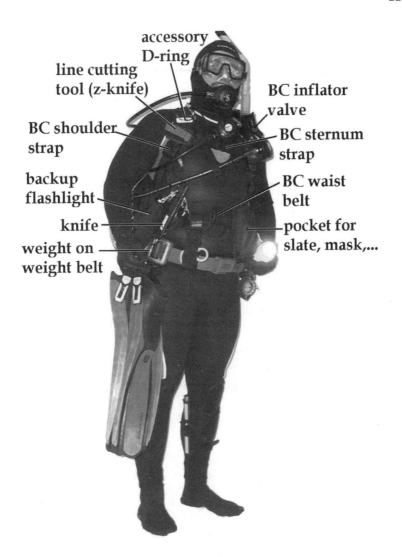

accessory
D-ring

line cutting
tool (z-knife)

BC inflator
valve

BC shoulder
strap

BC sternum
strap

backup
flashlight

BC waist
belt

knife

pocket for
slate, mask,...

weight on
weight belt

Figure F. SCUBA Equipment

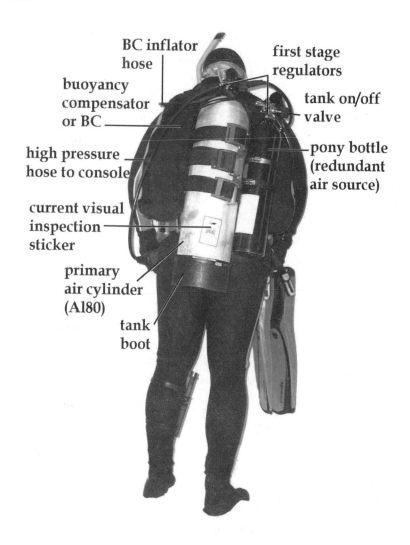

BC inflator hose

first stage regulators

buoyancy compensator or BC

tank on/off valve

high pressure hose to console

pony bottle (redundant air source)

current visual inspection sticker

primary air cylinder (Al80)

tank boot

Figure G. SCUBA Equipment (back view)

91. What equipment must I buy to become certified? Cost?

Different course providers offer different packages and some even include rental of all equipment during your certification course (see Question 70). Yet *in most cases, the minimal equipment you will need to buy to become certified is a facemask, a snorkel, fins, and probably booties (depending on fin type and water temperature). You will also want to purchase a good pair of gloves if you will be diving in cold water. The cost of the above equipment is $150 to $350,* depending on equipment quality, sales, and/or package deals offered by the dive shop. Then, even if you never get fully certified (if you have trouble equalizing your ears or doing some other underwater function), you can always use the equipment for snorkeling.

The dive shop is there to help you in your purchase of equipment, so ask them for assistance. When buying equipment remember that the number one thing to look for in equipment is proper fit. If the equipment does not fit, i.e., feel comfortable while affording you a full range of movement, then you are going to be uncomfortable or your underwater activities will be hindered.

In order to see underwater, you will need a facemask. It is particularly important to get a facemask that fits properly. The mask must form a good seal around your face in order to avoid constant leakage (which can be really annoying, particularly in saltwater). You will learn how to fit a mask in your SCUBA class or by asking an employee of the dive shop. If you wear prescription eyeglasses (see Question 64), you may also want to consider getting a prescription mask.

I had been using a low volume, clear mask without a purge valve (SeaQuest Vision), but I am now trying out a higher volume, peripheral vision, clear mask (Aqua Lung Hawaii 3), still sans purge valve. I think I like my old mask better, but I am not giving up on the new one quite yet. Ask your equipment salesperson for the pros and cons of each mask type, style, and color vs. clear plastic. Note that the SCUBA facemask covers the diver's eyes and nose because this allows for both underwater vision and the equalization of air pressure within the mask.

This paragraph is for men only. If you sport a mustache, finding a mask that fits without leaking can be a chore, if not impossible (depending on your moustache). You can try smearing your mustache with globs of Chap Stick®, bear grease, or waterproof wheel bearing grease {just kidding about the bearing grease ... I think}. I have heard that high concentration petroleum products are discouraged because they eat the plastic of the mask. Other things to try are keeping it trimmed short, trying different masks (I understand the Apollo frameless mask works well), use food grade silicon on the moustache, or get a high volume mask with a purge valve. As I sport a mustache, I initially tried Chap Stick®. I soon got fed up with the mess and now I just keep an area below my nose shaved and the mustache trimmed to a reasonable length. The mask is reasonably watertight and I retain the mustache.

Your fins are your primary source of locomotion underwater. They should fit you as well as a pair of shoes. Full-foot fins enclose the heel like a shoe and generally work best on the surface or in warm water environments. Adjustable or open heel fins are the preferred fin type for SCUBA in colder water and are generally worn over a bootie. If you will be wearing booties, then you will obviously need to try on the fins while wearing the booties.

Booties are essentially neoprene socks with soles that keep your feet warmer and absorb some of the friction between feet and fin. Fins also come in a number of sizes and shapes. Take into account your physique when buying fins. You do not want them to be so short that you over power them and visa versa. A good fitting pair of fins will enable you to maximize your propulsion while minimizing the effort you expend.

Snorkels come in many different types and styles. They come with or without a purge valve and with different tube shapes and tips. Be sure to pick one with a large diameter tube for easier breathing. Snorkels are energy savers as they enable you to breathe on the surface without having to lift or turn your head. Snorkels come in handy if you want to make a surface swim (to save air) out to the dive area from the shore or boat. Snorkels are also useful if you must make a surface swim back to the shore or boat.

Some divers believe the snorkel is more trouble than it is worth and do their surface swims on their backs.   Other divers securely store the snorkel in the BC or under their leg knife straps for use if needed, thereby avoiding possible entanglement of the snorkel when it is attached to the facemask.   I was trained with a snorkel attached to the facemask strap, and that is where I keep it ready to use.   Yet, most of my long surface swims are primarily done on my back, as it seems that I can make better progress that way.   Someday I will experiment with storing the snorkel off my mask, but for now it is attached to my mask strap, unless I am doing a penetration dive.

A Diver's Candy Store
A well stocked dive store will have the necessities: mast, snorkel, booties, and fins .. and so much more!

92. Do I have to buy more equipment after getting certified?

If desired, you may continue to rent most of the equipment you will need for diving after becoming certified. You really do not absolutely have to buy much more. Realistically though, *if you want to own the minimal amount of equipment for diving in warm water, you should purchase a knife (or two), a light pair of gloves, a dive slate with pencil, a whistle, and an underwater flashlight for a total of approximately $175+.*

You can rent regulators, a BC (buoyancy compensator), weights and weight belt, an exposure suit, and tanks at many dive sites around the world (see Question 114). As most dive operators take reasonably good care of their rental equipment, they will usually function properly. In fact, even if you own all your own equipment, there may be times you can not or do not want to bring it along and decide to rent instead. If you do not dive enough to justify buying, then renting is a good option. The down side of renting is that the BC may not always fit just right, the functionality of the various components may differ from dive to dive, and the hassle of obtaining and returning the equipment (see Question 19).

Yet if you decide to buy additional equipment, then a dive bag, BC (see Question 95), regulators (see Question 97) and gauges (pressure, depth, and compass) should top that list. There is nothing like knowing where that BC and regulator have been and what condition they are in. A good dive bag to carry everything in, will set you back about $80, regulators and gauges about $400-$800+, and a buoyancy compensator will cost $250-$700+.

BCs differ as to type, fit, amount of buoyancy provided, and the type of diving for which they are best suited. Just one last thing I will mention here. Remember the first rule of buoyancy control: never use your BC as a lift bag (see Question 44), particularly with you in it!

Additional diving equipment you may consider investing in are:
- an exposure suit and hood for $200-$2,000+,
- a dive computer for $225-$750+,
- additional set of thicker gloves ($30-$50),

- a secondary dive light for night diving ($30-$100),
- bug (lobster) bag ($20+),
- weights (about $100), and
- tanks ($130-$300 each).

Because of the initial expense and yearly maintenance fees, most divers do not buy tanks unless they will be doing a lot of local diving. If you really get into diving, then there are all sorts of specialties to become trained in. Of course, with the specialties often comes the necessity of purchasing additional equipment. The bottom of the ocean and your piggy bank are the limits. SCUBA diving is a great avocation for the gadget guy (male or female), but remember, more is not necessarily better in diving. When diving, try to minimize looking like a peddler with all sorts of stuff dangling off your BC. Dangling equipment decreases swimming efficiency by increasing drag. Additionally, dangling equipment can become entangled, damage sensitive ecosystems, get dinged up against rocks or plugged up on muddy bottoms, and it is just hard to find something when it is just dangling. Minimize the dang dangles.

93. How about a basic open water equipment checklist?

As you become a more proficient diver, expanding the variety and complexity of your dives, your equipment checklist will also expand. Figure H on the next page is an equipment checklist from which you can start one of your own and populate your possibles kit (see Question 110). You can copy the Figure H page or print a basic or expand list from **http://www.ehpublishing.com/scubaequipcklist.html**.

235

Figure H. Open Water Equipment Checklist.

Basic	Spare	Accessories
__gear bag(s)	__tank(s)	__game bag
__fins	__weights	__slate & pencil
__mask	__straps (fin/mask)	__marked line/tape
__snorkel	__O-rings	__primary dive light
__exposure suit	__tools / wrenches	__back-up dive light
__hood	__suit cement/patch	__tank light/glow stic
__booties	__regulator hp plug	__marker-buoys
__gloves	__reg. mouthpiece	__buddy line
__BCD	__snorkel keeper	__camera w/ strobe
__regulator	__high/low pres. hoses	__film
__safe second	—	__spear
__depth gauge	—	__lift bag
__pressure gauge		__knife(s)
__compass	**Personal Items**	__line cutter/scissors
__dive computer	__certification cards	__batteries (camera/
__watch	__current log book	light/computer)
__temp. gauge	__dive tables	__spare air source
__tanks	__swim suit	__float/dive flag
__weights & belt	__towel	__first aid kit
__tank(s) (filled?)	__jacket	__oxygen cyl/mask
__knife(s)	__deck/swim shoes	__zip ties
__whistle	__garbage sacks (dry)	__abalone iron
__adrift/possibles bag	__extra clothes	__hvy thread/needle
__extra mask	__tickets	__instant heat packs
__mask defogger	__fishing license	—
__silicone grease	__money/credit cards	—
—	__seasickness meds/swim-ear medication	
—	__aspirin/gauze/neosporin/water proof tape	
	__white vinegar for stings	
	__sunglasses/sunblock	
	__toilet articles/cotton swabs/resealable bags	
	__filet knife	
	__eating utensils	
	__lunch	
	__ice chest/thermos	
	__sleeping bag/pad	
	__tent	
	—	
	—	

94. Should I buy equipment via mail order, dive shop, or ?

There are a number of sources from which you can purchase SCUBA equipment, e.g., dive shop, mail order, garage/yard/tag sales, fellow divers, etc. For the reasons stated in Listing AH, it is *my opinion that the best place for the novice diver to get their equipment is from their local dive shop.*

Listing AH. Why the Beginning Diver Should Purchase Equipment from a Dive Shop.

- *If you are buying life-support equipment, then the dive shop should, as part of the sale, verify that you have been trained/certified to the level that you know how to use it,*
- dive shops are a good place to *get advice regarding equipment* as store personnel are most often dive professionals,
- you can *look at and try the gear on before purchasing,*
- *dive shops are often the only place to get adequate dealer prep of life-support equipment,*
- the *dive shop should be able to support you on repairs and maintenance* of the equipment with manufacture authorized parts and service, and
- *dive shops support you by providing safe air refills* (which do not pay the overhead), *having rental equipment available, providing a convenient place to get that last-minute item before a dive, provide travel and dive packages, often they support a local dive club, they are a place to hang out and talk SCUBA with like-minded individuals and look at cool new stuff.*

Of course the experienced, technical and commercial divers will argue that mail order is often cheaper, sometimes faster, and the dive shop may not carry the needed item(s). All valid statements. Yet points three through six above still apply to even the experienced diver.

I have purchased the great majority of my equipment via dive shops (no, I do not own one nor am I affiliated with one). I will continue to do so unless there is a good reason not to. Of course, you are encouraged to shop around for the best price and purchase needed items during periodic shop sales. Hey, even SCUBA divers have kids to put through college.

Unless you know what you are doing or the item is not life supporting, then I recommend that you stay away from garage/yard/tag sales. Purchasing from fellow divers is an obvious mixed bag where caveat emptor (buyer beware) applies. It does not appear to me that it is worth losing a dive buddy over an argument regarding your purchase of a piece of their equipment.

Standard Military Issue

Rough Rider

U.S. Divers

Aqua-Lung
Royal Aqua-Master

Most dive ships do not carry equipment from the 70's.

95. What is a Buoyancy Compensator?

A buoyancy compensator, or BC, is just that, a device that is worn on the upper torso (see Question 90) to help control a diver's buoyancy. Additionally, most BCs incorporate a 'backpack' to hold your SCUBA cylinder or tank and many have pockets and D-rings for storing or attaching additional equipment. Integrated-weight BCs have pockets in which you can place weights as opposed (or in addition) to using a weight belt. As you can see, a BC is a very functional piece of equipment.

A BC provides buoyancy by the inflation of its internal air bladder(s) either orally (via your mouth) or from a low-pressure inflator (which in some designs can also serve as a safe-second) (see Question 97). This low-pressure inflator is attached to the first stage regulator (see Question 90), which in turn is threaded into your SCUBA tank. Thus the low-pressure inflator obtains air to inflate your BC from the tank. Deflation (thus enabling you to sink) of the BC is accomplished manually by either pressing another button on the low-pressure inflator, or by pulling open one of the pressure-relief valve(s) built into the BC. One of the important skills you will learn in your open water course and from experience is buoyancy control, which in part, involves your BC.

The three general types of BCs are front-mounted, jacket-style, and back-mounted with the jacket-style BC being the most popular. Going into detail regarding BCs is beyond the scope of this text, but you should be given additional information on their usage and care in your open water course. You can get BC purchase recommendations from dive shop personnel, product reviews in SCUBA magazines, your Instructor, and fellow divers. The important thing is to get the best fitting BC you can which meets the needs of your diving interests. You can always rent a BC until you decide upon the model best for you and give yourself the time to save up the $250 to $700+ that a new BC will set you back.

For all-around diving I am happy with my Zeagle Ranger BC. Talking to other Ranger owners, they also seem to be happy with it. Other BCs you should consider include, but certainly are not limited to, Mares Frontier Expedition, Oceanic Baja,

Poseidon Power Lift Photic, Scubapro Classic NT, Scubapro Tradewind, Sea Quest Spectrum 1, and Sea Quest Spectrum 2.

Women's Jacket Style BC

Men's Jacket Style BC

'Back Plate' Style BC

96. Tanks a lot for info on SCUBA cylinders.

The tanks or cylinders that are in common use in recreational SCUBA are predominantly made of steel or aluminum. Until 1970, all sport diving tanks were made of steel, but since then the most common size in the U.S. has become the aluminum 80, or Al80 for short. Listing AI displays some of the more common SCUBA tanks used in the U.S.

Listing AI. Common SCUBA Tanks Used in the U.S.

☐ the Al80 tank, when filled to 3014.7 psia (pounds per square inch absolute) at 70° F at sea level, contains 80 cubic feet (cf) of air (about the amount of uncompressed air in a 3.4 feet x 3.4 feet x 7 feet phone booth),

☐ the 71.2 cubic-foot steel cylinder which holds 71.2 cf at 2,475 psi (overfilled by 10 percent) or 65 cf at 2,250 psi (after second hydrostatic test),

☐ the 50 cf aluminum cylinder filled to 3,000 psi, and

☐ the 103.5 (or 104s or 100s) cf steel tank filled at 2,400 psi.

The Al80 tank weighs about 33 pounds, the 71.2 steel about 29 pounds, the Al 50 about 21 pounds, and the 103.5 steel about 44 pounds. The actual tank weights are dependent upon the tank manufacturer. You should be instructed in tank handling and care in your basic open water course.

As long as we are talking about tanks, some of the pros and cons of aluminum compared to steel SCUBA cylinders are listed in Listing AJ.

Listing AJ. Some Pros and Cons of Aluminum vs. Steel Tanks.

✎ *Both aluminum and steel cylinders are susceptible to corrosion,* but steel tanks are much more susceptible to becoming uncertifiable due to rust than aluminum tanks are to damage by aluminum oxide. Yet, with proper care, a steel tank will last for many years.

✎ *Steel is harder than aluminum, thus it takes banging and scraping abuse better.* Cavern, cave, wreck, and ice divers regularly bang their cylinders against solid surfaces and steel would take this abuse better. In recreational SCUBA diving, all that usually gets scraped up is the paint on the tank (thus some divers use unpainted tanks or plastic meshes that cover the cylinder).

- *Steel weighs more than aluminum,* but since aluminum is not as strong as steel, the aluminum tanks tend to be physically bigger than comparable steel ones.
- *Since aluminum tanks are bigger than steel ones, they displace more water, becoming more buoyant when emptied.* Thus aluminum tanks when drawn down, generally require a few more pounds of lead added to the weight belt or BC (buoyancy compensator). Alternately, steel tanks are more likely to be neutral or negatively buoyant when empty (depending on size and manufacturer of the tank).
- *Aluminum tanks are more susceptible to becoming uncertifiable due to cracks in the neck of the tank.*
- *Aluminum cylinders tend to be more readily available than steel ones in the U.S., whereas the reverse tends to be true in Europe.*
- *Steel cylinders are more expensive than aluminum ones.* Recent prices for a ScubaPro Steel 72 with valve is about $300 and a low-pressure steel 95 is about $200. An Al80 with valve and boot (goes around the bottom of the tank so the tank stands up more securely) is only about $130.

With all that said, unless there are other special considerations, you should size your tank for the diving you do and the amount of air you consume (see Question 35), not just the material it is composed of.

I have two unpainted Al80s that I use for my 'everyday' diving and another two unpainted 'go to meetin' Al80s especially cleaned for Nitrox diving (see Question 85). Additionally, I have a 19 cf pony tank and a 3.0 cf spare air unit which I use as a redundant air sources (see Question 99). As tanks tend to get scratched up, that slick-looking paint job soon looks rather ratty, thus I opted for the 'natural brushed aluminum' look for my Al80s. To help keep your painted tanks looking good, you can purchase plastic netting that slips over the tank. Having two tanks enables two dives for myself, or one dive apiece for a tank-challenged buddy and myself, before refilling.

97. It takes a regulator to pass gas. What is a regulator?

In the SCUBA context (vs. government regulators which also pass a lot of gas), regulators are one of the necessary pieces of equipment that makes SCUBA diving possible (see Figures E and F in Question 90). *The primary function of regulators is to take air at tank pressure (ranging from 0 to 3,000+ psi (pounds per square inch) or over 200 times atmospheric pressure) and deliver it to the diver upon demand at near ambient (surrounding) pressure at depth.*

I said regulators because, in reality, a recreational SCUBA diver dives with two types of regulators, the first stage and the second stage. Regardless, you will most commonly hear them called the first and second stage of your regulator. Additionally, the first stage has two types of air ports (holes), high and low pressure ports. The first stage regulator is what is attached to the SCUBA tank's valve. When the valve is opened this regulator reduces the tank's high pressure down to about 140 psi over ambient pressure. The air then passes through a low-pressure port down a low-pressure hose to a second stage regulator or low-pressure inflater. There is also a high-pressure port in the first stage that is typically used to pass gas (air) down the high-pressure hose to your instrument console (pressure gauge or dive computer) at tank pressure.

The two basic designs of the first stage are either piston or diaphragm. Certainly, arguments can be made for the pros and cons of either, but quality first stages are made in both designs. First stage regulators, are said to be balanced or unbalanced. The balanced first stage regulator tends to deliver air at a relatively constant pressure regardless of tank pressure. The unbalanced first stage requires harder breathing (inhalation) with lower tank pressure ranges. There are pros and cons to either system, though I prefer the balanced design.

The second stage regulator is the device to which the mouthpiece is attached (in conventional non-full-face mask designs) and is what we generally think of when divers talk about regulators. *Second stage regulators are either "downstream" or "upstream" in design.* In essence, a downstream design means the second stage regulator will free flow (leak air though the mouthpiece) if the controlling valve in the second stage fails. Upstream regulators, upon valve failure, would not free flow and thus not deliver air.

In my opinion, in the rare event of a second stage regulator failure, it is preferable to have a free flow (from which you can still breathe) than no air flow. Finally, some of the second stage regulators can be tuned during a dive to match personal breathing needs.

Recreational SCUBA divers generally carry two second stage regulators, their primary regulator and a safe-second or octopus (see Figures E and F in Question 90). These regulators are identical in purpose (provide air to the diver upon demand) and are attached to the first stage regulator by separate low-pressure hoses. You will likely be trained that the octopus is your spare (second stage) regulator that can be used by your buddy or yourself in an emergency. In this scenario, the octopus is attached loosely to the BC (buoyancy compensator). You or your buddy, are supposed to grab the octopus off the BC and breathe from it in an emergency. However, in real life emergencies, most divers simply go for the primary second stage in their buddy's (or nearest diver's) mouth. This leaves the diver with the air searching for their octopus or safe-second.

To avoid the above problem, some divers attach the spare second stage (octopus) to an elastic cord around their neck and hang it just below their chin. In an emergency, their buddy takes the primary second stage out of their mouth and the diver with the air simply places the other second stage' mouthpiece (which is hanging around their neck) into their mouth. If hung correctly, the octopus can be obtained without the use of the divers' hands.

Another configuration is to have the safe or spare second stage integrated with your BC inflator/deflator, e.g., Octo+. This configuration eliminates one of the low-pressure hoses but raises other issues (ask your Instructor for their advice). Whichever configuration you adopt, just make sure your buddy is aware of which regulator they are 'supposed' to acquire in the rare event of an emergency. Make sure that you can respond safely to whichever one they actually do grab.

If there were only two pieces of SCUBA equipment on which I could splurge, one would be my regulators (I would also splurge on a good warm exposure suit if I dove in cold water - which I do). I want to make sure I have air at depth regardless of conditions (though most regulators will work fine under a wide range of conditions). To that end I own a Zeagle environmental enclosed first stage and a ScubaPro Mk 20 first stage. My second stages are a Zeagle Tech-50D, a couple of ScubaPro G250s, and several SeaQuest Mirage's. I use the Zeagles and ScubaPros for the majority of my diving. Additional regulators that you might consider for inclusion in your long list of regulators to investigate buying are the: Beuchat VXT-8, Mares MR 12 AKROS, Mares V12XL, Oceanic Delta II PX2, Oceanic Delta II DX4, Oceanic Gamma PX2, Oceanic Gamma DX4, and Scubapro MK14 R380.

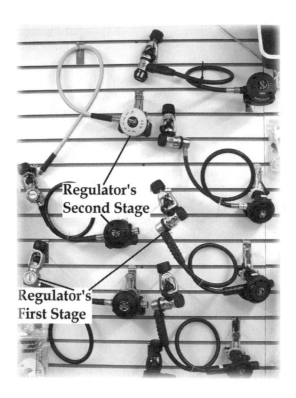

98. How much air do I need to make a safe ascent?
Ok, you are at depth and the air in your primary tank, for whatever reason, becomes unavailable (you would never actually run out of air would you?) *The question becomes how much air do my buddy and I need to make a normal (safe) ascent (not greater than 60 feet per minute) from depth? No one can guarantee that you will never have a DCS (decompression sickness) or an AGE (arterial gas embolism), regardless of how carefully you follow the rules and dive tables. However, let us assume you and your buddy intend to make a 'normal' ascent and that you desire to minimize the likelihood of getting a DCS or AGE hit.*

Given the above assumptions, the table in Figure I is an attempt to answer the question posed. The table was calculated and initially produced by Dave Waller and published on the rec.scuba newsgroup. The table shows calculated air consumption rates (cubic feet per minute) for ascents from various depths (without and with a 3-minute, 15-foot safety stop). These rates are based on a diver's Surface Air Consumption (air consumption at sea level). For the calculation of your SAC (Surface Air Consumption) see **http://www.ehpublishing.com/scubasac.html**.

It has been stated that the "average" diver consumes air at a surface consumption rate of about one cubic foot (cf) per minute. If your primary tank runs dry at depth, then you are likely to be surprised and a bit stressed (see Question 35), thus your air consumption rate would probably increase (another reason to remain calm!). Thus if your surface air consumption (SAC) were 1.0 cf/minute, then maybe using the 1.5 cf/minute column would be more conservative.

Do the following to determine the amount of air that you will use for an ascent. Determine if you want to exclude (first half of the table) or include (second half of the table) a 3-minute, 15-foot safety stop, then find your SAC rate and go down that column to the depth in feet (row) from which you will ascend. The number in that cell is the amount of air (in cubic feet) you are calculated to consume. For example, let's use a diver with a SAC of 1.0 (we will use 1.5 to be more conservative) wanting to do a 3-minute, 15-foot safety stop. If they were ascending from a depth of 130 feet, they would consume 16.6 cubic feet of air, or 623 psi (from an Al80), before breaking the surface.

Figure I. Dave Waller's Table on Air Consumption.

	Consumption w/o 15' safety stop				Consumption with 15' safety stop			
Depth	Consumption Rate (cubic ft/min)				Consumption Rate (cubic ft/min)			
SAC-0	**0.5**	**1.0**	**1.5**	**2.0**	**0.5**	**1.0**	**1.5**	**2.0**
60	1.7	3.3	5.0	6.6	2.8	5.5	8.3	11.0
80	2.3	4.7	7.0	9.3	3.4	6.8	10.3	13.7
100	3.1	6.2	9.3	12.4	4.2	8.4	12.6	16.8
130	4.5	8.9	13.4	17.8	5.5	11.1	16.6	22.2
150	5.5	11.0	16.4	21.9	6.6	13.1	19.7	26.3

Note: Total air consumption includes 30 seconds at the indicated depth and a 60 feet/minute ascent rate (which is too fast for most computers and some certifying agencies). Because of inactivity, the table assumes your air consumption rate is halved during the 3 minute, 15 foot safety stop (this may or may not be the actual case). The 150-foot depth is shown only for reference, as you never dive deeper than 130 feet without additional training (see Question 82).

Think about it. These numbers should be sobering. If you experience an OOA (out-of-air) situation at depth, then it is likely your buddy is low on air. With both of you breathing off the one tank at depth (say 130 feet) and both of you having a SAC of 1.5 (stressful situation?), then your buddy better have at least 1,005 psi (13.4 (no safety stop) *2*37.5 psi/cf) in the tank (assuming Al80s). Otherwise, you will both end up doing a swimming emergency ascent at some point.

Note that what is showing on the pressure gauge attached to the aluminum 80 tank does not count, it is what is in the tank. Further, we are assuming all 1,005 psi in the tank is breathable. And how accurate is that gauge between 500 and 0? And that 1,005 psi assumes no safety stop!

Of course, you might ask if both have a SAC of 1.5, how is it that one diver has 0 psi and the other 1,005 psi. This points out just one of a number of variables that must be considered when determining the amount of air needed. Did one of you exert yourselves more than the other? What is your metabolic rate for the day? Are you male or female? What is your body build? How do you feel, physically? Did you have an equipment malfunction? If you are diving with a consumer of mass quantities of air (a hoover), then you better take that into account when calculating the amount of air you both would need to arrive safely at the surface.

Other things to consider are:
? How accurate are the pressure gauges {typically within 5 percent}?
? How stressful will the situation be and how will that affect air consumption?
? Is it a shore or boat dive?
? How long can you remain conscious underwater without breathing (in fact exhaling while ascending)?
? How many breaths can you get from your own tank/regulator as you ascend? Etc.

Without beating the subject to death and trying to include all possible factors, I calculate the amount of air my buddy and I need to make a safe ascent on normal (no special factors, e.g., penetration, extreme dive conditions, etc.) dives as follows. Note that your calculations and parameters may be different. If you dive, based on these calculations and parameters, then you do so at your own risk. If your Instructor recommends other figures then consider using them.

I assume we (my buddy and I) must always get back on to the boat or shore with at least 8 cf (cubic feet) (300 psi in an Al80 tank) for each of us. We must break surface with at least 14 cf (500 psi in an Al80) for each of us. Note that the gauges will be assumed to be reasonably accurate (my pressure gauge is tested once a year). We will assume a SAC of 1.5 for each diver (having dove with those ranging from less than 0.5 to some 2.0 SACs, 1.5 is a compromise and will be adjusted upward if diving with a known heavy breather).

Every dive I make will be made with a redundant air source available (bailout bottle or pony) (see Question 99). The redundant air source will enable my buddy and me to ascend 'normally' (with a safety stop) from depth assuming one of our main air sources is still functional. That is, there will always be at least three tanks of air upon descent and both divers can ascend normally breathing from any two. Thus, when diving with single Al80s and one 19 cf pony bottle, we will not dive deeper than 140 fsw. If either Al80 completely fails, then we can still make the surface with a safety stop, but we will begin a 'normal' ascent ASAP.

Under normal circumstances, we begin the ascent based on the psi remaining in the least full Al80. The formula I use is: depth-40*5+700. For a depth of 130 fsw (feet seawater): 130-40*5+700=1,150 and rounding up to the nearest 100 gives 1,200 psi. Therefore, we must start our ascent at 1,200 psi in the Al80, which shows the lowest psi. After a 3-minute safety stop, we will be at the surface with approximately 500 psi (for an Al80 there is approximately 37.5 psi/cf or 0.027 cf/psi). To verify the formula, (as per Waller for a 130 foot dive with safety stop and SAC of 1.5) use 16.6 cf of air needed times 37.5 psi/cf giving 623 psi. Rounding up gives 700 psi minus the 1200 psi at the start of the ascent leaving 500 psi at the surface.

Remember temperature, breathing rate, rate of ascent, depth of safety stop (some recommend stopping at 20 feet in rough seas because of the change in depth due to wave action), accuracy of your pressure gauge, altitude, etc. can all potentially affect your psi. Note also that it is likely one of the divers will have more than 500 as they did not start their ascent at 1,200 psi but at some greater value.

The formula: depth - 40 * 5 + 700 (operating left to right) will only work for Al80s and 1.5 cubic feet per minute surface consumption rate (note that at the surface you will have 500 psi as 0-40*5+700=500). Regardless, if you adopt it, then you do so at your own risk. Do not adopt it if your SAC is greater than 1.5.

This concept of breathing from any two of three tanks to get back is similar to that used by cave divers. When cave divers are diving with a buddy, they turn around and start back when they have used one-third of their air. This, hypothetically, enables them to buddy-breathe the entire way out (based on equal air consumption and similar use of air on the way out, i.e., not fighting a current etc.). In my scenario above, *we always have a redundant source of air (not just an octopus) which would enable both divers to make the surface safely.* Of course, part of your dive planning is determining how deep you will dive and thus at what psi you and your buddy should begin your ascent.

Palau

99. Redundant breathing systems. Should I get 1 or 2 or ?

I use the term "redundant breathing systems" to mean total independence from the diver's primary air source. Thus, the octopus or safe second (see Question 97) or an alternate-air-source inflator is not a redundant system, as air is still obtained from the primary tank. Additionally, a tank Y valve is not a redundant system because a burst disk could rupture or an O-ring could fail, exhausting the entire air supply. Now I am not implying that an octopus, etc. are not of value. They are. However, redundant is just that, redundant.

Your dive buddy can be thought of as a redundant system (assuming they are within reach). Yet, without a redundant system, if you are low on air (getting ready to ascend), at 130 feet, and either your or your buddy's system totally fails, then both of you will be breathing off the one tank. Assuming the Al80 has 1200 psi of air left and both of you have SACs (Surface Air Consumptions) of 1.5, then there will only be 600 psi or 16.0 cf of air per diver remaining at that moment. Referring to Dave Waller's table in Question 98, you can see that from 130 feet you have almost enough air to make a 3-minute, 15-foot safety stop and then you are totally empty. Not taking a safety stop will get you to the surface with about 200 psi remaining and that is cutting it close. Of course the above assumes normal air consumption.

One of my Instructors tells the story of his recent dive on a wreck in Lake Erie. He and his buddy were down deep when his buddy's dive computer started going into the deco range (indicating that they would have to a decompression stop upon ascent). This freaked his buddy out, so even though they immediately started their ascent, his buddy breathed at twice his normal rate. His rate doubled just because he was stressed. Imagine a low-on-air or out-of-air situation and your increase in air consumption.

Of course you might ask, "If I suffer an OOA (out-of-air) situation, then my buddy is within reach, right?" The correct answer is, "not always". Even assuming they are within reach, imagine the potential confusion ensuing as you swim to them asking for or simply grabbing their secondary. Yes, they have an octopus or safe second, which the OOA diver is supposed to acquire. Yet the facts are that most OOA divers go for the regulator in their buddy's mouth. It obviously works, it is immediately visible, and it is accessible. After sorting all that out, now do a controlled ascent while buddy breathing at a normal rate.

Of course, some recreational SCUBA divers do successfully buddy breath to the surface, divers do make successful controlled emergency swimming ascents from 60 feet and deeper. In fact, Dr. George Bond in the early '60s was exiting submarines at greater than 250 feet without breathing apparatus and successfully making controlled exhaling ascents.[Q] Additionally, as you ascend you will likely be able to get another hit or two of air out of your regulator (be sure not to hold your breath!). If all goes by the book and you have practiced those ascents and you feel comfortable doing them in any situation regardless of your physical condition and nitrogen loading, then do it.

Instead of going through all that, why not just carry a redundant air source sized to your current dive parameters (depth, temperature, exertion, return swim, etc.) That said, a diver should not become complacent, should always practice safe diving, and should not depend on the alternate air source except in the rare event of the failure of their primary air source. To extend a dive (time, depth, exertion, etc.) knowing you have an alternate source entirely defeats the purpose of the redundant source.

Given the above, I now always dive with a totally redundant breathing system. If my buddy or I ever have to use the redundant source, then what a difference a normal (relaxed) ascent with a "by the book" safety stop will make. A normal ascent compared to a rushed, will we make it, let's hold our breath and panic (see Question 22), and no safety stop ascent. It is those DCS and AGE hits in concert with panic and drownings that yearly contribute to over one third of the diver fatalities.

If the case for a redundant air source has not been made by now, then forget reading the rest of this answer and please just do not dive deep or in overhead environments.

There are three principal systems of redundant air that are currently on the market: bailout bottles, pony bottles, and doubles.

Looking at bailout or self-contained ascent bottles first, the primary manufacturer is Submersible Systems, Inc. producing a product called Spare Air, which costs about $300 plus some fittings. These bottles are small, can easily be attached to your BC (buoyancy compensator), and come with their own balanced single-stage regulator. As of this printing, Spare Air models come in 1.7 cf (cubic feet), 3.0 cf, and twin 6.0 cf models (all at 3000 psi <u>when completely filled</u>). Looking at Dave Waller's table, you can see that if you go deeper than 60 feet with a SAC of 1.0 or greater and you are depending on the Spare Air with 3.0 cf to get you comfortably to the surface, then good luck.

Some people have tested bailout bottle ascents from as deep as 100 fsw, but it is important to note that the tests are generally not done under stressful conditions. Additionally, the diver is usually already neutrally buoyant, ready to ascend, and with the bailout bottle in hand. Referring to Waller's chart, it can be seen that a diver with a SAC of 0.5 could make it up from about 90 fsw without a safety stop. Yet do you want to be zooming up from 90 fsw wondering if every breath is your last with no safety stop and do you have a SAC of 0.5? Additionally, the bailout bottle gives you no time to solve problems and little or no air to make yourself positively buoyant. Finally, the bailout bottle may give you a false sense of security. Do not dive deeper than you can safely ascend from. Bailout bottles used in shallow dives are fine and could save your bacon.

Another system is the pony bottle. These bottles range from approximately 13 cf on up to 40+ cf. The pony bottle is basically just a smaller SCUBA tank on which standard regulators (first and second stages) are attached. Most divers attach inexpensive regulators to the pony, but before you do that, stop and ask yourself if you want to depend on breathing from that in any environmental condition. The pony is usually mounted either to the BC (buoyancy compensator) in front of you or to the primary tank on your back. Ponies start at about $100 plus the regulators and small pressure gauge. I use a 19 cf pony (at 3000 psi) with a ScubaPro Mk 20 primary and G250 secondary attached to the primary tank with a total package price of about $600, which is definitely high end, cost-wise.

Mr. Bill High in his book <u>Beneath The Sea</u>,[R] made a very valid observation (via personal experience) regarding redundant air supplies that deliver air off similar or same models of secondary regulators. This observation particularly applies to pony bottles thus is included here. One of his four opportunities to live beneath the sea as an Aquanaut was in the Edalhab positioned at 50 fsw (feet salt water). As he was living at depth his body was completely nitrogen saturated and an ascent to the surface without a long decompression would result in an assured DCI (decompression illness) and probably death. For underwater activities, the Aquanauts wore double 72 cf cylinders with a single secondary and what amounted to a pony with its own regulator.

Obviously the pony was to be used in an emergency OOA situation, ascending was not a viable option. On one occasion he donned his tanks and started about his underwater business with two other divers. In a relatively short time he was out of air. He took his tanks off to make sure all the valves were turned on then started breathing off the pony's regulator. He was still out of air! Fortunately a buddy saw his predicament and offered assistance and they made it back to the habitat.

It was later learned that Bill had mistakenly started breathing off the pony tank rather than the doubles. When that air was exhausted he took off the tanks, made sure all the valves were on, and again started trying to breath off the pony. As he had assumed his doubles were empty he figured the pony was full! So again he got no air! If you are going to use a pony then be sure the regulator on that tank is clearly marked or it is obvious which regulator is from your main tank(s) and which is from your pony.

I also highly recommend a pressure gauge on the pony set-up. On a recent boat dive trip, I was making my second dive of the day and asked the Divemaster to turn on my air after I donned my BC (I should have done it before hand). He thought the pony's valve turned on like there was no air in the tank. He inquired if there was supposed to be air in the tank. I responded affirmatively and asked him to check the small pressure gauge attached to the pony's primary regulator. It read empty. Sometime between my first dive and the start of my second dive, the pony's air had been exhausted while sitting on the deck of the boat. To date I have not been able to determine the cause. Always ensure you have air in your pony, just as you do with your main tanks(s).

Anyway, referring to Waller's table, with a 19 cf pony bottle and a SAC of 1.0 (increased to 1.5 for conservative usage), I can safely dive to 140 fsw, switch to the pony, stick around another 30 seconds, ascend and do a 3 minute safety stop at 15 fsw. Even with that dive profile I would still have a few breaths left upon surfacing. The downside of a pony is the added weight, expense, plumbing, carrying it aboard airlines, and getting it filled at a remote or primitive site. People who prefer bailout bottles to a pony say that a pony bottle is too cumbersome to transport and wear, thus it is usually not worn, thereby defeating its purpose.

The independent twin tank system is a good option for certain specialty dives, such as wreck and cave penetrations, extreme deep diving, rescue dives, etc. They will not be discussed here, as they are infrequently used by the novice diver in basic recreational SCUBA diving. You will obviously want to get training in using them before depending on them. Note that twins/doubles may require the purchase of another BC and backplate.

When you dive, look at your fellow enthusiasts. Most of them do not carry a redundant source of air. Those few who do, might not use it properly (using it as a dive extender, not as a backup) and fewer still practice using it. Getting comfortable using your equipment will decrease the incidence of panic.

The final judgement of what type of redundant system to use most appropriately depends on your SAC and the type-of-diving you do. If your SAC is about average and you plan on diving between 15 and 50 feet (as many divers do), and never deeper than 60 feet, do not go into overhead environments, or other 'advanced' dives, then maybe the 3.0 cf bailout bottle would be sufficient. However, if you are a heavy breather, want that extra measure of security, or plan on diving deeper than 60 fsw, then the pony bottle, in my opinion, is a better choice. {Spare Air defenders: do not spend your time writing me (I own one too), go diving with your Spare Air instead – to each their own!}.

80 cu ft (A180)

19 cu ft Pony

3 cu ft Spare Air

100. An exposure suit sounds kinky. What is it and how much?

Simply stated, an exposure suit protects you from exposure, whether that exposure be from cold, contaminated water, jellyfish and coral stings, or the sun's ultraviolet rays. The broad category of exposure suits can be divided into dive skins, wet suits, and dry suits.

Dive skins are typically made of Lycra® or some other stretchy fabric. Because water saturates the suit and circulates freely over your body, the warmth retained wearing a dive skin is minimal. Typically, they are used to prevent stings from nematocysts (stinging cells) of jellyfish, accidental coral contact, and sunburn. Divers tend to wear skins in water warmer than 80° F and under wetsuits so they slide on easier. Note: if you are self conscious about that less-than-perfect physique, then maybe a one-eighth inch thick wet suit or several months at the gym would be more flattering.

A Darlexx® suit is next in the warmth continuum. Darlexx is a suit that is similar to a diveskin, but is made out of a fabric that slows water flow, thus is a cross between a dive skin and wet suit. Aeroskin® is similar to Darlexx and uses polypropylene and Lycra. Depending upon how warm-blooded you are, you probably can wear Darlexx down to about 70° F.

Next is the ubiquitous wet suit. Wet suits are typically made of closed-cell (impregnated with air bubbles) neoprene rubber and serve to retard water circulation over your skin. This enables your body to warm the water within the wet suit (thus its name). Additionally, because of the air bubbles in the neoprene, the closed-cell neoprene helps insulate you from the cold water outside the suit. A poorly fitting wet suit can make your dive miserable by letting too much water flow through the suit, or be so tight that it cuts off your circulation or restricts your movements.

If an off-the-shelf wet suit does not fit, then by all means buy a custom made one. Custom wet suits are only marginally more expensive, but fit perfectly (if tailored correctly). Expect to pay somewhere around $300 to $600 for a quarter inch farmer john (bib overall style) with top wet suit (long sleeved). Other wet suit styles are the shorty (a one piece vest or short sleeve top with a shorts length bottom) and the full wet suit (one piece, generally long sleeved top with full length bottoms).

Farmer John   **Shorty**   **One Piece Long Sleeve**

Figure J. Wet Suit Styles

Wet suits come in two popular thickness': eighth inch (2-3 mm) and quarter inch (6-7 mm) (see 'Conversion Index' section). You can wear different combinations of shorties, full, and two-piece suits and suits of different thickness to keep you warm in a wide range of water temperatures. Wet suits are generally worn when water temperatures are between 45° F and 75° F. You can dive in near-freezing water for a time if you <u>warm</u> up some water and pour it in your wet suit (be extremely careful not to scald!).

Probably the most versatile exposure suit is the dry suit. It, in combination with additional undergarments, can be worn relatively comfortably in water varying from 29° F to 70° F. It keeps you warm by insulating you from the cold water via the dry air trapped between you and the suit. Some divers even use argon as the primary gas in the dry suit because of its heat retaining properties. As your depth increases, a dry suit, unlike a wet suit which compresses, can maintain up to 85 percent of its ability to retain heat.[E] As a precautionary note, if you plan on diving in very cold water (below 40º F) be sure your regulators, inflators, etc. are up to the task. Ask a dive professional and get special training.

The drawbacks of dry suits are increased expensive ($1,200 to $2,500+), you need special training on their use, added bulkiness, increased maintenance, and they can leak while you cannot (without Depends®). On the other hand, it is definitely luxurious coming out of cold water being dry and warmer than your wet-suited peers who are shivering and struggling to get dry in the cold wind.

Neoprene   Tri-laminate Shell   Rubberized Canvas

Figure K. Dry Suit Styles

Dry suits can be divided into four general categories: foam neoprene suits, nylon or tri-laminate shell suits, vulcanized rubber suits, and crushed neoprene.

Foam neoprene dry suits, since they are made from air-impregnated neoprene, are very similar to wetsuits. If they are flooded, they have a greater tendency to retain their insulating ability and buoyancy than other dry suits. At the shallower depths, they are typically the warmest dry suits and require the least amount of additional undergarments. On the down side, like wetsuits at depth, the neoprene is compressed, thereby causing a reduction in thermal protection and buoyancy. Neoprene dry suits also take a long time to dry, tend to be more difficult to repair, and lose a portion of their insulating ability after repeated dives (300, give or take).

Nylon or tri-laminate (shell) suits are constructed of various types of nylon. These suits are typically very durable, light, dry quickly, easy to repair, and easy to don. They do not have much stretch in them, thus they tend to be pretty baggy, which results in a little more drag while you swim. Additionally, nylon or tri-laminates provide little or no thermal protection so you will have to wear more air trapping undergarments for added thermal protection.

Vulcanized rubber dry suits have many of the same pros and cons as nylon dry suits. In general, the thicker the rubber the more durable the suit, but also the more bucks you will have to shell out. These suits excel when used in contaminated water as they are relatively easy to clean and patch. Of course, you do not dive in contaminated water without special training and equipment!

The final general category of dry suits is the crushed neoprene suit. These suits do not lose buoyancy or insulation at depth, are relatively flexible, have a reasonably low drag coefficient, take fewer under garments than other dry suits to keep you warm, and they are durable. On the other hand, they tend to be heavy, take a long time to dry, and can be time consuming to repair.

Dry suits can be obtained with attached boots (recommended), internal suspenders, a protective zipper over the watertight zipper, gloves, and latex or neoprene neck and arm seals. Latex seals are recommended for general use, though wars have been fought over less.

In addition to your exposure suit, you will want several pairs of gloves of different thickness, depending upon the water temperature and the tasks you expect to perform underwater. A thin pair with synthetic leather palms, an eighth inch and a quarter-inch pair, tend to cover most temperature ranges. A pair of neoprene mittens work well in really cold water. If your exposure suit does not come with boots attached and you do not have booties, then you probably should buy a pair to protect your feet and for thermal protection.

Finally, do not forget the hood. Your head makes up only 9 percent of your body's surface area but is responsible for the loss of almost 50 percent of your body heat. In cold water, a good neoprene hood with tuck in neck flaps is well worth the expense.

Seek help from your local dive shop when you get around to purchasing an exposure suit. They will want to know what type of diving you will be doing most. If you plan on a lot of photography, then multi-colored exposure suits can add or detract from photos, depending upon your purpose. If you are like a lot of us, you will end up owning skins, an eighth-inch one-piece wet suit, a quarter-inch farmer john and jacket wet suit, and a dry suit. But hey, I make up for it by having only one "Sunday, go to meetin' suit". One has to have ones priorities straight.

Diving in relative comfort with a dry suit in a PA quarry.

101. He ain't heavy.. Why do divers wear weights?

As most people float, particularly when wearing a buoyant exposure suit, the typical diver must wear varying amounts of weight in order to descend and control buoyancy. In fact, the wearing of weight that can be easily jettisoned to become buoyant in an emergency is a safety factor. Some divers, when diving warm water locations with heavy gear and steel tanks, do not need added weight to descend. However, in my opinion, if you are open water diving and do not have easily dropped weights, which facilitates positive buoyancy, then you are not diving as safely as you could be. On the other hand you must guard against the new diver's tendency to be over weighted. Cave divers often use steel doubles and therefore may not wear weight belts. Yet for them, ascending in an emergency is not usually an option, as they would just get plastered up against the cave ceiling.

The two basic weighting systems are weight belts/harness and integrated BCs (buoyancy compensators). In weight belt systems, weights are treaded onto, wrapped around (lead shot in packets with Velcro), or placed inside a weight belt. In integrated BC systems, the weights are placed inside two pockets (one on either side of the BC) with quick release mechanisms. The weights, in combination with the BC (or dry suit if used), form the divers gross buoyancy control mechanism.

There are pros and cons to either system. Integrated BC systems tend to give improved swimming trim, less strain on the back, and eliminates the belt (which some divers cannot effectively wear). Weight belts offer a lower center of gravity, do not make the BC as heavy to don, and can be easier to remove separately from the BC thus making getting into some boats easier. Some divers, yours truly included, wear a combination of both a weight belt and integrated weight BC, with the necessary weights distributed to the diver's liking.

One of the most important features of a weighting system is the release. If the diver needs to ascend quickly in an emergency, then jettisoning their weight system will give them positive buoyancy and assist in their ascent. In most fatalities where the outcome may have been different, the diver retained their weights. Though usually a last ditch effort, the quick removal of a diver's weights could have saved their life. Because of their importance, you will certainly be instructed in weighting and buoyancy control in your open water course.

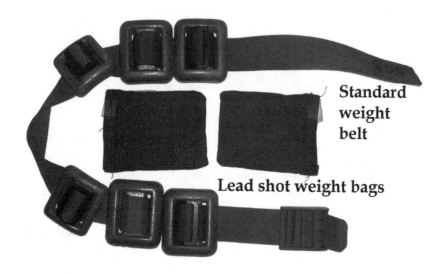

Standard weight belt

Lead shot weight bags

102. What are dive tables?

Our bodies are designed for living on land and breathing air (which is 78 percent nitrogen) at atmospheric pressures. Based on that design, our bodies do a great job. As nitrogen is eliminated via our lungs during respiration, its accumulation at atmospheric pressures is normally not a problem. However, when we dive to depths with increased pressures and breathe compressed air, the level of nitrogen increases in our bodies. Upon our ascent from depth, the ambient pressure decreases and the level of nitrogen increases faster than our bodies can eliminate (off-gas) it. If too much nitrogen is accumulated within our bodies, it can cause a DCI (decompression illness) (see Question 39).

Using dive tables, we can calculate the quantity of nitrogen in our bodies so that safe concentration limits are not exceeded. Manual dive tables enable us to calculate nitrogen concentration based on the depth of the dive, time at depth, and residual nitrogen remaining from previous dives (within 6-12 hours, depending on agency). Dive computers go through the same process, but can take more variables into account, e.g., multi-level diving, more tissue compartments (different tissues absorb nitrogen at different rates), etc.

As the calculation of nitrogen levels in the human body is not an exact science, there are a number of different dive tables in use. For example, dive tables are produced by the U.S. Navy (see Figure L), many of the certifying agencies, and there are technical and commercial tables. During your classroom instruction, you will be instructed on the use of the tables recommended by your certifying agency. The tables are not difficult to use, but do take practice and periodic use. Your continued good health could be predicated upon your knowing how to use them and safely applying the information.

As stated above, dive tables are not exact and their application to you can vary depending on your state of hydration, physical fitness, etc. (see Question 39). On one extreme, if you never dive, you will likely never get a DCI hit and on the other, you can conduct a dive so as to practically guarantee a hit. As a DCI could either incapacitate a diver or worse, knowing that the tables are not exact, and they cannot guarantee that you will

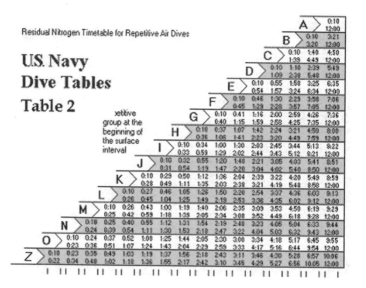

No-Decompression Limits and Repetitive Group Designation Table For No-Decompression Air Dives

Depth feet / metres	No-Deco Limits (min)	A	B	C	D	E	F	G	H	I	J	K	L	M	N	O
10 3.0		60	120	210	300											
15 4.6		35	70	110	160	225	350									
20 6.1		25	50	75	100	135	180	240	325							
25 7.6		20	35	55	75	100	125	160	195	245	315					
30 9.1		15	30	45	60	75	95	120	145	170	205	250	310			
35 10.7	310	5	15	25	40	50	60	80	100	120	140	160	190	220	270	310
40 12.2	200	5	15	25	30	40	50	70	80	100	110	130	150	170	200	
50 15.2	100		10	15	25	30	40	50	60	70	80	90	100			
60 18.2	60		10	15	20	25	30	40	50	55	60					
70 21.3	50		5	10	15	20	30	35	40	45	50					
80 24.4	40		5	10	15	20	25	30	35	40						
90 27.4	30		5	10	12	15	20	25	30							
100 30.5	25		5	7	10	15	20	22	25							
110 33.5	20			5	10	13	15	20								
120 36.6	15			5	10	12	15									
130 39.6	10			5	8	10										
140 42.7	10			5	7	10										
150 45.7	5			5												
160 48.8	5					5										
170 51.8	5					5										
180 54.8	5					5										
190 59.9	5					5										

U.S. Navy Dive Tables Table 1

Residual Nitrogen Timetable for Repetitive Air Dives

U.S. Navy Dive Tables Table 2

Figure L. U.S. Navy Dive Tables (Sides 1 and 2)
(courtesy of U.S. Navy and Aquaholics at www.aquaholics.com)

not get a hit even if followed, I tend to dive conservatively. On the bright side, I have never had a DCI hit nor do I know anyone who has. Only about 1 in 25,500 dives results in a DCI hit (see Question 39).

There are also tables and computer algorithms for calculating oxygen toxicity and other inert gas levels (besides nitrogen) used in more advanced diving. Oxygen toxicity is normally not a problem for the recreational SCUBA diver, thus use of oxygen toxicity tables is not taught. You will get training in their use if you become nitrox certified.

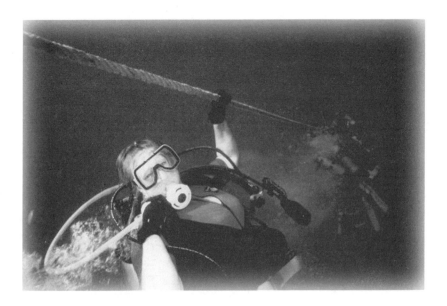

103. Can I stay down a bit longer with a dive computer?
The purchase of a dive computer will definitely take a "byte" out of your wallet. Yet, due to multi-level time allowances vs. manual dive tables, they will give you more accuracy in no decompression bottom time calculations (see Question 84). Bits and bytes aside, a full-function dive computer is a fairly expensive piece of equipment, starting at about $225. On the other hand, *dive computers can make your diving less of a hassle and if properly maintained and used, argumentably safer.* Additionally, the data from the dive computer could be used by medical personnel to determine the best course of treatment if the diver were to get a DCI (decompression illness) hit.

The multi-level time allowance (time at different depths or levels during your dive) enables the calculation of a diver's nitrogen absorption based on multi-level profiles, rather than the total time at the deepest depth. Dives are seldom truly square in profile. That is, you seldom dive straight down, stay at that level the entire dive then ascend straight up. Yet using manual dive tables (see Question 102), that is how you have to calculate your nitrogen absorption.

Oceanic DataMax
Pro Plus

As profiled in Listing AK, dive computers can additionally supply you with a lot of functions which can make your dive more interesting and safer, e.g., alarms for turnaround time, bottom time limits, ascent rates (see Question 98), etc. As this market continues to mature, you will see increasing functionality and reliability, decreased cost, and increased diver utilization.

Listing AK. Functions/Information Available from Most Dive Computers.

- *Date and time of dive* for future reference (in case you forget to log it in your log book!),
- *maximum depth reached, as well as current depth,*
- *temperature* (including average temperature) of the water,
- *elapsed bottom time,*

- *profiles next and previous dives,*
- *surface interval time,*
- *cylinder pressure* at the beginning and ending of the dive,
- *air consumption rate,*
- *time remaining,*
- *no decompression dive violation warning (see Question 84),*
- *rate of ascent and timing of safety stop,*
- *time to fly* (time needed to off-gas before getting on a plane)
- *PC interface,* and
- *nitrox capability.*

Dive computers are usually worn on the wrist or placed in the instrument console (see Question 90). Dive computers worn on the wrist may be at greater risk of getting lost than those in the console. 'On the other hand', wrist mounted computers may be easier to view. However, wearing the computer on the wrist means you must view the instrument console and wrist-mounted computer separately, rather than having all your instruments in one place. Having my dive computer in my instrument console works best for me.

It is my opinion that the student should not immediately go out and buy a dive computer for some of the same reasons they should not go out and buy all the other dive equipment the first day of class. After you dive for awhile and become more knowledgeable as to your type and frequency of diving, you will be in a much better position to select the appropriate equipment, computer included.

Additionally, while being trained in your basic open water class, you will most likely be using non-computerized equipment (analog depth gauge and pressure gauge). Also, most certifying agencies (though not all) train divers using dive tables to calculate nitrogen absorption. Finally, most rental dive gauges are analog and you should know how to use the dive tables. Someday this will no doubt change, but for now I believe it is important for the student to become competent in using the dive tables.

Owning and using a dive computer really makes sense for those who dive frequently, particularly those making consecutive day multi-dives (live aboards or dive vacations). A wise diver will always bring along their analog gauges and dive tables for backup (and remember how to use them).

Due to the dynamic nature of the market, reviewing all the pros and cons of the various dive computers would soon be dated and is beyond the scope of 'SCUBA Scoop'. For more information on dive computers read current reviews in SCUBA magazines, surf the net, ask your Instructor and diving friends what works for them, and ask your local dive shops for suggestions. As I do not want to leave you totally wondering where to start, you might include in your long list of dive computers to consider the: Aeris 100S, Aeris 750GT, Aeris Atomos Sport, Mares Surveyor, Mares Tutor, Oceanic DataMax Pro Plus, Oceanic Data Plus 2, and Suunto Spyder.

104. Time flies while diving. Can I get a slower dive watch?
Dive watches are available in analog, digital, or a combination of both. The standard dive watch for years was the water-resistant analog model with rotating bezel. Aligning the 0 on the bezel (see 'Glossary' section) with the minute hand at the start of the dive and then noting at which number on the bezel the minute hand points to at the end of the dive will give the dive length in minutes. Obviously for dives over 59 minutes you will need to add 60 to the number on the bezel.

Digital dive watches generally have a stopwatch function you start and stop by pushing a button. Digital dive watches generally cost less, but also may be more difficult to operate with gloves on. Additionally, the small numbers (as compared to an analog watch's minute hand) may be difficult to see at depth unless it is backlit or you shine your flashlight on it. Some watches combine analog and digital displays. There are also mechanical and electronic timers available, though my experience with them is nil.

In the higher quality watches look for the features presented in Listing AL. You will pay more, but they should last longer and have greater functionality.

Listing AL. Features to Look for in a Quality Dive Watch.
- A *notched bezel* which only rotates counterclockwise. Thus if the bezel accidentally moves during a dive it will give a more conservative bottom time.
- A *bezel designed so that it is easy to turn when wearing gloves.*
- A *depth rating of at least 660 feet.* This is important because some manufacturers use static pressure when rating their watches. You will be moving around, there may be currents, changes in temperature, bumping the watch against things, using the buttons, etc. This activity causes more dynamic pressure, which could flood your watch. For instance, Casio 50m watches are fine for showering but can flood if used in SCUBA. Their 100m watches are fine for snorkeling, but get the 200m watch for SCUBA diving. {Once again I used metric because that is how they are commonly thought of (see 'Conversion Index' section).}
- A *flat or recessed crystal* is less likely to get scratched.

🕐 *Be sure that strap you use is made for diving.* One popular method is to have a continuous loop of fabric with either a Velcro® or buckle closure that passes through both watch body pins. That way if one pin breaks the watch and band will remain in place. Another type that seems to work is the heavy-duty expandable plastic-like band. Remember, your watch band may need to be adjusted to fit your wrist for tropical dives and be expand to fit a dry suit for that arctic dive.

My current time pieces consist of a Citizen Aqualand Divers 660 feet which is a combination analog and digital watch. The digital component automatically keeps track of dive time, maximum depth, average depth, temperature, date of the dive, etc. for up to four dives. I love it. On the negative side, replacing the batteries (after less than a year's use) cost me $35 and 2 weeks time. I believe this watch cost me about $300.

The first watch I bought was a Casio Illuminator 600 feet model and it is entirely digital. It has a back light, but is hard to operate at depth with gloves on. It cost me about $125. If you have the dough I recommend the Aqualand. Citizen also makes a Hyper Aqualand from which you can download your dive data to your desktop computer. Kewl stuff. Ask your dive shop or Instructor for their advice on watches. If you pinch pennies, then wait for sales before buying or buy from discount outlets.

Even if you decide to eventually get a computer, you should also have a watch (or timer) as a backup. Purchasing a decent dive watch is not wasted money. If you do not have a dive computer and the watch floods at depth, then you should abort the dive so get a quality time piece.

105. Get to the point! What kind of dive knife should I buy?

Based on the number of knives I have found, a knife is likely the item you will end up losing the most. They frequently fall out of their sheaths or are dropped by divers. *So unless you have a special purpose for that very expensive knife, do not buy it. Instead, lightly coat the blade of a relatively inexpensive stainless steel one with silicone and make sure it fits its sheath securely.*

Of course, you will want the knife to work for the job intended. If you are looking for a monofilament (fishing line) cutter, then get a pair of snips in addition to a knife. If you need to cut thick line, then a larger serrated blade works best. A pointed tip knife works best if you need to bore a hole in something. A blunt tipped knife can be used for a light duty pry or as a broad tipped screw driver. {I know, I know, you should not use a knife that way but sometimes when all you have is a knife you have to make do}. Another benefit of the blunt tip is that you are less likely to puncture yourself or your BC (buoyancy compensator) upon re-sheathing.

Try to buy knives that have a line cutting grove in them, with one side of the blade serrated and the other smooth. At least one of the knives you carry should have a hard steel butt at the end of the handle to bang on a tank, or to pound with if you are using the knife butt as a hammer. Buy and carry several knives, placing them in different easy-to-reach locations on your body and BC.

I am a firm believer in Murphy's Law and an Eagle Scout. I therefore carry two small knives (one with a 4 inch blade on my BC's strap and one with a 3 inch blade on the BC belt). I also carry a pair of scissors (Sea Snips) and a hooked, razor bladed, fishing line cutting tool (Z Knife). That way, if I drop or lose a knife or my buddy needs one, then I still have a backup (or two). If the dive is going to involve diving among kelp, other potential entanglements, or a 'hostile' environment, then I will also wear a larger knife (4.5 inch blade) on the inside of my leg. Finally, unless you plan on underwater combat, leave the Booey knife and machete at home. Reasonably sized knives cost and weigh less and are easier to handle.

Most of the time, you will use your knife for tasks that are not dive-related, such as cutting that after-dive, peanut butter and banana sandwich in half. However, when you need one on a dive (entangled in monofilament), then they are worth more than their weight in gold.

106. It can be dark at 130 feet. Enlighten me on dive lights.

In my opinion, the well-dressed diver should always carry at least one dive light. A dive light is very handy for illuminating the nooks and crannies the diver finds underwater, to render more vividly the true colors of the flora and fauna, and as an attention getting and/or signaling device. When you use your light, be sure to not shine it in other diver's eyes, particularly at night. To get your buddy's attention, use a horizontal back and forth movement on some rocks or structure where they are or will be looking. A vigorous up and down movement of your light is the standard signal that something is wrong. I suggest taking the Advanced Open Water certification or Night Diving Specialty to learn more about the use of underwater light signals.

For night dives, a diver should have at least two hand-held lights plus a tank light or Cyalume Lightstick® (also known as Chemlights®, Snaplights®, and Glowsticks®). Rather than tying your tank light to your tank valve where it is more likely to get entangled with something, you might try taping it (with waterproof tape) to your regulator hose near the first stage.

The styles and types of dive lights are vast and a book could be devoted solely to the topic {yawn}. Regardless, a few key things to look for in a dive light are presented in Listing AM.

Listing AM. Some Key Characteristics of a Dive Light.
 ⋛ *The dive light should optimally be positively buoyant at the surface and neutrally or negatively buoyant at depth.* If the light is not already so configured, then this can be achieved by placing a neoprene (wet suit material) 'jacket' around the light. Since the neoprene compresses at depth, it will lose some of its buoyancy and thereby become neutrally buoyant.
 ⋛ Choose a *light with a round, narrow beam.* Water will disperse the light beam.

≳ A rechargeable (ni-cad) primary light and a carbon-zinc battery back-up light are preferred by some divers. The rechargeable batteries last about an hour then dim quickly (but cost less in maintenance if used frequently). The carbon-zinc batteries will dim slowly but cost more over the long run. If you do not do much night diving, then probably alkaline battery powered lights are the way to go (lower maintenance). Of course, cave and deep penetration wreck divers have specialized lights with longer lasting power supplies.

≳ Get lights that can be *switched on and off with one hand.*

≳ Be careful with attaching the light to you with a strong lanyard (see Glossary). A better idea is either substituting rubber tubing for the lanyard. Or, as cave divers do, securely attach a brass or stainless steel quick release clip to the light. You can then snap it to your BC when not in use.

I have found it convenient to use a smaller four C-cell light (Princeton Tec 400) as my sole shallow, day dive light. Anything less than four batteries is just not bright enough for night work. For deeper, darker, or night diving, my four C-cell light becomes my second backup. I use a Princeton Tec 8000 with eight D-cells as my primary light and a six C-cell Princeton Tec 600 light as my first backup. For a tank light, I have a two AA-cell Princeton Tec Sport Flare (but would like to try a small strobe). I also carry an OmniGlow Cyalume Lightstick (inactivated) just in case. A couple of other decent smaller lights at the time of this printing are the Ikelite PCa and Underwater Kinetics SL4.

Be sure you purchase lights that are designed for diving. My Advanced Open Water Diver training included my first night dive. It was my tenth dive and I had previously purchased my four C-cell Princeton Tec 400 light. The training dive was in Strawberry Quarry near Pittsburgh, Pennsylvania. I do not remember why now (I was probably trying to save a buck), but I started the dive with simply a 'water-proof' light that seemed to work fine. Fine that is until about 25 feet where it flooded and I was left in the dark (though my instructor had a light). I then resorted to my Tec 400. Though more expensive than 'water-proof' lights, lights built specifically for diving are the only way to go. Do not even bother with anything less, because in more hostile environments it could lead to trouble.

In the final analysis, as with knives, which lights to purchase boils down to how they are going to be used, the environmental demands, cost, and personal preference. Review product comparison articles in dive magazines, ask your dive shop personnel, Instructor, and other divers for further recommendations.

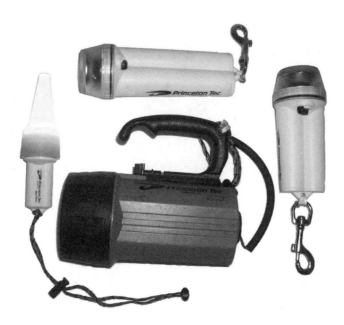

107. Can I use a GPS (Global Positioning System) underwater?

The typical consumer hand-held GPS (Global Positioning System) with integral antenna will not work underwater. The signal strength is not strong enough to penetrate but a thin layer of water. Military units with floating antennas work underwater and are more accurate than commercial units, but are not currently available to the public.

Regardless, a GPS can be useful for entries into your dive log (see Question 111) as to approximate dive location and to help find a specific site in the future. You could even put one in a water- and pressure-proof container with your marine radio as a means of contacting the Coast Guard with your location if you were to float away from your dive boat (see Question 109). I have yet to see anyone go to this extreme, but it may not be a bad idea on drift dives. Regardless, it makes a great excuse to buy one to play with!

108. What type of underwater homing devices are there?

Homing devices can range from sophisticated electronic devices used by commercial and military divers, to banging on the bottom of the boat, to the angle and direction of the sun's rays in the water. *As I am using the term, a homing device is anything that enables you to find your way to some goal, e.g., the dive boat or shore.*

As we use our five senses to collect homing 'device' information, we can divide the 'devices' into categories based upon how we collect the homing data. The categories are then grouped by tactile (touch), olfactory (smell), taste, auditory (hearing), and sight.

Tactile homing devices include guide lines laid down by cave divers, the rope that the ice diver is attached to, the line used in some search and recovery patterns, the anchor or dive line, etc. Using a rope or line in most open water recreational diving is not necessary and may actually cause more entanglement issues than solving your homing problem. Yet a wise diver eventually gets training and experience in laying and using dive lines.

Using our sense of smell and taste underwater is rather problematic and likely of little homing value for humans. Some exceptions that come to mind is smell or taste in polluted waters (but why are you diving there?) and maybe assisting in finding the mouth of a river flowing into an ocean (though current and water turbidity might be better devices.)

As water is about 770 times as dense as air, sound travels some four times faster (4,400 feet per minute) in water. This is because sound wave energy transfers easier in the denser medium. We can hear relatively well underwater, up to 15 miles.

The problem is that the sound is traveling so fast it seems like it is coming from all around us. Thus determining where a noise is coming from with the unaided human ear is difficult. Yet sound is a good attention getting device (unless you are hearing impaired). You may hear your dive boat give a predetermined sound signal indicating an emergency or "everyone outta the water it's time to go".

Our sense of vision can be a very effective collector of homing device information. On drift dives, the boat is able to follow you via a homing 'device' such as your bubbles or the dive buoy being towed by the Divemaster or group leader. Desert Star Systems makes two relatively inexpensive ($250 and $500), compact models of SONAR (SOund NAvigation and Ranging) transmitters/receivers good for a range of some 4,000 feet. They are quick to state these units are not 'life support gear' and you should have at least one other navigation aid (see http://www.desertstar.com for more details). {I placed the above SONAR example under vision as the read out for the diver is visual.}

Flashing underwater strobes are very good homing devices at night to the limit of our vision. Diver's hand-held lights and tank lights can also help us keep track of our buddy at night or in limited light situations. Other sight related homing devices are environmental. These include the direction of the current, the ripples in the sand caused by waves, the position of the sun overhead, slope of the seabed, etc. Then of course, the proficient use of your compass may actually be one of your best homing devices. You will be given training regarding use of environmental 'homing' devices and compass use in your open water course.

The best plan is to pre-plan your dive, always know where you are, and how to return or reach your goal. This is otherwise known as "plan your dive, then dive your plan". Be attentive and use the best homing device available. It resides inside your head.

109. Can I use an EPIRB while diving?

An Emergency Position Indicating Radio Beacon (EPIRB) is an emergency radio beacon device used primarily in lifeboats and by downed aircraft to signal their location in the water. Commercial divers working in strong currents also use them. EPIRBs can be used by recreational divers who are concerned about becoming separated from their dive boat.

When activated, an EPIRB emits an emergency signal which is picked up by satellites and transmitted via land-based receivers to rescue services, i.e., the Coast Guard. Class B EPIRBs transmit on the 121.5 MHz and 243.0 MHz (military) frequencies. These frequencies are not stored by the satellites, therefore it is possible to find yourself in "dead zones" where no one will hear the signal. This effectively limits the 121.5 MHz EPIRBs to coastal use.

These class B EPIRBs are manually activated and released and have an accuracy of approximately 10 miles. On the negative side, due to the many false alarms with the 121.5s, apparently the Coast Guard (at least in California) will wait a minimum of four hours before commencing a search.

A newer technology is the 406 MHz EPIRBs which have an accuracy of 3 miles and no dead zones. The satellite stores the signal location and transmits it when it is within range of a receiver. The 406 MHz EPIRB can be registered to a specific boat or user. The down side is that these units are much larger than the 121.5s.

A newer technology, the GPIRB (Global Position Indicating Radio Beacon), takes an active role in determining its position. When activated, the internal GPS finds its position and then broadcasts its identity and position on 406 MHz. After broadcasting, it shuts down to conserve power and repeats the process every 20 minutes. The advantages of a GPIRB are that an accurate fix is almost instantly available and its frequent update enable authorities to compute drift more accurately.

Several models of 121.5 MHz EPIRBs to consider are the ACR Mini B2, Litton Micro B, and GME MT310. They sell for approximately $250. The ACR Mini B2 weighs 9.2 ounces and will fit in a BC pocket. The factory rates the unit as waterproof to 33 feet, though some divers claim deep immersion of the unit. The batteries need to be replaced by the factory every six years.

If you are diving outside the U.S., you should check with the local coastal marine authorities to determine if licensing is required and whether they will even respond to the signal should you activate the EPIRB.

Mini B2

110. What is a possibles kit?

When the U.S. was young, the frontier mountain men always carried a leather possibles bag with them. The possibles bag often contained flint and steel, shot, twine or leather thong, nails, needles, small tools, medicines, or basically any item necessary for their survival or to make life a little easier in the wilderness. Taking a clue from our ancestors, we SCUBA divers should also take along a possibles kit which could save a dive or our bacon.

A possibles kit could include a tackle box (I am told that an empty cat litter pail works good too) and a bag or pouch. The pouch would be stocked from the tackle box depending upon what was needed for the dive at hand and be carried with us on the dive. That possibles bag would only take a few minutes to stock for the dive. The bag could then be attached to your BC (buoyancy compensator) or placed in a BC pocket. A possibles bag could make your diving a little easier and safer.

Items placed in the tackle box could include some of the items on your open water equipment checklist (see Question 93). For search and recovery dives (see Question 44), the possibles bag might contain a lift bag, a surface float, a 'Spare Air' unit, line and reel, etc. On open water drift dives, you may want to carry an inflatable safety sausage, mirror, whistle, telescoping signal flag or signal buoy, and a small strobe light. In the relatively rare event of not being immediately picked up by the dive boat, then you would be better prepared to help the boat or search team in finding you.

A story told by a friend, who was on the dive boat, is of the time a group of divers were diving the Bahamas. The dive boat was anchored near some of the walls the area is famous for. Apparently two divers were diving the wall and went deeper than they should have. While they were down a strong current came up (which is not unusual for the area). As they had gone deeper than they should have, they opted to do a five-minute safety stop at about 20 feet. Of course the current then proceeded to carry them into open water (you do not feel the current when you are drifting within it).

When they surfaced they found they were nearly a half-mile from the dive boat. They subsequently drifted for another half mile and were found by a fishing boat that just happened to be trolling in the area. The fishing boat radioed the divers position to the dive boat and they were picked up. Those divers were fortunate! Better dive planning would include knowing the currents, staying closer to the boat, not going so deep, and coming up the anchor line of their dive boat. Carrying flares and inflatable dive weenie, the divers might have avoided the adrenaline rush they no doubt experienced.

If you should ever find yourself adrift, the first things to do are: establish buoyancy, signal for assistance, conserve your energy and heat, and unless close enough to swim to shore or another boat, then minimize activity. For a diver, establishing buoyancy is as easy as the inflation of the BC (buoyancy compensator). Signaling can be done with whistle, mirror, inflated safety sausage, flares, and strobe light or flashlight.

If you find yourself adrift, hypothermia will likely be one of your primary concerns (see Question 28). To minimize your body heat loss, get out of the water if at all possible (into a raft or floating debris), cover your head, keep your wet suit on and zippered up, avoid swimming (it will pump out the warmed water), huddle with your buddy, and go into a HELP. The Heat Escape Lessening Position (HELP) is implemented by holding your knees to your chest, wrapping your arms around your legs, clasping your hands together, and keeping your head up.

After you have taken all the actions you can to maximize the likelihood of survival, you can do one other very important thing. Be determined to make it through the experience. Do not give up. Your will to live is one of your most powerful weapons for survival.

111. Isn't a dive log heavy? Why should I keep one?

Your dive log is an important piece of documentation that you should make every effort to keep current.
Most of us would rather spend the time between dives swapping dive stories with buddies in the galley than writing in our log books. Regardless, you should take the five minutes and update your log after each dive. Even if you have a dive computer, you should keep a dive log (see Question 112) and keep it current for the reasons delineated in Listing AN.

< Not a Dive Log

Listing AN. Some Reasons for Maintaining a Current Dive Log.

- *The dive log should contain emergency contact information, dive insurance carrier, and personal information such as blood type and drug allergies,*
- *it could be very helpful in accident maintenance if you ever have a DCI* (decompression illness),
- it *documents your dives for review by those needing to verify that you have done specific dives,* particularly for proof-of-experience for leadership training. Of course, like most log books, dive logs can be falsified. But ask yourself who are you endangering? It is not worth it.
- tracking your diving experience in a log book is good insurance *in case that far, far away dive operator has any doubts about your certifying agency or experience.*
- *it is good for going back to review weighting, air consumption, dive profiles, environmental conditions,* etc.,
- you can *review it for good dive sites you have found* over the years or some unusual dive situations,
- you might be able to *find that long lost dive buddy* from the past if you include their contact information in the log (hopefully (s)he made it back on to the boat), and
- simply as a source of *nostalgia.*

112. What type of dive logs are available?

A dive log can range from a simple fill in the blanks formatted page (available from most dive shops and Figure M) to a spreadsheet to a computer multimedia event. The multimedia dive log could include voice, music, pictures, and complex statistical graphing. Which type of log you decide to use is up to you. In fact, you may wish to keep two logs. A simple paper log (manually or computer generated) to take on dives for documentation and another more complete computer multimedia log. One source of links to currently available dive logs can be viewed on the internet at **http://www.ehpublishing.com/scubalinks.html**.

If you choose to use a simple formatted page log, then it should minimally include: dive number, dive date, location, surface interval, pre-dive pressure group letter, dive depth, bottom time, post-dive pressure group, total bottom time to date, verification signature (buddy, instructor, other), and comments. Comments could include environmental conditions, equipment used, weighting, activities done, dive boat, GPS coordinates (see Question 107), underwater topography, flora and fauna seen, dive operator stamp, etc. A simple example of a basic dive log page is shown in Figure M.

Simple, single page logs are good for getting the facts down, monitoring your residual nitrogen, and a page which can be stamped (if they have one) by your dive buddy or dive operator. Figure N displays a few examples of some dive stamps from my log book.

Using a spreadsheet as a dive log is relatively simple. Each row could be a dive with columns for surface interval, beginning pressure group, depth of dive, bottom time, ending pressure group, water temperature, air temperature, visibility, buddy, etc. It is an easy process to then total the relevant columns and track dive time. The last row number (minus header and total rows) is the number of dives you have made. If you would like a simple Microsoft Excel spreadsheet template to track your dives, then just contact me at **ehp@ehpublishing.com** and I will e-mail you one.

Dive Log
Location: _____
Dive #: _____ Date: _____ Verified by: _____
Phone at: _____ Instr_____ DM_____ Buddy DO
DAN: (919) 684-2948 @: _____
Other Emergency #: _____

Air Temp: _____ Alt: _____
Weather: _____
Water Temp: S _____ D _____
Vis: S _____ D _____
GPS Co-ord: _____
Misc: _____

Bottom Time to Date: _____:____
SI: ____:____ BPG: ____
Depth: _____ BT: _____:____   - Stamp -
Stop: _____ EPG: ____
Total Time after Dive: _____:____   Tank Size: _____   Air In: _____
                                                            Air Out: _____
                                                            Air Used: _____
Wt Used: _____ Fresh / Salt Exposure Suit: _____
Body Wt: _____
Pre-Dive Plan: _____
_____
_____
_____

Actual Dive: _____
_____
_____
_____
_____
_____
_____

Other: _____

Figure M. Example of a Dive Log Page
(feel free to copy this figure for personal use)

Figure N. Examples of Stamps From Log Book.

If you really want to get into it, you can use some pretty neat software to track your dives. Some of the dive log software available at the time of this printing include (in no particular order):

A trial version of Dive Log can be downloaded from http://www.webdive.com/software and a fully functional version purchased for $30.00. This software stores images, tracks standard dive information, charts and prints records. The downloadable trial version is 1.9 KB in size (zipped).

The Sea Wolff Dive Log for Windows logs dives, photos, fish watching, and is a information management tool for diving equipment maintenance. Special features include Citizen HyperAqualand import of data, up to 10 pages of text per dive, detailed and summary report, Metric and Imperial support, database searches, and air consumption calculators. The Sea Wolff Dive Log can be found at http://www.seawolff.com/ and is available for $49.00.

The Diver's Log (v.1.2) is a Filemaker Pro based shareware dive log program for the PC and Mac and can be found at http://www.inf.ethz.ch/personal/rys/diving/sw/. Diver's Log features extensive logging of dives, Metric and Imperial measurements, automatic calculation of air consumption rate and surface interval. You will also need Filemaker Pro loaded on your system to make this software work.

The Diver Log Book can be downloaded as a 991KB zipped files from http://www.webdive.com/software/. This software tracks basic dive information and sorts dives by date, country, place, sea, site, depth, duration, and quality. It tracks multiple divers, but apparently has no provision for images (at least the version I downloaded).

The ProFile® Dive Log System is a full-featured interactive dive log and database that enables the logging of many aspects of a dive. ProFile can be found at http://www.anewwave.com/profile.html and is available in Air or Enriched Air versions. ProFile Dive Log runs on Macintosh, Power Mac, Windows 3.1, Windows 95 or Windows 98 platforms. The ProFile Downloader version imports data from the Hyper-Aqualand Dive Watch and is available on all the above platforms. Versions appropriate for the new diver run in price from $64.95 to $89.95.

The user-friendly <u>DiveMaster 2.0</u> dive log can be found at http://www.reefnet.on.ca/. This software is a Windows-based dive and equipment log that enables you to track equipment, equipment maintenance, personal information, and dive statistics. DiveMaster 2.0 can be purchased for $19.95.

The <u>Giant Stride Multimedia Divelog</u> can be downloaded from http://www.giantstride.com/. The thirty-day trial version is free, and the fully functional version is just $28.88. This dive log creates a multimedia slide show presentation as you maintain your dive log. You can attach photos, voice, and plain text in logging each dive. Other attributes include Metric and Imperial calculations, graphs and dive statistics, and numerous photo viewer effects.

Some other dive planners/logs that might be of interest are:
- Abyss Advanced Dive Planning Software at www.abysmal.com,
- Pro Planner at www.IANTD.com, and
- Voyager Desktop Decompression System at www.DiveVoyager.com.

One final word on dive logs. I personally do not use any computer software for tracking my dives, and other than downloading some of the above trial versions, I have not used any of the above software. My problem is that it is an effort just to log my dives in my paper log book let alone the computer. No doubt the above software makes for a much richer record of ones' dives not to mention having a backup in case the log book is lost. Maybe someday I will make the time.

113. Once I have my own equipment can I dive for $1?

Yes, if you have your own air compressor, live on a boat or are within walking distance to the dive site (see Question 115), do not include expendables (batteries, etc.), and the amortization of your equipment. Using your own compressor, it would take less than a buck's worth of gas (electricity may be even cheaper) to fill an Al80. Thus the couched affirmative answer to a buck a dunk.

More realistically for most of us and our accountants (spouses), the cost of diving includes the amortization and replacement of equipment at about $10 a week for the active diver, air fills at about $4 a tank and a few bucks in gas to get there. Thus shore dives near home might cost about $20 for two dives. Boat dives further from home will set you back starting at about $90 for two dives (including amortization, air, gasoline, and expendables).

If you own your own boat and use it for diving then God help you, unless you have friends who will split the expenses. Be careful you do not run afoul of any laws and liabilities using your boat and taking on paying passengers. Look into the regulations involved before proceeding.

114. I'm certified! What are the top worldwide dive sites?

Congratulations! You have earned your C-card and you are eager to go diving, but not just local diving. You have a week's vacation coming and the desire to dive one of the best diving locations in the world. In perusing the diving literature[GG] and talking to divers, a list of some of the better novice dive spots in the world are listed in Figure O. That does not mean that all the dives in these areas are meant for the newly certified diver but some of the best ones are!

Figure O. Some of the Better Novice Dive Locations in the World.

Caribbean/Atlantic locations

Bahamas	700+ islands just 50 miles east of Miami with sharks, dolphins, wrecks and long, sandy beaches
Bay Islands, Honduras	(Guanaja, Roatan, Utila) some of the most diverse Caribbean diving including reefs, wrecks, and walls with warm water and great vis
Bermuda	water temperatures vary from 65° F in the winter to the 80s in the summer with the best (100-foot+) visibility in the summer and fall
Bonaire	shore diving capital of the Caribbean with beautiful reefs, parts were devastated by hurricane Floyd in 1999
British Virgin Islands	most diving done on shallow ocean shelves with maximum depths of approximately 80 feet

Grand Cayman, Cayman Islands	home of Stingray City, where stingrays eat from your hands in shallow water and you thought your buddy was a hoover!
Curaçao	considered one of the best all-around dive destinations in the Caribbean
Looe Key, Islanmorada, Key Largo, and Tavernier, Florida Keys	wreck of the HMS Looe (1744) and other shallow wrecks, coral spurs separated by sandy grooves, Molasses Reef, good visibility, top rated family resorts and charters, variety of critters, and it is in the U.S.
Turks & Caicos	some of the best beaches, restaurants, reefs, and walls in the Caribbean and a humpback whale migration
U.S. Virgin Islands	With visibility in 80-foot+ range and water in the 80° F St. Croix, St. John, and St. Thomas offer shallow water wreck, coral, and tunnel diving

Pacific locations

Big Island, Kanuai, Maui, and Oahu, Hawaii	reefscapes that include lava tunnels, tubes, and wrecks and some 450 marine species
Cabo San Lucas, Baja, Mexico	party and dive hot spot for Gringos (but do not drink and dive!)
Catalina Island, California	kelp (the world's largest marine plant), sea lions, and Avalon, all only a short boat ride from LA
Cozumel, Mexico	among the world's best drift diving on coral-studded reefs and fish-filled walls, warm water and superb vis
Great Barrier Reef, Australia	at 1,200 miles long this is the planet's largest living thing and offers some of the best snorkeling and diving down under

Indo locations

Egyptian Red Sea	clear waters and abundant underwater life

A map pinpointing the locations of the above dive sites can be seen in Figure P.

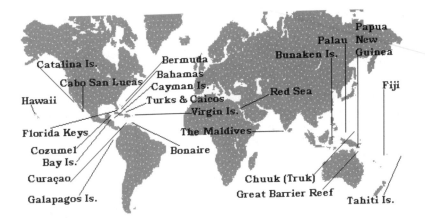

Figure P. Worldwide Dive Locations Map.

With the world being about 70 percent water, there are many great dive spots that can be regularly visited by divers. There are even more that seldom see a dive flag. After you gain some experience and explore the dive sites in Figure P, you may try any or (better yet) all the sites listed in Listing AO. Better yet, add your own and keep kickin'.

Listing AO. Additional Worldwide Sites to Whet Your Diving Appetite.

- Blue Corner, Palau
- Bunaken Island, Indonesia
- Chuuk (Truk) Lagoon, Chuuk
- Great White Wall, Fiji
- Galapagos Islands, Equador
- Papua New Guinea
- The Maldives, India

115. What are the best dive sites in my state?

To answer that question, 499 dive shops in the U.S. (approximately ten per state) were sent a survey asking them (the experts) where the good dive spots were in their state. Of those 499 surveys, 51 were returned address unknown or unable to forward and 128 were returned by the deadline, with the survey at least partially filled out. Of the surveys returned, all were usable, save one (which listed non-U.S. dive sites). A 28.6% return on deliverable surveys is excellent and shows the interest the dive shops had in compiling this data and their interest in SCUBA. A list of the responding dive shops can be found at the end of this question (Figure R). Note that the dive shops were selected at random from a business address CD. Therefore, just because your local dive shop is not listed does not mean they did not respond. They were most likely not included in the survey sample.

The results of the best dive sites survey has been compiled into the following tables by state (see Figure Q). The tables are presented in alphabetical order by state and alphabetical by dive site within the state's table. The #/# following the state heading is the number of survey respondents / number of surveys sent to dive shops in that state. A few states had no respondents. As to the tables, the '#' column is the number of shops designating that site as one of the top five within their state. The remaining column headings are self-explanatory. Note that there may be areas in a large state not represented in the tables since the dive shops were selected at random from an address CD and some shops elected not to participate.

Figure Q. Best Dive Sites by State

Note: This survey did not address the difficulty of the dive sites recommended. Some of the following dive sites are no doubt unsuitable for the novice diver. It is YOUR RESPONSIBILITY to ask dive shops in the locale you want to dive for an area orientation. During that orientation pay particular attention to potential hazards, which areas are the best to dive, relevant laws and regulations, aquatic life, etc. Who knows, you might find a dive buddy or two in the process. Have a great dive!

Alabama - 3/10

#	Dive Site	Description	Location Near
1	Alabama Point	channel dive - great dive for sea life	Gulf Shores

295

1	Anderson Reef	wreck - 90' depth	Gulf Shores
1	Military Tanks		Dolphin Island
1	Tensaw River Bridge Spans	metal spans of old bridge taken out & dropped for reefs	Mobile
1	Whiskey Wreck	100' depth	Gulf Shores

Alaska - 0/10

#	Dive Site	Description	Location Near

Arizona - 5/10

#	Dive Site	Description	Location Near
1	Apache Lake		Phoenix
3	Canyon Lake		East Mesa
3	Colorado River		Bullhead City
2	Lake Mohave		Bullhead City
2	Lake Pleasant		North Phoenix off I-17
3	Lake Powell		Page
1	Ringbolt Rapids		Hoover Dam
2	Saguaro Lake		East Phoenix - Beeline Hwy
1	Salt River		Phoenix
1	Willow Springs Lake		Payson

Arkansas - 4/10

#	Dive Site	Description	Location Near
2	Beaver Lake		Rogers
1	Buffalo River		Northern AR
2	Bull Shoals Lake		Mtn. Home
2	DeGray Lake – Iron Mtn. Marina		Arkadelphia
4	Greers Ferry Lake		Heber Springs
1	Lake Hamilton		Hot Springs
1	Lake Norfolk	55' Snap-on-Tool Truck	Mtn. Home
3	Lake Onchita		Hot Springs
1	Norfolk Lake		Mtn. Home
1	Ouachita Lake		Hot Springs

California - 6/20

#	Dive Site	Description	Location Near
1	Anacapa		Santa Barbara
1	Big Rock		Malibu
1	Blue Car Wreck		Catalina Island
1	Breakwater		Monterrey
1	Butterfly House		Carmel
1	Casino Point		Avalon, Catalina Is.
3	Catalina Island		Los Angeles
1	Eagle Reef		Catalina Island
1	East Rock Quarry		Catalina Island
2	Farnsworth Bank		Catalina Is.
1	La Jolla		San Diego
1	Leo Carillo State Beach		Malibu
1	Louers Point		Monterey
1	Monastery Beach		Carmel
1	Mono-Lobo Wall		Carmel
1	Point Dume		Malibu
2	Point Lobos		Carmel
1	Salt Point St. Park		Jenner
1	San Miguel		Santa Barbara
1	Santa Cruz		Santa Barbara
1	Santa Rosa		Santa Barbara
1	Shaws Cove		Laguna Beach
2	Ship Rock		Catalina Island

Colorado - 2/10

#	Dive Site	Description	Location Near
1	Blue Mesa Reservoir		Montrose
1	Grand Mesa	several lakes	Grand Junction
1	Island Lake	Top of Grand Mesa	CO
1	Lake San Cristobal		Lake City
1	Moles Lake		Silverton
1	Rifle Gap		Rifle
1	Taylor Park Reservoir		Gunnison

Connecticut - 3/10

#	Dive Site	Description	Location Near
1	Avery Point		Groton
1	Bartlett Reef		Bridgeport

1	Bigelow Hollow State Park		Union
1	Bluff Point Park		Groton
1	Candelwood Lake		Danbury
1	Eastern Point Beach		Groton
1	Greenfalls State Park Pond		Voluntown
3	Pleasure Beach		Avery Point
3	Stonington Point		Stonington
2	West Hill Pond		Torrington

Delaware - 2/7

#	Dive Site	Description	Location Near
1	Cherokee		Rohobeth Beach
1	Indian River		Rehobeth Beach
1	Marine		South Delaware
1	Moon Stone		Rohobeth Beach
1	Northern Pacific		Rohobeth Beach
1	S-5 Submarine		South Delaware

Florida - 4/20

#	Dive Site	Description	Location Near
1	Adolphus Busch Sr.		Florida Keys
1	Blue Grotto		Williston
1	Cayman Salvager		Key West
1	Deep Freeze		Miami Beach
1	Devils Den		Williston
1	Dwane		Key Largo
1	Ginnie Springs		High Springs
1	Kaptain Kurl Reef		Jupiter
1	Kedge Ledge		Key West
1	King Spring	manatees	Crystal River
1	Molasses Reef		Key Largo
1	Molassis/Elliot Key		Key Biscayne
1	Mulliphen	wreck	Stuart
2	Panama City		Panama City
1	Seagrove Beach		Panama City
1	Springs		Middle FL
1	Ten Fathom Ledge		Key West
1	Tenaco Towers		Dade/Broward Line

1	USS Rankin	wreck	Stuart
1	West Palm Beach		Palm Beach
1	Wreck Treck		Miami Beach

Georgia - 4/10

#	Dive Site	Description	Location Near
1	"G" Reef	Shipwrecks	St. Simons
1	"J" Reef	Shipwrecks	St. Simons
1	Altamaha River System		Vidalia
1	Etowah River		Allatoona
4	Gray's Reef Nat'l Marine Sanctuary		St. Simons
1	J Rudy		Sapelo Island
1	Lake Julliett		Forsyth
2	Lake Lanier		Atlanta
1	Ohoopee River		Vidalia
1	R2 Navy Towers		St. Simons

Hawaii - 5/10

#	Dive Site	Description	Location Near
1	1st Cathedral		Lanai
1	2nd Cathedral		Lanai
2	Back Wall of Molokini	crater	Maui
1	Black Rock		Kaanapali Beach
1	Breadloaf Cave		Opihihale
1	Cathedrals		Manele Bay, Lanzi
1	Hanauma Bay Nature Park	Shore Dive	KoKo Marina, Kai
1	Honolua Bay		Maui
1	Island Scuba		Kaanapali Beach
1	Kauna Point		Kauna
1	Mahi Shipwreck		Waikiki Honolulu
1	Makaha Caves		Waianae, Oahu
1	Manta Nite Dive		Kona
1	Marriott Reef		Kaanapali Beach
	Molokini Crater		Kihei, Maui

1	Old Airport Beach		Kaanapali Beach
1	Ono Rock		Papa Bay
1	Red Hill		Kihei, Maui
1	Shraks Cove & Three Tables	Summer Only	Oahu
1	The Finger		Kapua
1	Turle Canyon & Koko Craters		SE Coast of Oahu
1	Turtle Annaole		Honokohan Harbor
1	Turtle Reef		West Maui
1	YO-257 Shipwreck		Waikiki Honolulu

Idaho - 2/10

#	Dive Site	Description	Location Near
1	Bear Lake		Fish Haven
1	Blue Heart	Need boat to get to	Hagerman
1	Eagle Steam Tug		Cour d' Alene
1	Fire Hole on Snake River		Yellowstone Park
1	H&H Dive	26' deep pool w/fish	Pocatello
1	Harrison Steamship		Cour d' Alene
1	Palisades		Swan Valley
2	Red Fish Lake	Good visibility	Salmon
2	Ririe Reservoir	20', lots of crawfish	Idaho Falls
1	Sand Star	private yacht	Cour d' Alene
1	Seweewana	passenger boat	Cour d' Alene
1	Snake River	September only	Idaho Falls
1	Spokane Steamship		Cour d' Alene

Illinois - 3/10

#	Dive Site	Description	Location Near
2	Haigh Quarry		Kankakee
1	Morley Beach Access	wreck	Evanston
2	Pearl Lake		Beloit
1	Tacoma Tug		Chicago
1	Wells Burt		Evanston
1	Wreck of the George Molley		Evanston
1	Wreck of the Illinois		Chicago

1	Wreck of the Milwaukee		Zion
1	Wreck of the Wells Burt		Evanston
1	Wreck of the Wings of the Wind		Chicago

Indiana - 2/10

#	Dive Site	Description	Location Near
2	Blue Springs		Waldron
2	France Park		Logansport
2	Hidden Paradise		Rushville
1	Lake Maxinkuckee		Culver
1	Lake Wawasee		North Webster
2	Philips Quarry		Muncie
1	Sunset Park		Linton
1	White Rock Park		St. Paul

Iowa - 2/10

#	Dive Site	Description	Location Near
1	Banner Ship Mines		Indianola
2	Big Blue	Lester Milligan Park, 20' visibility in April	Mason City
1	Briggs Woods Co. Park		Webster City
1	Northwood Quarry		Northwood
1	West Lake, Okojoji		Spencer

Kansas - 1/10

#	Dive Site	Description	Location Near
1	Wilson Lake		Salina

Kentucky - 2/10

#	Dive Site	Description	Location Near
2	Cumberland Lake		Somerset
1	Dale Hollow Lake		Burkesville
1	Dive Cerulean		Cerulean
1	Grayson Lake	US Army Corp Lake	Greyson
1	Laurel Lake		London
1	Pointsville Lake	US Army Corp Lake	Pointsville
1	Yatesville Lake	US Army Corp Lake	Louisa

Louisiana - 0/10

#	Dive Site	Description	Location Near

Maine - 1/11

#	Dive Site	Description	Location Near
1	Cathedral Rocks		Rockport
1	Colony Beach		Kennebunkport
1	Folly Cove		Gloucester Harbor
1	Halibut Point		Rockport
1	Nubble Light		York
1	Plum Cove		Gloucester
1	Ships Cove, Ft. Williams		Cape Elizabeth
1	St. Ann's Beach		Kennebunkport
1	Wreck of Wandby		Kennebunkport

Maryland - 3/9

#	Dive Site	Description	Location Near
1	African Queen	80' - wreck	Ocean City
1	Bay Bridge		Annapolis
1	Calvert Cliffs State park	Shark Teeth	Lusby
1	Chesapeake Bay		Chesapeake Bay
1	Fenwck Shoals	22'-35' deep; 2 wrecks	Ocean City
1	Local Quaries/PA		Whiteford
1	Maxwell Wreck		Kent Island
1	Ocean City		Ocean City
1	Point Look Out		St. Mary's County
1	SS Washingtonian	100' - wreck	Ocean City
1	Tolley Point Oyster Bar		Annapolis
2	USS Blenny	submarine - 75'	Ocean City
1	USS Nina	75' deep - wreck	Ocean City

Massachusetts - 6/10

#	Dive Site	Description	Location Near
2	Back Beach	shore dive	Rockport
3	Cathedral Ledge/Rocks	surface 80' - only 100' from shore - shore dive	Rockport

5	Chester Poling	100' wreck dive	Gloucester Harbor
1	Dry Breakers	seal dive 60' max - boat dive	Rockport
2	Dry Salvages		Gloucester Harbor
2	Folly Cove	shore dive	Gloucester Harbor
2	Halfway Rock	surface 120' - boat dive	Gloucester
1	Halibut Point		Rockport
1	Loblolly Cove	shore dive	Rockport
1	Magnolia Rocks		Magnolia
1	Normans Woe	beach dive	Magnolia
2	Old Garden Beach		Rockport
1	Paddock Rock		Manchester
1	Pebble Beach		Rockport
1	Sandwich Town Beach		Sandwich

Michigan - 3/10

#	Dive Site	Description	Location Near
1	America	15'-90'	Isle Royal
1	Bermuda	30'	Munising
1	Cederville	100'	Michigan City
1	Ft. Barney	Wreck	Rogers City
2	Lake Huron	wreck	Lexington, Port Huron
1	Perserverance	Wreck	Rogers City
3	St. Clair River	treasure hunting	Algonac, Port Huron, St. Clair
1	USCGC – Mesquite	100'	Keweenaw Point
1	Wrecks of Hammond Bay		Rogers City
1	Wrecks of the Straits		Machinaw City
1	Wrecks of Thunder Bay		Alpena

Minnesota - 3/10

#	Dive Site	Description	Location Near
1	Bad Medicine Lake		Park Rapids
1	Big Cormorant Lake		Detroit Lakes
1	Big Sand Lake		Park Rapids
1	Crosby Mines		Crosby, Ironton
1	Lake 7 (aka Scalp Lake)		Frazee

1	Lake Sever		Frazee
1	Moose Lake		Deer River
1	Pickeral Lake		Detroit Lakes
1	Samuel P. Ely in Lake Superior		Two Harbors
1	Square Lake		Stillwater
1	Ten Mile Lake		Hackensack
1	The Madiera in Lake Superior		Silver Bay
1	Thomas Wilson in Lake Superior		Duluth
1	White Earth Lake		White Earth

Mississippi - 3/10

#	Dive Site	Description	Location Near
1	Bill Waller Wreck		Horn Island
1	Canyon Rigs	100 miles south of Biloxi	Biloxi
1	Dauphin Island	wrecks	Dauphin Island
1	FH-2		Horn Island
1	Horn Island	wrecks	Ocean Springs
1	Margarite Wreck		Horn Island
1	Military Tanks		Petit Bois
1	Oil Rigs of Gulf		Pascagoula
1	Rigs & Wrecks of Petit Bois Island		Dauphin Island
1	Triple Rigs		Petit Bois Island

Missouri - 3/10

#	Dive Site	Description	Location Near
1	Bennett Springs		Lebanon
1	Blue Water Quarry		Oronogo
1	Bonne Terre Mine		Bonne Terre
1	Bull Shoals Lake		Southern MO
1	Norfolk Lake		Southern MO
2	Oronoco Circle		Joplin
1	Roubiduex Spring		Waynesville
1	Scuba Adventure Dive Park		Jefferson City
2	Table Rock Lake		Branson

Montana - 2/7

#	Dive Site	Description	Location Near
1	Cemetery Island - Canyon Ferry		Helena
1	Coopers Lake		Missoula
1	Fire Hole River		Madison Junction/Yellowstone
2	Holland Lake - Rock Bay		between Missoula & Big Fork
2	McDonald Lake	Shovel Garden	Glacier Park
2	McGregor Lake		Kalispell
1	Missouri River Drive		Craig

Nebraska - 2/7

#	Dive Site	Description	Location Near
1	Bass Way Strip		Minden
2	Lake McConaughy		Ogalla
2	Sandy Channel State Rec. Area		Elm Creek

Nevada - 3/10

#	Dive Site	Description	Location Near
3	Boulder Islands	Lake Mead	Las Vegas
2	Black Canyon	Lake Mead	Las Vegas
2	Colorado River	Ringbolt Rapids	Hoover Dam
1	Hemingway Wall	Lake Mead	Las Vegas
1	Hole 33	Lake Mead	Las Vegas
3	Lake Mead	no specific dive site specified	Las Vegas
1	Narrows	Lake Mead	Las Vegas
3	Scuba Park	Lake Mead	Las Vegas

New Hampshire - 1/10

#	Dive Site	Description	Location Near
1	Clarke's Point		Wolfebero
1	Horse Barge		Bear Island
1	Lady of the Lake		Glendale
1	Old Navy Testing Site		Diamond Island
1	The Ledges		Newfound Lake

New Jersey - 2/10

#	Dive Site	Description	Location Near
1	Almirante	65' wreck dive	Atlantic City
1	City of Athens	110' wreck dive	Cape May
1	Great Isaac	90' wreck dive	Barnegat Bay
1	Jacob Jones	120' wreck dive	Cape May
1	Round Valley Recreational Area		Hwy 78 & 22
1	Seaside Park Pipeline		23rd Avenue
1	Shark River Inlet		Belmar
1	SS Mohawk	80' wreck dive	Brielle
1	The Pinta	wreck	6 mi. offshore
1	The Venturo & Army Tanks	wreck	1 mi. offshore

New Mexico - 1/10

#	Dive Site	Description	Location Near
1	Blue Hole		Santa Rosa
1	Conchas		Tucumcari
1	Elephant Butte		Truth or Consequences
1	Navajo		Farmington
1	Perch Lake		Santa Rosa

New York - 1/10

#	Dive Site	Description	Location Near
1	Islander		St. Lawrence
1	Keystorm		Alex Bay, St. Lawrence
1	Niagara River Drift		Niagara Falls/Buffalo
1	Roger Rock State Park		Lake George
1	Skeneattes Lake		Finger Lakes Region

North Carolina - 4/13

#	Dive Site	Description	Location Near
1	23 Mile Rock		Wrightsville
1	Aeolus	wreck	Beaufort
1	Asikabad		Morehead City
1	British Splendour		Hatteras

2	Caribe Sea	wreck	Beaufort
1	Cassimer	wreck	Beaufort
1	Dixie Arrow		Hatteras
1	Frying Pan Tower		Wrightsville Beach
1	Hesprides		Hatteras
1	Hyde		Wrightsville
2	John D. Gill WR-4		Wilmington
1	Kassandra		Hatteras
1	Lake Jocassee		Devils Fork State Park
1	Lobster Ledge		Wrightsville Beach
2	Papoose	wreck	Morehead City
1	Proteus		Hatteras
2	U-352	wreck	Morehead City

North Dakota - 1/3

#	Dive Site	Description	Location Near
1	Garrison Dam	tail race	Pick City
1	Lake Sakakawea	face of the dam	Pick City
1	Spiritwood Lake		Jamestown

Ohio - 4/10

#	Dive Site	Description	Location Near
1	Circleville Quarry		Circleville
1	France Lake		New Paris
3	Gilboa Quarry		Findlay
3	Lake Erie	wrecks	Cleveland
1	Long Lake		Lima
1	Nelson's Ledges		Niles
2	Plum Run	Adams Quarry	Peebles
3	Portage Quarry		Bowling Green
1	Salisbury Quarry		Maumee
3	White Star Quarry		Gibsonburg

Oklahoma - 6/10

#	Dive Site	Description	Location Near
3	Broken Bow Lake		Broken Bow
1	Grand Lake		Grand Lake Towne

3	Lake Elmer Thomas		Lawton
4	Lake Murray		Ardmore
1	Lake of the Arbucieles		Sulphur
5	Lake Ten Killer		Gore

Oregon - 3/10

#	Dive Site	Description	Location Near
2	Arch Rock		Newport
1	Big Cliff Reservoir	drift dive	Mill City
2	Clear Lake	300' visibility	Bend
1	Garibaldi	bar view jetty	Tillamook
2	Haystack Rock		Pacific City
1	Orford Reef		Port Orford
2	Pinnacles	off shore	Newport
1	Snake Island		
1	Three Pools		Lyons

Pennsylvania - 2/10

#	Dive Site	Description	Location Near
1	Bainbridge Quarry		Harrisburg
1	Blue Hole Quarry		Altoona
1	Dutch Springs		Bethlehem
1	Erie Bay		Erie
1	Kinjua Dam		Warren
2	Lake Erie	Wreck diving	Erie
1	Willow Springs		Richland

Rhode Island - 3/10

#	Dive Site	Description	Location Near
2	Beaver Tail State Park		Jamestown
3	Fort Wetherill State Park		Jamestown
2	Ft. Adams State Park		Newport
3	King' Beach	Ocean Dive	Newport
1	Lands End		Newport
1	Narragansett Pier		Narragansett
1	Pirate's Cove		Newport
2	U-853	German WWII U-Boat, wreck	Rhode Island Sound

South Carolina - 1/10

#	Dive Site	Description	Location Near
1	Bill Perry Artificial Reef	variety of fish (grouper, snapper, & tropical)	North Myrtle Beach
1	The City of Houston Wreck		North Myrtle Beach
1	The General Sherman Wreck	52' deep (multitudes of marine life)	North Myrtle Beach
1	The Governor Wreck	80' deep (southern stingrays & other fish)	North Myrtle Beach
1	The Hebe Wreck	90'-100' deep	North Myrtle Beach

South Dakota - 3/3

#	Dive Site	Description	Location Near
1	Coldbrook Reservoir		Hot Springs
2	Lake Francis Case/Ft. Randall Dam	Lake and tail race diving	Pickstown
1	Milbank Rock Quarry		Milbank
3	Oahe reservoir & Tail Race	250 mile lake diving and spear fishing	Pierre
2	Packtola Reservoir		Rapid City

Tennessee - 0/10

#	Dive Site	Description	Location Near

Texas - 3/20

#	Dive Site	Description	Location Near
1	Aquarena Springs	Comal River	San Marcos
2	Balmorhea State Park		Balmorhea
1	Blue Lagoon	quarry	Huntsville
1	Canyon Lake		Canyon
1	Lake McKenzie		Silverton
1	Lake Meredith		1 hr N. of Amarillo
2	Lake Travis	Windy Point	Austin
2	Possium Kingdom		Graford

Utah - 3/10

#	Dive Site	Description	Location Near
2	Bear Lake		Fish Haven
2	Blue Lake		Wendorer

#	Dive Site	Description	Location Near
1	Deer Creek Reservoir		Hebab (sp)
3	Fish Lake		Richfield
1	Homestead Crater		Midway
2	Lake Powell		
1	Mirror Lake		
2	Seabase		Grantsville

Vermont - 2/5

#	Dive Site	Description	Location Near
1	Ferris Rock – Lake Champlain		Colchester
1	The Burlington Bay Horse Ferry	wreck - 50' deep	Burlington Breakwater
1	The Coal Barge, A.R. Noyes	wreck - 80' to bow; 65' to stern	Proctor Shoal
1	The Diamond Island Stone Boat	wreck - 12'-25' depth	Diamond Island
1	The General Butler	wreck - 40' deep	Burlington
1	The Phoenix	wreck - 60' to bow; 110' to stern	Northern face of Colchester Shoal Reef
2	VT Underwater Historic Preserve	Wreck of O.J. Walker - Lake Champlain - Horse Ferry wreck	Burlington

Virginia - 2/10

#	Dive Site	Description	Location Near
1	Chenango		Virginia Beach
1	Chesapeake Bay Bridge Tunnel		Norfolk
2	Chesapeake Light Tower	wreck	Virginia Beach
1	Eureka		Virginia Beach
1	Gulf Hustler	wreck	Virginia Beach
2	John Morgan	wreck	Virginia Beach
2	Lillian Luckenbach	wreck	Virginia Beach
1	Marine Electric	wreck	Virginia Beach
2	Rawlings Quarry		South Hill

Washington - 2/10

#	Dive Site	Description	Location Near
1	Deception Pass		Fidalgo Island
1	Diamond Knot	wreck	Port Angeles

#	Dive Site	Description	Location Near
2	Edmonds Underwater Park		Edmonds
1	Harpers Fishing Warf		Port Orchard
2	Keystone Marine Park		Whidbey Island
1	KVI		Vashon Island
1	Octopus Hole		Lilliwaup
1	Rosario Beach		Deception Pass State Park
1	Salt Creek Park		Port Angeles
1	San Juan Island	boat dives	around San Juan Island
1	Tolmle Underwater Park		Nisqually Flats

West Virginia - 4/10

#	Dive Site	Description	Location Near
1	Cheat Lake		Morgantown
2	Ohio River		Huntington
3	Summersville Lake	20'-45' visibility	Summersville
1	Sutton Lake		Sutton
1	Tygart Lake		Grafton
3	Vepco Lake	15'-20' visibility; temp. approx. 80 degrees	Mt. Storm

Wisconsin - 3/10

#	Dive Site	Description	Location Near
1	Apostle Islands		Bayfield
1	Devil's Lake		Baraboo
1	ER Williams	100'; schooner	Door County
1	Flynns Quarry		Wactoma
1	Frank O'Connor	wreck	Baileys Harbor
1	Garrett Bay		Ellison Bay
1	Lake Lucerne		Crandon
1	Lake Owen		Cable
3	Lake Wazee		Black River Falls
1	Perch Lake		Hudson
1	Prinz William	wreck	Milwaukee
1	Red Granite Quarry		Wautoma
1	Round Lake		Hayward

Wyoming - 1/3

#	Dive Site	Description	Location Near
1	Flaming Gorge Lake		Rock Springs

1	Fremont Lake		Pinedale
1	Jenny Lake		Jackson Hole
1	Middle Piney Lake		Big Piney
1	Yellowstone Lake		Jackson Hole

Figure R. Dive Shops Participating in Best Dive Site by State
Survey

The 128 dive shops responding by the survey deadline date to
the 'Best Dive Sites in Your State' survey were:

Note that the dive shops were selected at random from a business address CD.
Therefore, just because your local dive shop is not listed does not mean they did
not respond. They were most likely not included in the survey sample.

Company Name	City	State
Gulf Coast Divers	Mobile	AL
Scubaventures Inc	Birmingham	AL
Sea Diver's Inc	Ozark	AL
Aquanauts Dive Ctr	Jacksonville	AR
J & T Dive Shop	Jonesboro	AR
Ocean Extreme	North Little Rock	AR
Papa Smurf's Dive Shop	Sheridan	AR
Aqua Sports	Phoenix	AZ
El Mar Diving Ctr	Mesa	AZ
Oasis Divers	Phoenix	AZ
Summit Divers & Watersports	Flagstaff	AZ
Water World Scuba Diving Ctr	Bullhead City	AZ
Aquatic Center	Newport Beach	CA
Cal Dive & Travel	Berkeley	CA
Malibu Divers	Malibu	CA
Monterey Bay Dive Ctr	Monterey	CA
Santa Barbara Watersports	Santa Barbara	CA
Scuba Luv Inc	Avalon	CA
Blue Mesa Scuba & Travel	Montrose	CO
Colorado Scubaventures	Grand Junction	CO
Aqua Sports Diving Ctr	Gales Ferry	CT
Central Sales Scuba	Thomaston	CT
New England Diving-	Wallingford	CT

Connecticut		
Blue Planet Divers	Wilmington	DE
First State Sports Inc	Wilmington	DE
Deep Six Dive & Watersports	Stuart	FL
Diving Locker	North Miami Beach	FL
Ginnie Springs Resort	High Springs	FL
Southpoint Divers	Key West	FL
Atlanta Divers & Scuba Club	Decatur	GA
Island Dive Ctr	Saint Simons Island	GA
South Georgia Scuba	Lyons	GA
Wet Set Scuba	Stockbridge	GA
Aloha Dive Co	Kailua Kona	HI
Aloha Dive Shop	Honolulu	HI
Dive & Sea Maui	Kihei	HI
Island Scuba	Lahaina	HI
Lahaina Divers Inc	Lahaina	HI
Iowa State Skin Diving Schools	West Des Moines	IA
Matt Leydens Dive Shop	Des Moines	IA
H & H Dive & Travel	Pocatello	ID
Inland Scuba Inc	Idaho Falls	ID
Tom's Diving Adventures	Coeur D Alene	ID
Elmer's Water Sports	Evanston	IL
Midwest Scuba Ctr	Champaign	IL
Underwater Safaris	Chicago	IL
Divers Supply Indy North	Carmel	IN
Leaird's Underwater Svc	Muncie	IN
Aquaventure Scuba	Topeka	KS
Divers Den	Somerset	KY
Dolphin Dive Ctr	Owensboro	KY
Aqua Shack	Marlborough	MA
Cape Ann Divers	Gloucester	MA
Central Massachusetts Scuba	Worcester	MA
Merrimack Aquatic Ctr	Methuen	MA
Scuba Center	Attleboro	MA
Undersea Divers Inc	Beverly	MA
Aqua Ventures Inc	Cockeysville	MD
Chesapeake Underwater Sports	Annapolis	MD

Divers Den Inc	Parkville	MD
Divers Locker	Alfred	ME
Anchor Bay Scuba Training Ctr	Fair Haven	MI
Great Lakes Divers	Rogers City	MI
M & M Diving	Menominee	MI
Northwest Divers	Moorhead	MN
Scuba Daddy's Dive Shop	Apple Valley	MN
Tri-State Diving Svc	Detroit Lakes	MN
Aquasports Scuba Ctr	Springfield	MO
Scuba Adventure	Jefferson City	MO
Scuba School & Travel	Joplin	MO
Deep South Scuba	Jackson	MS
Sea Urchins Dive & Travel	Hattiesburg	MS
Seaspace Dive Ctr	Gautier	MS
Great Northern Scuba Adventure	Great Falls	MT
Mrs J's Scuba	Helena	MT
Aquatic Safaris & Divers	Wilmington	NC
Bill's Scuba Inc	Raleigh	NC
Burlington Dive Ctr	Burlington	NC
Outer Banks Diving & Charters	Hatteras	NC
Scuba One	Mandan	ND
Heartland Scuba Ctr	Kearney	NE
Heartland Scuba Ctr East	Lincoln	NE
Fathom Divers Scuba & Wtrsprts	Laconia	NH
Atlantic Divers	Egg Harbor Township	NJ
Scuba Co	Albuquerque	NM
American Cactus Divers	Las Vegas	NV
Boulder City Divers	Boulder City	NV
Colorado River Divers	Boulder City	NV
Seafan Scuba Ctr	Endicott	NY
Diver's Paradise	Toledo	OH
Long Lake Scuba Inc	Lima	OH
Sub-Aquatics Inc	Reynoldsburg	OH
Underwater Dive Ctr	Elyria	OH
Aquasports Scuba Inc	Moore	OK

Broken Bow Scuba Svc	Broken Bow	OK
Dive Pro	Duncan	OK
Dive Site	Tulsa	OK
Oklahoma Scuba Shop	Norman	OK
Poseidon Adventures Ltd	Tulsa	OK
Horizon Water Sports Inc	Portland	OR
Hydrosports Dive & Travel	Salem	OR
Northwest Divers	Albany	OR
J & S Dive Shop	Erie	PA
Splash Water Sports Inc	Pittsburgh	PA
Bubbles Dive Ctr	Newport	RI
East Bay Aquanauts Inc	Barrington	RI
Ocean State Scuba	Jamestown	RI
Coastal Scuba	North Myrtle Bch	SC
Donovan's Scuba & Hobby Ctr	Sioux Falls	SD
Mick's Scuba Ctr	Rapid City	SD
Blue Dolphin Dive Ctr	Temple	TX
Dive West, Inc.	Plano	TX
Southern Scuba	Fort Worth	TX
Absolute Scuba	Orem	UT
Dive Utah-Holladay	Holladay	UT
Scuba Utah	Salt Lake City	UT
Chesapeake Bay Diving Ctr	Portsmouth	VA
Lynnhaven Dive Ctr	Virginia Beach	VA
Scuba Center	Richmond	VA
Waterfront Diving Ctr	Burlington	VT
Northwest Sports Divers Inc	Bothell	WA
Watermark Scuba	Auburn	WA
Aqua Center	Green Bay	WI
Divepoint Scuba Ctr	Stevens Point	WI
St Croix Scuba	Hudson	WI
Charleston Scuba	Saint Albans	WV
Huntington Sports & Diving Ctr	Huntington	WV
Sarge's Dive Shop	Summersville	WV
Scuba West Virginia Inc	Parkersburg	WV
Mountain Bay Scuba	Rock Springs	WY

Don't Miss Your Manners .. Diving Etiquette

Primary rule: when on a dive boat, listen to and follow the Divemasters' and crews' instructions and advice. They are there in part for your safety and to assist you.

Use your head and not the boat's. If you get seasick (see Question 62), then upchuck over the railing, down wind from everyone. In SCUBA circles, reverse peristalsis is also termed feeding the fish. Note that there are no fish in the boat's head to feed. Making a smelly, slimy mess in the lavatory is unnecessary and very bad form. Just because it is called a head does not mean that is where yours goes.

Do not put your weights on anything higher than what you want them to slide off of, and on to your toes. Or worse, your neighbor's toes! Particularly when your neighbor is twice your size. Not only can those weights break a toe but more importantly they could ruin the dive. If possible, keep those weights on the boat deck under your bench or otherwise out of the way and secure. Additionally, be sure to secure tank(s) as instructed by the crew or Divemaster. A loose cylinder on a pitching boat can be deadly; to everyone, including you.

One thing that many do not want to endure is listening to that braggart who has dove everywhere, knows it all, and damn well wants everyone to know it by loudly expounding on how wonderful they are. Dive stories and helping other divers are one thing, but just remember you are not the only one who paid good money to get on that dive boat. Be considerate, it makes for a better time for everyone.

On many dive boats, there is a table, bench, or other spot reserved for cameras. Do not leave open drinks in those areas. Spilling a sticky drink on a camera or having to work on your camera in an area where some stroke has spilled a drink is aggravating, if not expensive. Be considerate.

Another common blunder is for some newbie to spit or put defogger in their mask and then dip the mask in the camera rinse tank. Think about it. Underwater cameras can easily cost thousands of dollars and repairing them is expensive, not to mention maybe missing that shot for which someone (you?) paid good money to dive for. If you do not know which tank is for mask rinsing and which is for cameras, then ASK. If in doubt, do not dunk that mask. There's a whole ocean (see Question 15) just over the side of the boat!

While we are talking about photography. If you are into taking photographs, remember that once a photographer has chosen a photo opportunity, it is theirs until they voluntarily abandon it. Do not invade another's photographers photo set-up!

On a dive boat there are usually areas which are designated as dry. That does not mean you cannot drink there. It means do not invade that area when wet. Please dry off before entering those areas.

Tipping is a controversial subject among some divers, but Divemasters and the boat's crew are generally not independently wealthy. In my opinion, it is very good form to leave a gratuity, particularly if they have made your dive(s) go smoother and/or more interesting. What goes around, comes around.

If at all possible, it is generally accepted etiquette to return recovered dive gear to its owner. Over the course of your diving, you too will lose gear and will appreciate its return.

Touch as little as reasonably possible when diving. Humans are tactile animals, but putting that pinky on a blue ringed octopus could be the last less-than-brilliant thing you do. Touching aquatic creatures can also wipe away their protective coating of slime and leave them open to disease.

Buoyancy control is like gun control, except instead of placement of the bullet on a target, it is the positioning of your body in a water column. Learn how to keep yourself and your equipment from touching marine organisms and ecologically sensitive terrain.

Do not chase, harass, or kill our underwater buds unless it is legal to do so and you are going to use/eat the beast. Lobster (bugs) and shellfish in season taste great, and are themselves a good reason to dive, but use common sense and maintain your fishery. Shooting that huge Jew fish at a wreck may be legal in some places, but it might also be the reason some of your compatriots dive there. It is NOT sporting to take a fish that comes up to you to have their belly scratched! If you take game, PLEASE take it away from structures used for underwater sightseeing. Thank you!

Shore divers particularly take note. Do not change into your birthday suit where you can be seen. Even though you have a great looking, tanned body, there are shoreline residents who would rather not see it. Beachfront residents often have political clout (money). Keep your dive site open. Be considerate of the local inhabitants. That includes loud noises, particularly early in the morning, e.g., banging tanks, opening tank valves, yelling, honking, etc. And, for heavens sake, pick up after yourselves and do not mictrate (see Question 36) in the petunias! That really did not have to be said, did it?

Diving Deeper into SCUBA .. Other Resources

The resources for further information regarding SCUBA diving are extensive, varied, and growing. To continue your exploration into SCUBA diving, consult dive professionals, certifying agencies, dive Physicians, fellow divers, TV, periodicals, books, and the Internet.

The best sources for information about specific dives are *dive professionals*, i.e., Instructors, Divemasters, dive shop personnel, and other divers. Many dive shop owners are also instructors. These people live and breath diving and can be great sources of diving wisdom. The best part is, because of their love of SCUBA, they are usually willing to chat about it in great length. Additionally, some of the most current information about a dive site can be obtained from fellow divers. However, be aware that your fellow divers may not take into account your inability to safely do a specific dive on a particular day. You have to know your limits and stay within them! Ask an Instructor for additional training if you need it.

In addition to the dive business, the *SCUBA certifying agencies* (see Question 72) are also in the publishing business. They produce training manuals, CDs, videotapes, and materials and are an excellent source of additional information. Any of the certifying agencies can either answer your questions or direct you to the appropriate source.

Please see a knowledgeable *dive Physician* if you have health questions. See Question 65 for sources of knowledgeable dive Physicians in your area. You can also check out the web site **http://www.ehpublishing.com/scubalinks.html** for additional links to SCUBA web sites that may reference dive Physicians. The bottom line is, do not dive if you have any doubts. Live to dive another day!

If you have equipment-related questions then ask *your instructor, dive shop personnel, fellow divers, or pose a question on the rec.scuba newsgroup.* Caveat, not everyone on the Internet has your best interest at heart. Be careful in implementing suggestions obtained solely from the Internet. Just like in society, most people are great, it is just the inevitable few muck sucking worms that make life more difficult for everyone else.

Another entertaining source of information is just a click away on *TV*, e.g., Discovery Channel and Outdoor Life Network. They often have SCUBA-related programming that is interesting and informative, though generally not that technical. Caveat, get dive training from a SCUBA professional not TV.

Another SCUBA informational source is *periodicals*. Be aware that some of them have been accused of having a bias in their equipment and dive resort reviews based on advertising revenues. I have heard this accusation from several diving professionals, but I must reserve judgement, as I do not know first hand of any proven biases. Go to your local dive shop and browse their magazine rack. A non-exhaustive list of SCUBA periodicals can be found in the 'SCUBA Periodicals' section of 'SCUBA Scoop'.

Some of the resources that were used in the compilation of this tome can be found in the 'References' section of 'SCUBA Scoop'.

One of the best sources of current diving information can be obtained from the *Internet*. Because of the dynamic nature of the Internet, it would not be wise to put extensive lists of constantly changing URLs (Uniform Resource Locators or web site addresses) here. Instead, if you wish to access additional information using the Internet, then either do a search using your favorite search engine or access **http://www.ehpublishing.com/scubalinks.html** via your browser. The links you find there will be kept current and will also point you to additional SCUBA link directories. Kawabunga!

The History of SCUBA in Three Pages

Mankind has practiced skin diving (breath-hold) for centuries. In ancient Greece (circa 500 B.C.), breath-hold divers dove for sponges and Scyllis used a reed as a snorkel for his military exploits. However, because of the difficulty of inhaling against water pressure, a two-foot reed is about the maximum length for a snorkel. Air filled bags were also tried but rebreathing carbon dioxide was a problem limiting dive times.

In 1530 the first diving bell was invented. It was a stationary, open bottom bell that was lowered into the water a few feet from the surface. With air pumped in from the surface, a diver could stand on the lake, river, or ocean bottom with his head in the bell and dive until the air became fouled with carbon dioxide.

American Turtle

The first documented attack by a military submarine occurred in September 6, 1776 in the New York harbor with the American Turtle submarine vs. the British HMS Eagle.

In 1837, the German inventor, Augustus Siebe sealed a diving helmet to a watertight air-containing rubber suit. This was then connected to a surface air pump. The first documented cases of decompression sickness were in 1843 when divers used Siebe's suit to salvage the HMS Royal George in 65 feet of water. The salvage of the George was the first recorded instance of divers using the buddy system (see Question 45). In 1843, the first dive school was established by the Royal Navy.

In 1876 the Englishman Henry Fleuss developed the first workable, self-contained diving rig that used compressed oxygen rather than air. With this closed circuit SCUBA unit, a diver could stay down for several hours. Though it was not known at the time, the problem was that pure oxygen becomes toxic (1.6 ATA) at about 20 fsw (feet seawater).

In 1878, the Frenchman Paul Bert published the 1,000 page, report entitled <u>La Pression Barometrique</u>. This report showed that decompression sickness was due to nitrogen gas bubbles. Bert suggested recompression to relieve the pain.

1908 saw the publication of The Prevention of Compressed-Air Illness by Haldane, Boycott, and Damant. This publication, though based on hyperbaric experiments on goats, was the basis for the initial staged decompression, British Royal Navy, and U.S. Navy diving tables.

In the 1920s, the first experiments were conducted in the use of helium-oxygen mixtures in deep diving. In the early 1930s an American ex-aviator, Guy Gilpatric, pioneered the use of rubber goggles with glass lenses for skin diving. By the mid-1930s, facemasks, fins, and snorkels were widely used in diving, with fins being patented by the Frenchman Louis de Corlieu in 1933. Enlarging the facemask to include the nose occurred circa 1935 by Russian Kramarenko and Frenchmen Le Prieur and Forjot. In 1938, Gilpatric wrote the first book on amateur diving and underwater hunting entitled The Compleat Goggler.

In 1942 and 1943, French naval lieutenant Jacques-Yves Cousteau and Air Liquide engineer, Emile Gagnan worked on a regulator which would provide compressed air to a diver upon inhalation (upon demand). Except for the 1865 demand regulator designed by Rouquayrol and Denayruse, all other self-contained breathing apparatus used continuously supplied air or air which had to be turned off manually.

In January of 1943, Cousteau tested their regulator in the Marne River near Paris. This was the birth of the Aqua Lung, which was commercially marketed in France in 1946, Great Britain in 1950, Canada in 1951, and in the United States in 1952.

In 1951, the first issue of Skin Diver Magazine was printed. The 1950s saw dive stores start to open up around the United States. The International Diving Educators Association (IDEA) was formed in 1952. In 1957, the first segment of Sea Hunt aired on television with Lloyd Bridges starring as Mike Nelson. Sea Hunt inspired thousands to take up SCUBA diving {including my brother}.

In 1959, the YMCA began the first nationally organized course for SCUBA certification. In 1960, NAUI (National Association of Underwater Instructors) was formed, NASDS (National Association of Scuba Diving Schools) organized in 1961, and PADI (Professional Association of Diving Instructors) followed in 1966. In 1968, Jacques Cousteau began the TV series "The Underwater World of Jacques Cousteau" which ran for 8 years.

Advances in safety that started in the 1960's, become widely adopted in the 70's. The institution of a certification card (C-card) to signify basic training and get air fills was adopted. Divers changed from using the J-valve reserve systems to non-reserve K-valves. Submersible pressure gauges, buoyancy compensators (BC), and single hose regulators were also adopted.

K-Valve

In 1970, Scuba Schools International (SSI) was formed. Jacques-Yves Cousteau started the 'Cousteau Society' in 1974 to help protect ocean life. 1975 saw the incorporation of the Professional Diving Instructors Corporation (PDIC). In 1980, the Divers Alert Network (DAN) was formed at Duke University. The National Academy of Scuba Educators (NASE) was formed in 1982. 1983 saw the introduction of the first commercially available dive computer (the Orca Edge). IANTD (International Association of Nitrox and Technical Divers) was formed in 1985. Jacque Cousteau died on June 25, 1997, the same year the World Association of Scuba Instructors (WASI) was organized.

In 200_, you became SCUBA certified and began a lifelong journey of exploring our underwater world. Welcome to recreational SCUBA diving!

Off-Gassing (Glossary)

It seems that every unique human endeavor has it's own vocabulary? After all isn't that one of the big differences between us and a limpet {excluding Henry Limpet}? Think about the unique vocabulary of law enforcement, teaching, law {no one understands them anyway which, by the way, is not without purpose}, accounting, construction, etc. In this section I present a few of the more salient {kewl word, reminds me of saltwater thus diving} words as used in this book.

- A -

absolute pressure – the resulting pressure when atmospheric pressure is added to gauge pressure.

actual bottom time (ABT) – the total elapsed time in minutes from leaving the surface until final ascent is begun.

actual dive time (ADT) – the total time spent underwater from the beginning of the descent until breaking the surface at the end of the dive excluding the safety stop time.

aerotitis – middle ear squeeze.

AGE - see arterial gas embolism.

air - a gas mixture containing 21 percent oxygen, 78 percent nitrogen, and 1percent other gases (primarily argon); colloquial for the compressed air used for recreational SCUBA diving.

air compressor - a machine that compresses or pressurizes air. In SCUBA, air is compressed from the atmospheric level (14.7 psi at sea level) to the capacity of the tank, which is typically between 2500 and 3000 psi.

air embolism - see arterial gas embolism.

air pressure - the force per unit area exerted by the weight of a column of air. At sea level the air pressure is 14.7 psi. Air pressure decreases with altitude.

A180 - an aluminum SCUBA tank which holds 80 cubic feet/2,267 liters of air at 3014.7 psi (pounds per square inch)/203 bar at 70° F at sea level.

alternate air source – any device a diver can use in place of their primary air source in order to make a controlled ascent while breathing normally.

alveolus - the air sac at the end of a bronchus where oxygen and carbon dioxide transfer occurs (alveoli is the plural).

ambient pressure - the surrounding pressure. On land the ambient pressure comes from the weight of the atmosphere (see air pressure). At depth, the ambient pressure comes from the weight of the water plus the weight of the atmosphere.

analog instruments – instruments which use a needle or a hand moving around a dial to provide information vs. digital instruments whose output is electronically generated.

anemia - a reduction in the oxygen carrying capacity of the red blood cells.

anoxia – deficiency of oxygen.

anticoagulants - medications that reduce the clotting ability of the blood. Anticoagulants are of concern to divers due to the increased potential of barotrauma in air-filled body cavities.

Archimedes Principle – any object wholly or partly immersed in fluid is buoyed up by a force equal to the weight of the fluid displaced by the object – which is why you can float your boat.

argon - an inert gas that makes up less than 1 percent of air.

arrhythmias - irregularities in the rhythm and rate of the heart which potentially can be dangerous to divers due to the increased stress and varied pressures of the underwater environment.

arterial gas embolism (AGE) - the condition characterized by bubble(s) of air emitting from a ruptured area of the lung under pressure. The bubbles enter the pulmonary circulation and travel to the arterial circulation, where they may cause a stroke or 'heart attack'. The blockage of blood flow in the body by air bubbles escaping into the blood.

asthma - a relatively common condition caused by a narrowing of air passages within the bronchi of the lungs. One reason for the narrowing is excess mucous in the airways.

ATA - atmosphere absolute. Where 1 ATA is the atmospheric pressure at sea level as measured with a barometer.

atmosphere (atm) - the blanket of air surrounding the earth, from sea level to outer space. Also, a unit of pressure where "one atmosphere" is the pressure of the atmosphere at sea level, i.e., 760 mm Hg or 14.7 psi (1 bar=0.986 atmospheres).

atmospheric pressure - pressure of the atmosphere at a given altitude or location.

- **B** -

bailout bottle – see pony bottle.
bar - a measurement of pressure, 1 bar=100,000 newton/meter^2 or 14.5 psi
barometric pressure - same as atmospheric pressure.
barotrauma - any disease or injury due to unequal pressures between a space inside the body and the ambient pressure, or between two spaces within the body. Examples include arterial gas embolism, pneumomediastinum, and pneumothorax.
BC (BCD) – see buoyancy compensator (also termed buoyancy compensating device or BCD).
bends - a form of decompression sickness (DCS) caused by dissolved nitrogen leaving the tissues too quickly thus forming bubbles. 'The bends' are manifested by pain, usually in the limbs and joints.
bezel – a movable ring on a compass or watch that is inscribed with index marks. In watches, the ring should only be able to rotate in one direction and is used to measure elapsed time.
bleb - an abnormal pocket of air in the lungs, usually under the lining of a lung, that can rupture with ascent and lead to barotrauma.
bottom time (BT) - in square wave diving, the time between descending below the surface to the beginning of ascent. In multi-level diving, the time between descending below the surface and beginning the safety stop.
Boyle's Law - at constant temperature, the volume of a gas varies inversely with the pressure, while the density of a gas varies directly with pressure (PV=K).
bradycardia – slowness of the heart beat.
breakwater – an offshore structure erected to diminish the force of waves.
breath-hold diving - diving without an underwater life support apparatus, while holding one's breath.
bubble - a collection of air or gas surrounded by a permeable membrane through which gases can enter or exit.

buddy breathing – an emergency out-of-air (OOA) procedure where two divers share one second stage regulator while ascending.

buddy system – a requirement of recreational SCUBA diving such that you never dive alone and always have someone to assist you (if necessary).

bulla - similar to a bleb. An abnormal pocket of air or fluid.

buoyancy - tendency of an object to float or sink when placed in a liquid. Objects that float are positively buoyant, those that sink are negatively buoyant and those that stay where placed are neutrally buoyant. Buoyancy control is a very important factor in diving safely.

buoyancy compensator (BC) - an inflatable vest worn by the diver that can be inflated orally or via air from the SCUBA tank. Used to help control buoyancy.

burst disk – a thin copper disk held in place with a gasket and a vented plug which prevents the pressure in a scuba tank from exceeding the maximum tank pressure. Once burst it will have to be replaced by a qualified technician.

burst lung – see pulmonary baurotrauma.

- C -

CAGE - cerebral arterial gas embolism (see arterial gas embolism).

carbon dioxide (CO$_2$) - an odorless, tasteless gas that is a byproduct of metabolism and is excreted by the lungs in exhaled air. Carbon dioxide is important component in the body's control of respiration.

carbon dioxide toxicity - problems resulting from the buildup of CO$_2$ in the blood. These problems may range from headache and shortness of breath, all the way to sudden blackout.

carbon monoxide (CO) – an odorless, tasteless, highly poisonous gas given off by incomplete combustion of hydrocarbon fuels.

carbon monoxide toxicity - illness from inhaling excess CO. These problems may range from headache to unconsciousness and death.

C-card – SCUBA certification card.

ceiling – a minimum depth to which a diver may ascend without risk of decompression sickness, typically displayed by a dive computer.

certification card (C-card) – a card that a certifying agency award as evidence of completing required training.

certified – short for open water SCUBA certificate thus connoting a level of training which enables you get air refills and purchase additional equipment. A stepping stone to further SCUBA training.

cf - cubic feet.

chamber – see hyperbaric chamber.

Charles's Law - at a constant volume, the pressure of gas varies directly with absolute temperature (given a constant volume, the higher the temperature the higher the gas pressure).

chokes - a form of decompression sickness caused by bubbles entering the lungs to interfere with gas exchange. The chokes are manifested by shortness of breath and can be fatal.

chronic obstructive pulmonary disease (COPD) - terminal airway dilation and blockage from long-term smoking, infection or substances chronically inhaled. Dangerous to the diver due to possibility of 'burst lung' and a gas embolism.

ciguatera – a poisoning that results from eating certain fish which contain a poison (ciguatoxin). May be fatal.

clearing – the moving of air from the lungs to the other air spaces, such as ear and sinuses to relieve a squeeze.

closed circuit SCUBA - apparatus designed to allow divers to re-breathe exhaled air after removal of CO_2 and the addition of supplemental O_2. In contrast to "open circuit," closed circuit SCUBA is noiseless and produces few bubbles.

CNS - central nervous system. Composed of brain and spinal cord.

CO_2 retention - frequent cause of CO_2 toxicity which is usually due to skip breathing.

compartment - a theoretical division of the body into typically five or six compartments with an arbitrarily assigned half time for nitrogen uptake and elimination. Used in the calculation of dive tables.

console – a device that is designed to hold assorted gauges and instruments (including dive computer) around or in line with the submersible pressure gauge.

contraindications to diving – physiological, psychological, or environmental dive conditions that could preclude a person from diving safely.

coronary artery disease (CAD) - arteriosclerosis of the arteries supplying blood to the heart. Blockage causes heart failure and 'heart attacks'.

cyanosis – a bluish discoloration of the skin that results from an oxygen deficiency in the blood.

Cylume lightstick – a brand of chemical light stick which becomes a source of chemical light when two chemicals inside the tube are mixed. They are attached to the diver's tank valve, hose, or snorkel to facilitate being seen seen by other divers at night.

- D -

Dalton's Law - the total pressure exerted by a mixture of gases is equal to the sum of the pressures that would be exerted by each of the gases if it alone were present and occupied the total volume.

DAN (Diver's Alert Network) – a non-profit organization involved in diving research, diving emergency hot line, diving insurance, etc. If you SCUBA dive you should be a member.

decompression - any change from one ambient pressure to a lower ambient pressure. Decompression always results in a reduction of gas pressures within the body.

decompression dive - any dive where the diver is exposed to a higher pressure than when the dive began. The decompression occurs as the diver ascends.

decompression illness (DCI) - a relatively new term to encompass all bubble-related problems arising from decompression, including both decompression sickness (DCS) and arterial gas embolism (AGE).

decompression schedule - specific decompression procedures for a given combination of depth and bottom time.

decompression sickness (DCS) - a general term for all problems resulting from the formation of bubbles of inert gas, typically nitrogen, within the body of the diver when ambient pressure is lowered. Can be divided into Type I (musculoskeletal and/or skin manifestations only) or more seriously Type II (neurologic, cardiac, and/or pulmonary manifestations). DCS Type I involves muscle and joint

pain, fatigue and/or skin symptoms of itching or rash.
DCS Type II involves symptoms of the respiratory,
circulatory, and/or central nervous system. These
symptoms include: paralysis, shock, weakness, dizziness,
numbness, tingling, difficulty breathing, and varying
degrees of joint and limb pain.

decompression stop - the time a diver stops and waits at a
certain depth to allow nitrogen (or other inert gas)
elimination before surfacing. A decompression stop is
beyond what is taught in recreational SCUBA diving. A
decompression stop is not the same thing as a recreational
SCUBA safety stop. Used to decrease concentrations of
inert gas(es) in the body before continued ascent.

defog solution – a substance that is rubbed on the lens of the
mask to keep it free of condensation (cleans the glass so
condensation sheets off the glass rather than beads up).

dehydration - a condition where the water content of the body
is reduced. Dehydration is caused by immersion, alcohol,
medications, sweating, excessive loss of fluids from
vomiting and diarrhea or decreased intake of fluids.

density – mass per unit of volume.

depth - the maximum depth in fsw attained during a dive

depth gauge – an instrument or device that indicates depth.

dermatitis - inflammation of the skin.

descent/ascent line – a line suspended from a boat or buoy
which is used by a diver to control their rate of descent or
ascent and to provide a convenient means of doing a safety
stop.

diuretics - chemicals and medications that cause the kidneys
to excrete an increased quantity of fluids.

dive computer - a small computer, carried by the diver, that in
real time, measures water pressure (depth), rate of assent,
time, etc. Dive computers, based on pre-programmed
algorithms, calculate the tissue nitrogen uptake and
elimination based on theoretical compartmentalization of
the body.

dive flag – may be either a red rectangle with a diagonal white
stripe or a blue and white double tailed pennant (which
actually means boat's progress impeded). These flags are
used to warn other boaters away from the area.

dive tables - a printed collection of dive times for specific
depths, by which the diver can avoid contracting DCS.

Most tables are based on the Haldanian theory for nitrogen uptake and elimination.

dive time calculator – a rotary calculator containing the dive tables in a format that eliminates the mathematical calculations associated with the dive tables.

DPV (Diver Propulsion Vehicle) - underwater 'scooter'.

dry suit - a water-tight garment that keeps the diver's body warm by providing insulation with a layer of gas, e.g., air. Used for diving in waters that are too cold for comfortable wet suit protection.

dyspnea – difficulty breathing that results from increased depth.

- E -

EAD - Equivalent Air Depth.

EAN (EANx) - enriched air nitrogen or nitrox.

eardrum – the membrane that separates the middle and outer ears.

embolism, arterial gas - see arterial gas embolism (AGE).

emergency swimming ascent (ESA) – an independent, emergency ascent generally made due to depletion of the diver's air supply. Also referred to as an emergency out of air ascent or swimming ascent.

ENT - Ear, Nose and Throat diseases and conditions.

equalization - process of preventing and correcting squeezes by equalizing the air pressure between two air spaces, e.g., ears, mask.

Eustachian tube - a short, muco-cartilaginous tube connecting the back of the nose to the middle ear. The anatomy of this tube is such that it tends to close naturally when ambient pressure is higher than middle ear pressure (as on descent in a dive), and tends to open naturally when ambient pressure is lower than middle ear pressure (on ascent).

exposure suit – a suit worn by a diver to primarily help protect them from exposure to cold water and bites, stings, and scratches.

- F -

fathom – a nautical unit of measurement equivalent to six feet.

FFW - Feet of Fresh Water.

first stage regulator – a regulator attached to the SCUBA tank that lowers the tank pressure to ambient pressure plus a pre-determined pressure (typically 140 psi). The first stage regulator then connects via a hose to a second stage regulator.

foramen ovale, patent - Opening in the heart between the right and left atria that remains open in about 30 percent of people, allowing passage of bubbles into the arterial circulation creating symptoms of arterial gas embolism.

free ascent – an emergency method of getting back to the surface. It involves the diver breathing out all the way up.

free diving - in some usage, is diving without any SCUBA or other equipment and synonymous with breath-hold diving. In other usage, is diving without any attachment to the surface, and therefore includes SCUBA diving. I use the former definition within the context of this book.

FSW - feet of sea water; used to indicate either an actual depth or just a pressure equal to that depth, e.g., in a hyperbaric chamber.

- G -

Gag Reflex, Overactive - the inability to retain an object in the mouth without gagging or retching.

gas embolism - see arterial gas embolism.

gas laws - laws that predict how gases will behave with changes in pressure, temperature and volume. Four of the more important ones in SCUBA are Boyles, Charles, Dalton, and Henry's.

gastrointestinal - pertaining to the digestive tract.

gauge pressure - pressure exclusive of atmospheric pressure. When diving, gauge pressure is due solely to the water pressure.

glaucoma - abnormal condition of increased intra-ocular pressure, leading to blindness if uncorrected.

GUE - Global Underwater Explorers.

- H -

Haldanian - related to Haldane's theory that nitrogen is taken up and given off in exponential fashion during a dive and that there is some safe ratio of pressure change for ascent.

half time - half the time it takes for a dissolved gas in a tissue to equilibrate to a new pressure or to reach full saturation at a new pressure. Theoretical tissue half times are used in designing dive tables and algorithms for dive computers.

HBO chambers - hyperbaric chambers that lower (or raise) the pressures surrounding an individual, usually using periods of 100 percent oxygen for purposes of treating diving and other conditions.

hearing loss - a hazard of diving which is usually associated with the rupture of the round window or inner ear DCS.

heartburn (GERD) - reflux of acid gastric juice into the lower esophagus.

heat exhaustion – a condition resulting from overheating that is characterized by a pale, clammy appearance and a feeling of weakness.

heat stroke – a condition resulting from overheating that is characterized by hot, dry, and flushed skin. This is a life-threatening emergency.

heliox - mixture of helium and oxygen, used primarily for very deep diving.

helium - second lightest gas. Helium does not cause problems of narcosis seen with nitrogen and is therefore used for very deep diving.

Henry's Law - the amount of any given gas that will dissolve in a liquid at a given temperature is a function of the partial pressure of the gas in contact with the liquid and the solubility coefficient of the gas in the liquid.

hernia - a weakness of the abdominal wall through which the intestines or other intra-abdominal contents protrude. This condition is dangerous to a diver if a loop of air-containing intestine is trapped outside the abdomen.

holdfast – a structure which attaches seaweed's to the bottom or to other substrates.

hookah - a surface-supplied compressed air apparatus, for use in shallow diving in calm waters. The air is delivered to one or more divers through a long hose attached to a compressor or other air source on the surface.

hose protector – a piece of heavy plastic or rubber that fits over the end of a hose to relieve the stress that is caused by the weight of the equipment.

hydrogen - an inert gas and the lightest of all the elements. Hydrogen has been used in experimental deep diving.

hydrostatic pressure – the pressure exerted underwater by the surrounding water column.

hydrostatic test – a test that is required to ensure the safety of scuba tanks. This is a pressure test in which the tank is filled with water instead of air and raised to a pressure five thirds of the maximum working pressure, causing the water to expand and be displaced. If the levels of water displaced are within acceptable limits then the tank passes. If the tank does not pass the test then it can not be refilled.

hyperbaric chamber - air-tight chamber that can simulate the ambient pressure at altitude or at depth. Hyperbaric chambers are used for treating decompression illness.

hypercapnia (hypercarbia) - a higher than normal PCO_2 level in the blood.

hypertension - condition where the blood pressure is above 140/90.

hyperthermia - a body temperature warmer than normal. Hypertermia is less common in diving than hypothermia, but can occur from overheating in a wet or dry suit particularly while 'suiting up'.

hyperventilation - condition where an individual breathes too rapidly and has a lowered CO_2, lowered Ca^{++} with the production of tetany (rigidity). A condition usually due to panic.

hypothermia - a body temperature colder than normal (37°C/98.6°F). Severe hypothermic problems start to manifest when the body temperature reaches about 35°C (95°F).

hypoventilation (skip breathing) - under breathing to the extent that the blood carbon dioxide level is elevated which may be manifested by carbon dioxide narcosis.

hypoxemia (hypoxia) - lower than normal PO_2 level in the blood (insufficient oxygen in the blood).

hypoxia, latent - see shallow water blackout.

- **I** -

IANTD - International Association of Nitrox & Technical Divers.

IDEA – International Diving Educators Association.

immersion hypothermia – the lowering of body temperature by full body immersion in cold water. See hypothermia.

index marks – the points on a compass bezel that provide a place to aim the needle to stay on a desired course. Also marks on a dive watch indicating minutes.

inner ear - that portion of the ear in the petrous bone that has to do with hearing organs and balance.

integrated weight system – systems in which added weight is placed in pockets of the backpack or BC.

internal visual inspection – also known as the Tank Inspection Program (VIP) and the Visual Inspection Program (VIP). It is a procedure wherein the interior of the SCUBA cylinder is inspected for rust, corrosion, pitting, moisture, or any other problem. Most dive stores will not fill a cylinder that does not show evidence of having been tested annually.

isothermic – the isothermic water temperature for humans is 91° F. This is the temperature where an unprotected (no exposure suit) human can remain comfortable (temperature wise) in the water indefinitely.

- J -

J-Valve - a spring-loaded valve threaded into the scuba tank such that, if it is activated by low tank pressure (300 psi), it will shut off a diver's air supply. The diver then reaches back and pulls on a rod with re-opens the orifice for continued breathing while ascending.

- K -

knot – a nautical unit of speed equal to one nautical mile or about 1.15 statute miles per hour.

K-Valve – a simple on/off valve threaded into the scuba cylinder opened by turning a knob counter-clockwise.

- L -

lanyard - small diameter rope usually attached to the wrist and the item being secured.

latent hypoxia - a sudden unconsciousness, from hypoxia, that occurs among some breath hold divers. Often occurs near the surface after a deeper dive. Same as "shallow water blackout."

lee – the side of a ship, vessel, island, etc. that is farthest from the point from which the wind is blowing.

letter group designation – a letter that is used to designate the amount of residual nitrogen in the diver's system after a dive. Usually obtained from dive tables.

lice, sea - description of the condition (itching) caused by the nematocysts of the thimble jellyfish.

lifeline – see trail line.

liftbag – a bag-like device that is inflated with air and used to lift various objects from the bottom. Many models are designed with an overpressure relief valve to allow excess air to escape thus preventing damage to the liftbag.

live-aboard - a dive boat with sleeping and eating accommodations enabling for extended stay at dive sites. Commercial live aboards are usually between 50 and 130 feet long, and can carry anywhere from 10 to 30+ divers for a week or more.

live boat diving – a type of diving that utilizes a manned, unanchored boat.

log book – a journal that sets out each of diver's dives in detail, both as a personal and qualifying record.

low-pressure inflation device – a device that allows the flow of air from the SCUBA cylinder to the BC.

lubber line – the reference line on a compass. The stationary line that shows the direction of travel.

lung over-expansion injury – an injury to the lung tissues caused by a diver ascending too quickly or holding their breath upon ascent.

- M -

macro photography – close-up photography of a subject using special close-up accessories and lenses.

mal de mer - motion sickness or sea sickness.

Martini's Law – when diving to 100 feet seawater (fsw) a diver's reactions and reasoning capabilities will be affected as if they had just consumed one martini. Each 50 feet thereafter is the equivalent of an additional martini.

Maximum Dive Time (MDT) – the length of time that may be spent at a given depth without being required to stop during ascent to reduce the likelihood of decompression sickness.

mediastinal emphysema – the condition that exists when air from an over expansion injury escapes into the chest area near the heart.

MFW - Meters of Fresh Water.

MGR - Mixed Gas Rebreather, see closed circuit SCUBA.

middle ear - air-containing space of the ear bordered on one side by the tympanic membrane, which is exposed to any change in ambient pressure. Air pressure in the middle ear space can only be equalized through the Eustachian tube, which connects the middle ear to the back of the nose.

middle ear barotrauma - damage done to the middle ear due to the diver's inability to equalize the pressure differentials as they descend or ascend.

mitral valve prolapse - an incompetent (not fully closing) valve in the heart between the left atrium and ventricle.

mixed gas - basically, any non-air mixture (e.g., nitrox), although some divers use the term only for mixes that contain a gas in addition to (or in place of) nitrogen (e.g., helium, neon, etc.)

MOD - Maximum Operating Depth.

MSW - Meters of Salt Water.

multilevel dive – a dive characterized by progressively shallower dive depths.

multiple sclerosis (MS) – a demyelinating neurological illness causing symptoms similar to DCS.

Myer-Overton theory - any inert gas will cause an anesthetic effect if enough of it is dissolved in the fatty tissue of the nervous system.

- N -

NACD - National Association for Cave Diving.

narcosis - depressed mental state, anywhere from confusion or drowsiness to coma.

nasal congestion - swollen, blood-filled linings of the nose and sinuses, often due to allergies.

NASDS - National Association of Scuba Diving Schools.

NAUI - National Association of Underwater Instructors.

NDL (No Decompression Limit) - length of 'bottom time' without having to do a decompression stop.

negative buoyancy – that state that exists when an object tends to sink.

nekton – large, actively swimming marine animals, e.g., sharks, whales, marlin, etc.

neurologic problems - problems of the brain and spinal cord.

neutral buoyancy – the state that exists when an object neither floats nor sinks.

nitrogen - gas that makes up 78 percent of air. Nitrogen is inert in that it does not enter into any chemical reaction in the body but it can cause problems under pressure (see nitrogen narcosis and decompression sickness).

nitrogen narcosis - the narcotic effect nitrogen has at increased pressure. Manifestation of nitrogen narcosis usually, but not always, begins occurring below 80 fsw.

nitrous – N_2O, a dental anesthetic.

nitrox - any mixture of nitrogen and oxygen that contains less than the 78 percent of nitrogen as found in ordinary air.

NMFS – National Marine Fisheries Services.

NOAA - National Oceanic and Atmospheric Association.

no-decompression limits – see maximum dive time.

NSS-CDS - National Speleological Society - Cave Diving Section.

- **O** -

octopus – an extra second stage that is attached to the first stage regulator for use in out-of-air situations. An extra regulator.

OEA - Oxygen enriched air or nitrox.

Off-Gassing – removal of 'excess' inert gases (typically nitrogen by respiration).

one atmosphere – the force of the atmosphere on the earth taken as a constant of 14.7 psi or 1 bar.

open circuit SCUBA - apparatus used in recreational diving whereby exhaled air is expelled into the water as bubbles and no part is rebreathed by the diver.

open water diver course – the first course taken to become certified to scuba dive.

otitis - inflammation or infection of any part of the ear. Otitis media involves the middle ear and otitis externa the outer ear (ear canal).

overexpansion injury – injuries that are caused by the expansion of air in closed body spaces.

overpressure relief valve – a valve built into BCs which allows the escape of expanding gas without the loss of buoyancy or damage to the BC.

oxygen (O_2) - gas vital for all life on this planet; makes up 21 percent of air by volume. Too little oxygen is called anoxia and too much oxygen is called hypoxia which can result in oxygen poisoning.

oxygen therapy - administration of any gas, for medical purpose, that contains more than 21 percent oxygen.

oxygen toxicity - damage or injury from inhaling too much oxygen. Oxygen toxicity can arise from either too high an oxygen concentration or oxygen pressure. The first manifestation of oxygen toxicity while diving can be seizures which can result in drowning.

oxygen window - difference between total gas pressures in arterial and venous blood. The oxygen window exists because oxygen is partly metabolized by the tissues thus venous oxygen pressure is lower than arterial oxygen pressure.

- P -

PADI - Professional Association of Diving Instructors .

partial pressure - pressure exerted by a single component of a gas within a gas mixture or dissolved in a liquid.

partial pressure, carbon dioxide (PCO2) - pressure exerted by carbon dioxide in any mixture of gases or dissolved in a liquid.

partial pressure, nitrogen (PN2) - pressure exerted by nitrogen component in any mixture of gases or dissolved in a liquid.

partial pressure, oxygen (PO2) - pressure exerted by oxygen in any mixture of gases or dissolved in a liquid.

patent foramen ovale (PFO) - see foramen ovale.

pelagic – living or occuring in the open ocean.

phytoplankton – microscopic plant members of the plankton.

pneumomediastinum - abnormal collection of air in the middle part of the chest between the two lung hemispheres (mediastinum). Pneumomediastinum is often a consequence of barotrauma.

pneumothorax - abnormal collection of air outside the lining of the lung between the lung and the chest wall. A pneumothorax is often a consequence of barotrauma.

pony bottle - a small SCUBA cylinder, usually 40 cf or less, used as a redundant air source (bailout bottles tend to be 3 cf or less of air).

positive buoyancy – the state that exists when an object tends to float to the surface of the water.

prescription dive masks - dive masks produced especially for divers needing refractive correction.

pressure gauge – a piece of equipment that allows a diver to monitor the amount of air remaining in the SCUBA tank.

pressure relief disk – a safety device that is built into tank valves and prevents pressure from reaching dangerous levels. This is a one-time use device and must be replace if the disk bursts.

psi - pounds per square inch. A common measurement of air pressure.

psia – pounds per square inch absolute.

psig – pounds per square inch gauge.

ptitis externa - inflammation and infection of the external auditory canal - usually due to fungus and decreased acidity of the canal.

pulmonary barotrauma - rupture of the lung surface from increased pressure of ascent from depth. Usually due to closed glottis, pulmonary blebs or terminal airway disease. Causes arterial gas embolism (AGE), pneumothorax, pneumomediastinum.

pulmonary decompression sickness (chokes) - see chokes.

pulmonary edema due to diving - fluid accumulation in the lungs secondary to immersion and pressure changes.

purge – to evacuate the water from a regulator or snorkel so that air will flow unimpeded. There is a purge button on a regulator for this purpose.

- Q -

quick-release buckle – a buckle that is designed to be operated with one hand so that they can be opened quickly in an emergency.

- R -

rapture of the deep – see nitrogen narcosis.

RDP - Recreational Dive Planner.

recompression – the treatment for DSI by placing the diver/patient in a recompression or hyperbaric chamber and increasing the pressure based on specific protocols.

recreational SCUBA diving (RSD) - diving to prescribed limits which include a depth no greater than 130 fsw, using only compressed air, no decompression stop required, always done with a buddy, and there is always immediate access to surface.

reference line – the lubber line on a compass.

regulator - a device which changes air pressure from one level to a lower level. See first stage regulator and second stage regulator.

repetitive dive - any dive done within a certain time frame after a previous dive. With some tables any dive within 12 hours of a previous dive is considered repetitive. When using a computer, any dive whose profile is affected by a previous dive is considered repetitive.

residual nitrogen - nitrogen that remains dissolved in a diver's tissues as a result of a dive within the past 24 hours.

residual nitrogen time (RNT) - the time it would take to off-gas (remove via exhalation) any extra nitrogen remaining after a dive. In dive tables, RNT is designated by a letter A through Z with A being the least amount of residual nitrogen. Residual nitrogen time should always be taken into consideration in determining the safe duration for any repetitive dive.

residual volume – the quantity of air remaining in the lungs after a forceful exhalation.

reverse squeeze/block - pain or discomfort in enclosed space (e.g., sinuses, middle ear, inside face mask) on ascent from a dive.

RNT - Residual Nitrogen Time.

RSTC – Recreational Scuba Training Council.

Rule of Thirds – a rule used primarily by wreck and cave divers which states that exiting the enclosure should begin by or before 1/3 of the available air is consumed.

- S -

SAC-Rate – surface air consumption rate

safety stop - on ascent from a dive, a specified time (3 minutes typical) spent at a specific depth (15 feet typical), for purposes of nitrogen off-gassing. By definition a safety stop is not mandatory for safe ascent from the dive and is not the same thing as a decompression stop.

saturation - the degree to which a gas is dissolved in the blood or tissues. Full saturation occurs when the pressure of the gas dissolved in the blood or tissues is the same as the ambient (surrounding) pressure of that gas.

SCUBA - self-contained underwater breathing apparatus.

sea lice/seabather's eruption - dermatitis (skin rash) secondary to being stung by nematocysts of the thimble jellyfish.

second stage regulator - the regulator that follows, connected with a low pressure air hose, the first stage regulator, and delivers compressed air on demand (upon diver's inhalation) at ambient pressure. Attached to the regulator is a mouth piece which is placed in the diver's mouth.

service pressure – the working pressure of the scuba tank. It is stamped on the shoulder of the tank, e.g., "CTC/DOT-3ALxxxx-S80" where xxxx is the service pressure.

shallow water blackout - a sudden unconsciousness, from hypoxia, that occurs among some breath hold divers. Often occurs near the surface after a deeper dive, hence "shallow water." Same as 'latent hypoxia'. Occurs due to a lack of oxygen. To avoid shallow-water blackout do not hyperventilate more than three breaths before free diving.

shot line – a vertical line that extends between a surface buoy and the sea bed and thus fixes a position.

SI - Surface Interval; the length of time between consecutive dives.

single dive - any dive conducted at least 12 hours after a previous dive.

signs – observable

sinuses - air spaces within the skull that are in contact with ambient pressure through openings into the back of the nasal passages.

SIT – see surface interval.

skin diving - another term for breath-hold diving.

skip breathing – a potentially dangerous practice of taking a breath and holding it for as long as possible before taking another or of skipping a full exhale before the next inhale.

slurp gun – a cylindrical device equipped with a plunger and used underwater to collect small animals.

SPG - Submersible Pressure Gauge.

square profile dive – a type of dive that involves staying at one particular depth for the entire dive and then ascending directly to the surface.

squeeze - pain or discomfort in an enclosed space (sinuses, middle ears, inside a face mask) caused by shrinkage of that space which occurs on descent. See reverse squeeze.

SSI - SCUBA Schools International.

standing currents – currents that are regular and steady.

surface air consumption (SAC) - the amount of air (in cubic feet per minute or liters per minute) used by a person at sea level in 'normal' respiration. An excellent article on SAC calculation by Dr. Larry "Harris" Taylor can be accessed via the URL http://www.ivydene1.demon.co.uk/dive/gascalc.htm. The same material can also be obtained from the Jan/Feb 1995 issue of SOURCES and NAUI's Mastering Advanced Diving manual.

surface interval - length of time on the surface between two consecutive dives.

surface marker buoy (SMB) – a buoy that attaches to a diver marking their position.

symptoms – felt by the patient.

- **T** -

tachycardia – excessive rapidity of the heart beat.

tag line – see trail line.

TDI - Technical Diving International.

TDT - Total Dive Time.

test date – a date that is stamped on the scuba tank indicating the date of the last hydrostatic test.

thermocline – the intersection between two layers of water of that are of decidedly different temperatures. A diver can easily feel a thermocline which may also affect visibility in the thermocline.

tissue - a part of the body characterized by specific characteristics, such as muscle, bone, or cartilage. The term is also used to refer to any part of the body with a specific half-time for loading and unloading nitrogen.

TMJ Syndrome - in SCUBA usage it is the jaw and ear pain associated with the transmandibular joint (attachment of mandible (lower jaw) to the maxilla (upper jaw)) due to clamping the teeth around a second stage regulator's mouthpiece.

total nitrogen time (TNT) – the sum of residual nitrogen time and actual dive time following a repetitive dive.

toxicity, Oxygen - the condition caused by oxygen at depth (increased pressure) which usually includes convulsions. Drowning is possible.

trail line – a line that is used while boat diving. It is let out from the stern (back) of the boat with a float attached to aid divers returning to the boat (also called lifeline and tag line).

trimix - mixture of helium, nitrogen and oxygen, used for very deep diving.

tympanic membrane - the thin ear drum between the outer ear and the middle ear which is visible to the examiner with an otoscope.

- U -

UHMS – Undersea and Hyperbaric Medical Society.

- V -

valsalva maneuver – the attempted exhalation against a closed nose and mouth that ordinarily opens the Eustachian tubes, allowing equalization. Other ear squeeze maneuvers which are easier on the ears should be used before using Valsalva maneuver.

vertigo - Dizzy, unbalanced feeling often caused by diving problems with the inner ear.

VGE - Venous Gas Embolism.

visual inspection – a periodic inspection of the scuba tank that checks for corrosion to ensure the integrity of the tank. Also called the VCI (visual cylinder inspection) or VIP (visual inspection program).

- W -

water pressure - force per unit area exerted by the weight of a water column. Each 33 feet of sea water exerts a pressure equivalent to one atmosphere or 14.7 psi.

wave height – distance from the lowest portion of a wave (trough) to the highest portion (crest).

wet suit - any suit that provides thermal protection in water by trapping a layer of water between the diver's skin and the suit.

windward – the direction from which the wind blows, opposite of leeward.

SCUBA Periodicals

Alert Diver Magazine
Divers Alert Network
Box 3823
Duke University Medical
Center
Durham, NC 27710
(919) 684-2948

Asian Diver Magazine
Tanglin, P.O. Box 335
912412
Singapore
(65) 733-2551
www.asian-diver.com

Calypso Log
Cousteau Society
870 Greenbrier Circle, Ste.
402
Chesapeake, VA 23320
(800) 441-4395

Discover Diving Magazine
Watersport Publishing
Company
P.O. Box 83727
San Diego, CA 92138
(619) 697-0703
www.scubatimes.com

Dive Business International
Scuba Schools International
(SSI)
2619 Canton Ct.
Fort Collins, CO 80525
(303) 482-0883

Dive Report
Watersport Publishing, Inc.
P.O. Box 83727
San Diego, CA 92138
(800) 776-3483

Dive Training Magazine
201 Main St.
Parkville, MO 64152
(407) 731-4321
www.divetrainingmag.com

Dive Travel Magazine
P.O. Box 1388
Soquel, CA 95073
(800) 676-7254

Immersed
F.D.R. Station
P.O. Box 7934
New York, NY 10150
(718) 545-1325

Ocean Realm Magazine
P.O. Box 6953
Syracuse, NY 13217
(800) 681-7727

Pressure
Undersea & Hyperbaric
Medical Society
10531 Metropolitan Ave.
Kensington, MD 20895
(301) 942-7804

Rodale's Scuba Diving
Magazine
6600 Abecorn St., Suite 208
Savannah, GA 31405
(912) 351-0855
www.scubadiving.com

Scuba Times Magazine
33 Music Square West, Suite
104A
Nashville, TN 37204
(615) 726-4832
www.scubatimes.com
Skin Diver Magazine
6420 Wilshire Blvd.
Los Angeles, CA 90048
(323) 782-2960
www.scubatimes.com

Sport Diver
World Publications
330 W. Canton Ave.
Winter Park, FL 32789
(800) 394-6006

Sources, The Journal of
Underwater Education
National Association of
Underwater Instructors
(NAUI)
4650 Arrow Hwy, Ste. F-1
P.O. Box 14650
Montclair, CA 91763
(909) 621-5801

Sport Diver Magazine
330 W. Canton Ave.
Winter Park, FL 32789
(407) 628-4802

Squid
Handicapped Scuba
Association
1104 E. Prado
San Clemente, CA 92672
(714) 498-6128

Sub Aqua Journal
150 Marine St.
City Island, NY 10464
(718) 885-3332

The Undersea Journal
Professional Association of
Diving Instructors (PADI)
1251 E. Dyer Rd., Ste. 100
Santa Ana, CA 92705
(800) 729-7234

References

A. Clark, Eugenie, Ph.D., Rodale's New Diver Magazine, Premier Issue, p. 28.

B. Divers Alert Network, Report on Decompression Illness and Diving Fatalities, 1999 edition, p. 13.

C. Divers Alert Network, Report on Decompression Illness and Diving Fatalities, 1999 edition.

D. Franklin, Regina, Executive Director of the Diving Equipment and Marketing Association (DEMA), http://www.dema.org.

E. Graver, Dennis, 100 Best Scuba Quizzes, Aqua Quest Publications, Inc., New York, 1997, p. 138.

F. ibid, p. 160.

G. ibid, p. 24.

H. ibid, p. 52.

I. ibid, p. 100.

J. ibid, p. 100.

K. ibid, p. 102.

L. ibid, p. 102.

M. ibid, p. 106.

N. ibid, p. 118.

O. ibid, p. 170.

P. ibid, p. 176.

Q. High, William (Bill) L., Beneath The Sea, Best Publishing Co., Flagstaff, AZ, 1998, p. 15.

R. ibid, p. 26.

S. http://newfrontier.iinet.net.au/safety.htm

T. http://www.diveweb.com/uw/archives/arch/tragedy.html

U. http://www.gulftel.com/~scubadoc/fitage.htm

V. http://www.gulftel.com/~scubadoc/hzrdmrnlf.html

W. http://www.gulftel.com/~scubadoc/moresea.htm

X. http://www.gulftel.com/~scubadoc/rskwomdiv.htm

Y. http://www.newdiver.com/learntodive/trainagency

Z. http://www.padi.com/news/stats/default.stm.

AA. http://www.padi.com/news/stats/demographics.stm

BB. http://www.padi.com/news/stats/topten_cert.stm

CC. http://www.scubadiving.com/training/medicine/age&dive.
    shtml

DD. http://www.scubadiving.com/training/medicine/highanxie
    ty.shtml

EE. Martin, Lawrence, M.D., Scuba Diving Explained,
    Questions and Answers on Physiology and Medical Aspects
    of Scuba Diving, Best Publishing Company, Flagstaff, AZ,
    1997.

FF. ibid, Section B.

GG. Rodale Staff, Top 100, Readers Rate Destinations, Diver
    Operators, Live-Aboards, & Resorts, Rodale's Scuba Diving
    Magazine, January/February 1999, pp. 60-65.

HH. Taylor, David, Caution: Paradigm Shifts Ahead, Rodale's
    Scuba Diving, November/December 1999, p. 6.

II. Taylor, Dr. Larry "Harris", A Few Things Your Sport Diving
    Instructor May Not Have Told You About Deeper Diving,
    SOURCES, Nov/Dec. 1991, pp. 63-68.

JJ. Von Maier, Robert, Solo Diving, The Art of Underwater Self-
    Sufficiency, Watersport Publishing, Inc., San Diego, CA,
    1993.

KK. Webster's New Collegiate Dictionary, A Merriam-Webster, Springfield, MA, 1973.

Index

358

362

Readers' Notes

Order Form

USPS: **Ernest Hill Publishing**
12056 Mt. Vernon St., #234
Grand Terrace, CA 92313-5116

Toll Free Phone: 1-800-582-1882

FAX: (978) 389-6110

Internet: http://www.ehpublishing.com

Please send me the following books. I understand that I may return any of the books for a full refund, no questions asked, as long at the books are received by Ernest Hill Publishing in re-salable (as new) condition.

		Price	
Title	Qty	Unit	Total
SCUBA Scoop	___	16.95	_____
Winging Through America	___	10.95	_____
_____	___	____	_____

Sales Tax: _____

Shipping and Handling: _____

Total Enclosed: _____

Sales tax:
Please add 7.25% for books shipped to California addresses.
Shipping and Handling:
Book rate: $2.25 for the first book and $1.50 for each additional book. (Surface shipping may take three to four weeks.) Air Mail: $4.75 per book.

Ship to:
Name: _____

Address: _____

City: _____ State: ___ Zip: _____

Order Today!

Also written by Gary Shumway:

Winging Through America, A Motorcyclist's Solo Journey Through the 48 States

Ride along! A modern day "Easy Rider" takes to the road, riding through the 'Lower 48'. Not only a moving and humorous personal adventure but a compendium of traveling tips, historical info, and a comprehensive appendices of roads traveled, places to see, and contacts. A must read book for the rebel in all of us!

Reader Comments:

"What an adventure, both for Gary and the reader. I read it twice and it kept my interest both times, unusual for me...and I'm not a 'rider'." - Roland Barnes, Journalist

"Gary's description of his journey through the 48 states makes you feel like you are traveling right along with him." - Bob Wheeler, Photographer

"Reading Winging Through America makes you feel like you are riding with Gary; pegging out around the curves, shivering in the cold, and sweating in the heat. A quite enjoyable book." - Lonnie Casper, Goldwing Rider

"... is not only extremely witty and entertaining but also informative ... Gary's unique, yet down to earth, portrayal of his adventure will kindle the desire to enjoy just such a rich experience." - Dr. Anderson, Dentist

Winging Through America is... a real adventure story!

Order Form

USPS:	**Ernest Hill Publishing**
	12056 Mt. Vernon St., #234
	Grand Terrace, CA 92313-5116

| Toll Free Phone: | 1-800-582-1882 |

| FAX: | (978) 389-6110 |

| Internet: | http://www.ehpublishing.com |

Please send me the following books. I understand that I may return any of the books for a full refund, no questions asked, as long at the books are received by Ernest Hill Publishing in re-salable (as new) condition.

		Price	
Title	Qty	Unit	Total
SCUBA Scoop	___	16.95	_____
Winging Through America	___	10.95	_____
_____	___ ___	_____

Sales Tax:	_____
Shipping and Handling:	_____
Total Enclosed:	_____

Sales tax:
Please add 7.25% for books shipped to California addresses.
Shipping and Handling:
Book rate: $2.25 for the first book and $1.50 for each additional book. (Surface shipping may take three to four weeks.) Air Mail: $4.75 per book.

Ship to:
Name: _____

Address: _____

City: _____ State: ___ Zip: _____

Order Today!